Realizing a New Global Cyberspace Framework

Rolf H. Weber

Realizing a New Global Cyberspace Framework

Normative Foundations and Guiding Principles

Springer

Rolf H. Weber
Faculty of Law
University of Zurich
Zurich, Switzerland

Co-Publication with Schulthess Juristische Medien AG

ISBN 978-3-7255-7093-5.
www.schulthess.com
Published by Springer-Verlag GmbH Berlin Heidelberg 2015

ISBN 978-3-662-44676-8 ISBN 978-3-662-44677-5 (eBook)
DOI 10.1007/978-3-662-44677-5
Springer Heidelberg New York Dordrecht London

Library of Congress Control Number: 2014950795

Printed on acid-free paper

Springer is part of Springer Science+Business Media (www.springer.com)

Preface

In many respects cyberspace has created a new world. The online phenomena encompass social, cultural, economic, and legal facets. The information society's regulatory framework has gradually crystallized under the term of "Internet governance". However, the focus should be broader addressing all aspects of the invisible, intangible world of electronic informational processes stored at multiple interconnected sites with manifold possibilities for interaction. Cyberspace does include the exchange of people, businesses and other entities over computer networks.

Notwithstanding intensive discussions about the normative foundations and guiding principles of a global cyberspace framework the theoretical grounds still partly seem shaky. This book attempts to outline a model for a general legal framework enshrining key principles of human society. Such a framework could then be complemented by additional polycentric regulations developed through multistakeholder participation in a multi-layer regime.

The book has benefited from many inputs and encouragements that I am deeply grateful for. Valuable exchanges have often taken place within GigaNet, the academic network for Internet governance; furthermore, my stays at the Max Planck Institute in Munich and at the Institutt for Rettsinformatikk of Oslo University have provided opportunities for meaningful discussions. The most wonderful support was always granted by Prof. Dr. Christine Kaufmann (University of Zurich). Furthermore, I am grateful to my research assistant Ulrike I. Heinrich for her support in the completion of the book and to Miriam Frisenda for the review of the manuscript.

Any comments and suggestions from readers would be highly appreciated (rolf.weber@rwi.uzh.ch).

Zurich, June 2014 Rolf H. Weber

Contents

Bibliography

All weblinks have last been checked on June 30, 2014. Many additional references to specific topics are cited in the footnotes.

A

ABBOTT/SNIDAL, 2000. Kenneth W. Abbott/Duncan Snidal, Hard and Soft Law in International Governance, International Organization 54 (2000) 421–456

ALTWICKER/DIGGELMANN, 2014. Tilmann Altwicker/Oliver Diggelmann, What Should Remain of the Critical Approaches to International Law? International Legal Theory as Critique, Schweizerische Zeitschrift für internationals und europäisches Recht 24 (2014), 69–92

AMSTUTZ, 2011. Marc Amstutz, Mechanisms of Evolution for a Law of the Future, in: SAM MÜLLER/STAVROS ZOURIDIS/MORLY FRISHMAN/LAURA KISTEMAKER (eds.), The Law of the Future and the Future of Law, Oslo 2011, 395–405

ANTONOVA, 2008. Slavka Antonova, Powershape of Internet Governance, Saarbrücken 2008

B

BALDWIN/CAVE/LODGE, 1999. Robert Baldwin/Martin Cave/Martin Lodge, Understanding Regulation: Theory, Strategy, and Practice, 2nd ed., New York 2012

BALDWIN/SCOTT/HOOD, Robert Baldwin/Colin Scott/Christopher Hood, A reader on regulation, Oxford 1998

BARR/MILLER, 2006. Michael S. Barr/Geoffrey P. Miller, Global Administrative Law: The View from Basel, The European Journal of International Law 2006, 15–46

BAXTER, 1998. Hugh Baxter, Autopoiesis and the "Relative Autonomy" of Law, Cardozo Law Review 19 (1998), 1987–2090

BEAL/CORIDEN/GREEN, 2000. John P. Beal/James A. Coriden/Thomas J. Green (eds.), New Commentary on the Code of Canon Law, New York/Mahwah 2000

BENHABIB, 2006. Seyla Benhabib, Another Cosmopolitanism, Oxford 2006

BENKLER, 2011a. Yochai Benkler, Network Theory: Networks of Power, Degrees of Freedom, International Journal of Communication 5 (2011), 721–755

BENKLER, 2011b. Yochai Benkler, The Penguin and the Leviathan: The Triumph of Cooperation over Self-Interest, New York 2011

BENKLER, 2006. Yochai Benkler, The Wealth of Networks: How Social Production Transforms Markets and Freedom, New Heaven/London 2006

BENKLER, 2004. Yochai Benkler, Sharing Nicely: On Sharable Goods and the Emergence of Sharing as a Modality of Economic Production, Yale Law Journal 114 (2004), 273–358

BENKLER, 2000. Yochai Benkler, Net Regulation: Taking Stock and Looking Forward, University of Colorado Law Review 71 (2000) 1203–1261

BERMAN, 2007. Paul Schiff Berman, Global Legal Pluralism, Southern California Law Review 80 (2007), 1155–1237

BERNSTEIN/CASHORE, 2007. Steven Bernstein/Benjamin Cashore, Can non-state global governance be legitimate? An analytical framework, Regulation & Governance 1 (2007), 347–371

BESSON, 2005. Samantha Besson, The Morality of Conflict: Reasonable Disagreement and the Law, Oxford/Portland 2005

BEYDOGAN, 2010. Turgut Ayhan Beydogan, Interoperability-Centric Problems: New Challenges and Legal Solutions, International Journal of Law and Information Technology 18 (2010), 301–331

BIEGEL, 2001. Stuart Biegel, Beyond Our Control?, Confronting the Limits of Our Legal System in the Age of Cyberspace, Cambridge Mass. 2001

BLACK, 2008. Julia Black, Constructing and contesting legitimacy and accountability in polycentric regulatory regimes, Regulation & Governance 2 (2008), 137–164

BLACK, 1996. Julia Black, Constitutionalizing Self-Regulation, The Modern Law Review 59 (1996), 24–55

BOWRY, 2005. Kathy Bowry, Law and Internet Cultures, Cambridge 2005

BRAITHWAITE, 2008. John Braithwaite, Regulatory Capitalism, How it works, ideas for making it work better, Cheltenham 2008

BRAITHWAITE/DRAHOS, 2000. John Braithwaite/Peter Drahos, Global Business Regulation, Cambridge 2000

BREINING-KAUFMANN, 2005. Christine Breining-Kaufmann, The Legal Matrix of Human Rights and Trade Law: State Obligations versus Private Rights and Obligations, in: THOMAS COTTIER/JOOST PAUWELYN/ELISABETH BÜRGI (eds.), Human Rights and International Trade, Oxford 2005, 95–136

BREYER, 1982. Stephan Breyer, Regulation and Its Reform, Cambridge MA 1982

BROUSSEAU/MARZOUKI/MÉADEL, 2012. Eric Brousseau/Meryem Marzouki/Cécile Méadel (eds.), Governance, Regulations and Powers on the Internet, Cambridge 2012

BROWN/MARSDEN, 2013. Ian Brown/Christopher T. Marsden, Regulating Code: Good Governance and Better Regulation in the Information Age, Cambridge MA/London 2013

BROWNSWORD, 2012. Roger Brownsword, The shaping of our on-line worlds: getting the regulatory environment right, International Journal of Law and Information Technology 20 (2012), 249–272

BROWNSWORD, 2008. Roger Brownsword, Rights, regulation and the technical revolution, Oxford/New York 2008

BRUMMER, 2014. Chris Brummer, Minilateralism, Cambridge 2014

BRUMMER, 2012. Chris Brummer, Soft Law and the Global Financial System, Rulemaking in the 21st Century, Cambridge 2012

BRUMMER, 2011. Chris Brummer, How International Financial Law Works (and How it Doesn't), The Georgetown Law Journal 99 (2011), 257–327

BURK, 2011. Dan L. Burk, Law as a Network Standard, Yale Journal of Law and Technology 8 (2005), 63–77

BURKERT, 2012. Herbert Burkert, Balancing informational power by informational power *or* Rereading Montesquieu in the internet age, in: BROUSSEAU/MARZOUKI/MÉADEL, 2012, 93–111

BYGRAVE, 2014. Lee A. Bygrave, Data Privacy Law. An International Perspective, Oxford 2014

BYGRAVE/MICHAELSEN, 2009. Lee A. Bygrave/Terje Michaelsen, Governors of the Internet, in: BYGRAVE/BING, 2009, 92–125

BYGRAVE/BING, 2009. Lee A. Bygrave/Jon Bing (eds.), Internet Governance: Infrastructure and Institutions, Oxford 2009

C

CAMPBELL, 1999. Angela Campbell, Self-Regulation and the Media, Federal Communications Law Journal 51 (1999), 711–772

CANEY, 2006. Simon Caney, Justice Beyond Border: A Global Political Theory, Oxford 2006

CASSESE, 2005. Sabino Cassese, Administrative Law Without the State? The Challenge of Global Regulation, New York University Journal of International Law and Politics 37 (2005), 663–694

CHAYES/HANDLER CHAYES, 1998. Abram Chayes/Antonia Handler Chayes, The New Sovereignty: Compliance with International Regulatory Agreements, Cambridge MA 1998

CHENOU/RADU, 2013. Jean-Marie Chenou/Roxana Radu, Global Internet Policy: a Fifteen-Year Long Debate, in: ROXANA RADU/JEAN-MARIE CHENOU/ROLF H. WEBER (eds.), The Evolution of Global Internet Governance, Zürich 2013, 3–19

CHIK, 2010. Warren B. Chik, "Customary Internet-ional Law": Creating a Body of Customary Law for Cyberspace. Part I: Developing Rules for Transitioning Custom into Law, Computer Law & Security Review 26 (2010), 3–22

CLARK, 2005. Ian Clark, Legitimacy in International Society, New York 2005

COTTIER, 2009. Thomas Cottier, Multilayered Governance, Pluralism, and Moral Conflict, Indiana Journal of Global Legal Studies 16 (2009), 647–679

COTTIER/HERTIG, 2003. Thomas Cottier/Maya Hertig, The Prospects of 21st Century Constitutionalism, Max Planck Yearbook of United Nations Law, Vol. 7, Hamburg 2003, 261–328

D

DANY, 2008. Charlotte Dany, Civil Society Participation under Most Favorable Conditions: Assessing the Deliberative Quality of the WSIS, in: Jens STEFFEK/CLAUDIA KISSLING/PATRIZIA NANZ (eds.), Civil Society Participation in European and Global Governance, Paul Grave 2008, 53–70

DAVIES, 2011. Jonathan S. Davies, Challenging Governance Theory: From Networks to Hegemony, Bristol 2011 de Búrca/Keohane/Sabel, 2014. Gráinne de Búrca /Robert O. Keohane/Charles F. Sabel, Global Experimentalist Governance, British Journal of Political Science 2014 (forthcoming), now available at http://papers.ssrn.com/sol3/papers.cfm?abstract_id=2423810

de la Chapelle, 2011. Bertrand de la Chapelle, Multistakeholder Governance, MIND No. 2, September 2011, 14–25

Demchak/Dombrowski, 2011. Chris C. Demchak/Peter Dombrowski, Rise of a Cybered Westphalian Age, Strategic Studies Quarterly 2011, 32–61

DeNardis, 2014. Laura DeNardis, The Global War for Internet Governance, New Haven/ London 2014

DeNardis, 2011. Opening Standards: The Global Politics of Interoperability, Cambridge MA 2011

DeNardis, 2009. Laura DeNardis, Protocol Politics: The Globalization of Internet Governance, Cambridge MA 2009

DeNardis/Raymond, 2013. Laura DeNardis/Mark Raymond, Thinking Clearly About Multistakeholder Governance, GigaNet, November 2013, available at http://papers.ssrn.com/sol3/papers.cfm?abstract-_id=2354377

Diggelmann/Altwicker, 2008. Oliver Diggelmann/Tilmann Altwicker, Is There Something Like a Constitution of International Law?, Zeitschrift für ausländisches öffentliches Recht und Völkerrecht 68 (2008), 623–650

Doria, 2013. Avri Doria, Use [and Abuse] of Multistakeholderism in the Internet, in: Roxana Radu/Jean-Marie Chenou/Rolf H. Weber (eds.), The Evolution of Global Internet Governance, Principles and Policies in the Making, Zürich 2013, 115–138

Drake, 2011. William J. Drake, Multistakeholderism: Internal Limitations and External Limits, MIND No. 2, September 2011, 68–72

Duss, 2012. Vanessa C.Duss, Vom "Taking Rights Seriously" zum "Thinking Law Globally" – ein "Cultural Shift"?, in: Annja Mannhart/Silja Bürgi (Hrsg.), Die Zukunft des Rechts, Zürich 2012, 21–38

Dutton/Peltu, 2007. William H. Dutton/Malcolm Peltu, The emerging Internet governance mosaic: connecting the pieces, Information Polity 12 (2007), 63–81

E

Easterbrook, 1996. Frank H. Easterbrook, Cyberspace and the Law of the Horse, The University of Chicago Legal Forum 1996, 207–216

Ellickson, 1991. Robert C. Ellickson, Order Without Law: How Neighbors Settle Disputes, Cambridge Mass. 1991

European Commission, 2014. European Commission, Communication from the Commission to the European Parliament, the Council, the European Economic and Social Committee and the Committee of the Regions, Internet Policy and Governance, Europe's role in shaping the future of Internet Governance, COM(2014) 72 final of February 12, 2014

F

FINNIS, 1980. John Finnis, Natural Law and Natural Rights, Oxford 1982

FLYVERBOM, 2011. Mikkel Flyverbom, The Power of Networks: Organizing the Global Politics of Internet, Cheltenham 2011

FOUCAULT, 1978/79. Michel Foucault, Naissance de la biopolitique: Cours au Collège de France (1978–1979), Paris 2004

FRANCK, 1995. Thomas M. Franck, Fairness in International Law and Institutions, Oxford 1995

FRANKEL, 1998. Tamar Frankel, The Internet, Securities Regulation, and Theory of Law, Chicago-Kent Law Review 73 (1998), 1319–1354

FRANKLIN, 2013. Marianne I. Franklin, Digital Dilemmas. Power, Resistance, and the Internet, Oxford 2013

FRASER, 2005. Nancy Fraser, Reframing Justice in a Globalizing World, New Left Review 36 (2005), 69–88

FRYDMAN, 2012. Benôit Frydman, Comment penser le droit global?, in: JEAN-YVES CHÉROT/BENÔIT FRYDMAN (eds.), La science du droit dans la globalization, Brussels 2012, 17–47

FRYDMAN, 2004. Benôit Frydman, Coregulation: A Possible Legal Model for Global Governance, in: BART DE SCHUTTER/JOHAN PAS (eds.), About Globalisation: views on the trajectory of mondialisation, Brussels 2004, 227–242

FUKUYAMA, 2004. Francis Fukuyama, Governance and the Order in the Twenty First Century, London 2004

G

GADBAW, 2010. R. Michael Gadbaw, Systemic Regulation of Global Trade and Finance: A Tale of Two Systems, Journal of International Economic Law 13 (2010), 551–574

GIBBONS, 1997. Llewellyn J. Gibbons, No Regulation, Government Regulation, or Self-Regulation: Social Enforcement or Social Contracting for Governance in Cyberspace, Cornell Journal of Law and Public Policy 6 (1997), 475–551

GIBSON, 1984. William Gibson, Neuromancer, New York 1984

GOLDSMITH, 1998. Jack L. Goldsmith, The Internet and the Abiding Significance of Territorial Sovereignty, Indiana Journal of Global Legal Studies 5 (1998), 475–491

GOLDSMITH/WU, 2006. Jack L. Goldsmith/Tim Wu, Who Controls the Internet? Illusions of a Borderless World, Oxford 2006

GREWLICH, 1999. Klaus W. Grewlich, Governance in „Cyberspace“, The Hague/London/Boston 1999

GROTIUS, 1916. Hugo Grotius, The freedom of the seas or the right which belongs to the Dutch to take part in the East Indian Trade: a dissertation, ed. by James Brown Scott, New York 1916

GUZMAN/MEYER, 2010. Andrew T. Guzman/Timothy L. Meyer, International Soft Law, Journal of Legal Analysis 2 (2010), 171–225

H

HABERMAS, 2006. Jürgen Habermas, Does Constitutionalization of International Law still Have a Chance?, in: JÜRGEN HABERMAS (ed.), The Divided West, Cambridge 2006, 93–115

HABERMAS, 1992. Jürgen Habermas, Faktizität und Geltung, Frankfurt 1992

HART, 1997. Herbert L.A. Hart, The Concept of Law, 2nd ed., Oxford 1997

HENKIN, 1979. Louis Henkin, How Nations Behave: Law and Foreign Policy, 2nd ed. New York 1979

HILL, 2013. Richard Hill, Internet Governance: The Last Gasp of Colonialism, or Imperialism by Other Means?, in: ROXANA RADU/JEAN-MARIE CHENOU/ROLF H. WEBER (eds.), The Evolution of Global Internet Governance. Principles and Policies in the Making, Zürich 2013, 79–94.

HOBBES, 1651. John Hobbes, Leviathan or the Matter, Forme & Power of a Common-Wealth Ecclestiasticall and Civill, London 1651

HOOD, 1994. Christopher Hood, Explaining economic policy reversals, Buckingham 1994

HOWSE/TREITEL, 2010. Robert L. Howse/Ruti Treitel, Beyond Compliance: Rethinking Why International Law Really Matters, Global Policy 1 (2010), 127–136

HÜPKES, 2009. Eva Hüpkes, Regulation, self-regulation or co-regulation?, Journal of Business Law 5 (2009), 427–446

I

J

JACKSON, 2003. John H. Jackson, Sovereignty-Modern: A New Approach to an Outdated Concept, American Journal of International Law 97 (2003), 782–802

JOHNSON/POST, 1998. David R. Johnson/David G. Post, The New 'Civic Virtue' of the Internet, firstmonday 3 (1998), http://uncommonculture.org/ojs/index.php/fm/article/view/570

JOHNSON/POST, 1996. David R. Johnson/David G. Post, Law and Borders – The Rise of Law in Cyberspace, Stanford Law Review 48 (1996), 1367–1402

JØRGENSEN, 2013. Rikke Frank Jørgensen, Framing the Net. The Internet and Human Rights, Cheltenham 2013

K

KAKU, 2011. Michio Kaku, Physics of the Future, New York 2011.

KAUFMANN, 2011. Christine Kaufmann, International Law in Recession – The Role of International Law when Crisis Hits: Food, Finance and Climate Change, in: ULRICH FASTENRATH/RUDOLF GEIGER/DANIEL-ERASMUS KHAN/ANDREAS PAULUS/SABINE V. SCHORLEMER/CHRISTOPH VEDDER (eds.), From Bilateralism to Community Interest, Essays in Honour of Judge Bruno Simma, New York/Oxford 2011, 1189–1206

KAUL/GRUNBERG/STERN, 1999. Inge Kaul/Isabelle Grunberg/Marc A. Stern (eds.), Global Public Goods: International Cooperation in the 21st Century, Oxford 1999

KELSEN, 1952. Hans Kelsen, Principles of International Law, New York 1952

KINGSBURY/CASINI, 2009. Benedict Kingsbury/Lorenzo Casini, Global Administrative Law Dimensions of International Organizations Law, International Organizations Law Review 6 (2009), 319–358

KLEINWÄCHTER, 2011. Wolfgang Kleinwächter, A new Generation of Regulatory Frameworks: The Multistakeholder Internet Governance Model, in: ROLF SETHE ET AL. (eds.), Kommunikation, Festschrift für Rolf H. Weber, Bern 2011, 559–580

KLIMBURG, 2013. Alexander Klimburg, The Internet Yalta, Center for a New American Security, http://www.cnas.org/theinternetyalta

KOH, 1997. Harold H. Koh, Why Do Nations Obey International Law?, Yale Law Journal 106 (1997), 2599–2659

KOOPS, 2006. Bert-Jaap Koops, Should ICT Regulation be Technology-Neutral?, in: BERT-JAAP KOOPS ET AL. (eds.), Starting points for ICT regulation: Deconstructing prevalent policy one-liners, The Hague 2006, 77–108

KOSKENNIEMI, 2007. Martti Koskenniemi, The Fate of Public International Law: Between Techniques and Politics, The Modern Law Review 70 (2007), 1–30

KOSKENNIEMI, 2006. Martti Koskenniemi/International Law Commission, Fragmentation of International Law: Difficulties Arising from the Diversification and Expansion of International Law, UN Doc. A/CN.4/L.682 (April 13, 2006)

KOSKENNIEMI, 2005. Martti Koskenniemi, From Apology to Utopia: The Structure of International Legal Argument, Cambridge 2005

KROES, 2010. Neelie Kroes, How to get more interoperability in Europe, Address at the Open Forum Europe 2010 Summit: Openness at the heart of the EU Digital Agenda, Speech 10/300, Brussels 2010

KULESZA, 2012. Joanna Kulesza, International Internet Law, London/New York 2012

KULESZA/BALLESTE, 2013. Joanna Kulesza/Roy Balleste, Signs and Portents in Cyberspace: The Rise of Jus Internet as a New Order in International Law, Fordham Intellectual Property, Media & Entertainment Law Journal 23 (2013), 1311–1349

KURBALIJA, 2012. Jovan Kurbalija, Internet Governance, 5th ed., Geneva 2012

L

LANE, 2013. Jan-Erik Lane, On the Growth of Normativity in International Relations, Journal of Politics and Law 6 (2013), 15–23

LANIER, 2013. Jaron Lanier, Who owns the future?, London 2013

LA RUE, 2011. Frank La Rue, Report of the special rapporteur on the promotion and protection of the right to freedom of opinion and expression, Human Rights Council, Seventeenth Session, Agenda Item 3, A/HRC/17/27, May 2011, available at http://www2.ohchr.org/english/bodies/hrcouncil/docs/17session/A.HRC.17.27_en.pdf

LESSIG, 2008. Lawrence Lessig, Remix: making art and commerce thrive in the hybrid economy, London 2008

LESSIG, 2006. Lawrence Lessig, CODE Version 2.0, New York 2006

LESSIG, 2004. Lawrence Lessig, Free culture: how big media use technology and the law to lock down culture and control creativity, New York 2004

LESSIG, 2001. Lawrence Lessig, The Future of Ideas, New York 2001

LESSIG, 1999a. Lawrence Lessig, Code and Other Laws of Cyberspace, New York 1999

LESSIG, 1999b. Lawrence Lessig, The Law of the Horse: What Cyberlaw Might Teach, Harvard Review 113 (1999), 501–549

LIPTON, 2012. Jacqueline D. Lipton, Cyberlaw 2.0, in: SAM MULLER/STAVROS ZOURIDIS/MORLY FRISHMAN/LAURA KISTEMAKER (eds.), The Law of the Future and the Future of Law: Volume II, The Hague 2012, 141–149

LOCKE, 1689. John Locke, Two Treaties of Government, published anonymously, London 1689

LUHMANN, 1997. Niklas Luhmann, Die Gesellschaft der Gesellschaft, 2 Bde, Frankfurt 1997

LUHMANN, 1993. Niklas Luhmann, Das Recht der Gesellschaft, Frankfurt 1993

LUHMANN, 1990. Niklas Luhmann, Verfassung als evolutionäre Errungenschaft, Rechtshistorisches Journal 9 (1990), 176–220

LUHMANN, 1975. Niklas Luhmann, Legitimation durch Verfahren, 2. Aufl. Darmstadt/Neuwied 1975

M

MACKINNON, 2012. Rebecca MacKinnon, Consent of the Networked: The Worldwide Struggle for Internet Freedom, New York 2012

MAHLER, 2014. Tobias Mahler, A gTLD-right? Conceptual challenges in the expanding internet domain namespace, International Journal of Law and Information Technology 22 (2014), 27–48

MAIER-SCHÖNBERGER, 2008. Viktor Maier-Schönberger, Demystifying Lessig, Wisconsin Law Review 2008, 713–746

MAJOR, 2000. April Mara Major, Norm Origin and Development in Cyberspace: Models of Cybernorm Evolution, Washington University Law Quarterly 78 (2000), 59–111

MALCOLM, 2008. Jeremy Malcolm, Multi-Stakeholder Governance and the Internet Governance Forum, Perth 2008

MATHIASON, 2008. John Mathiason, Internet Governance: The new frontier of global institutions, London/New York 2009

MCLUHAN, 1962. Marshall McLuhan, The Gutenberg Galaxy: The Making of Typographic Man, Toronto 1962

MEHRA, 2011. Salil K. Mehra, Paradise is a walled garden? Trust, antitrust and user dynamism, George Mason Law Review 18 (2011), 889–952

MOROZOV, 2011. Evgeny Morozov, The Net Delusion: The Dark Side of Internet Freedom, New York 2011

MUELLER, 2010. Milton Mueller, Networks and States. The Global Politics of Internet Governance, Cambridge MA 2010

MUELLER, 2002. Milton Mueller, Ruling the Root: Internet Governance and the Taming of Cyberspace, Cambridge MA 2002

MURRAY, 2010. Andrew D. Murray, Nodes and Gravity in Virtual Space, Legisprudence 5 (2010), 195–221

MURRAY, 2007. Andrew D. Murray, The Regulation of Cyberspace: Control in the Online Environment, Milton Park 2007

MURRAY/SCOTT, 2002. Andrew D. Murray/Colin Scott, Controlling the New Media: Hybrid Responses to New Forms of Power, The Modern Law Review 65 (2002), 491–516

MUSIANI, 2013. Francesca Musiani, Nains sans géants, Architecture décentralisée et services Internet, Paris 2013

N

NADAKAVUKAREN, 2014. Krista Nadakavukaren, Rethinking Sources of International Law: as Politics, as Law and the Difference it Makes, Weblaw Jusletter of March 31, 2014

NEGROPONTE, 1995. Nicholas Negroponte, Being Digital, New York 1995

NORTH, 1990. Douglass C. North, Institutions, institutional change and economic performance, Cambridge 1990

NUNZIATO, 2000. Don C. Nunziato, Exit, Voice, and Values on the Net, Berkeley Technology Law Journal 15 (2000), 753–775

O

OGUS, 2004. Anthony Ian Ogus, Regulation: legal form and economic theory, Oxford 2004

OII-PAPER, 2014. Oxford Internet Institute (OII), Enhanced Cooperation in Governance, Forum Discussion Paper (written by SAMANTHA DICKINSON/WILLIAM H. DUTTON/ MARILIA MACIEL/DÉSIRÉE MILOSHEVIC/VLADIMIR RADUNOVIC), University of Oxford, 7 January 2014, available at http://papers.ssrn.com/sol3/papers.cfm?abstract_id=2376807

OST/VAN DE KERCHOVE, 2002. François Ost/Michel van de Kerchove, De la pyramide au réseau? Pour une théorie dialectique du droit, Bruxelles 2002

P

PALFREY/GASSER, 2012. John Palfrey/Urs Gasser, Interop: The Promise and Perils of Highly Interconnected Systems, New York 2012

PALFREY/GASSER, 2008. John Palfrey/Urs Gasser, Born digital: Understanding the first generation of digital natives, New York 2008

PAUWELYN, 2011. Joost Pauwelyn, The Rise and Challenges of "Infomal" International Law-Making in: SAM MÜLLER/STAVROS ZOURIDIS/MORLY FRISHMAN/LAURA KISTEMAKER (eds.), The Law of the Future and the Future of Law, Oslo 2011, 125–141

PETERS, 2006. Anne Peters, Compensatory Constitutionalism: The Function and Potential of Fundamental International Norms and Structures, Leiden Journal of International Law 19 (2006), 579–610

PETERSMANN, 2011. Ernst-Ulrich Petersmann, International Economic Law, "Public Reason" and Multilevel Governance of Independent Public Goods, Journal of International Economic Law 14 (2011), 397–411

PLATO, 1892. Plato, Phaedrus, in: BENJAMIN JOWETT (ed.), The dialogues of Plato, Oxford 1892

PLATO, 1942. Apology – Crito – Phaedo – Symposium – Republic: five great dialogues, ed. by LOUISE ROPES LOOMIS, New York 1942

POGGE, 1994. Thomas Pogge, Cosmopolitanism and Sovereignty, in: CHRIS BROWN (ed.), Political Restructuring in Europe: Ethical Perspectives, London 1994, 85–118

POLANSKI, 2007. Przemyslaw P. Polanski, Customary law of the internet: in the search for a supranational cyberspace law, The Hague 2007

POOL, 1984. Ithiel de Sola Pool, Technologies of Freedom, Cambridge MA 1984

POST, 2009. David G. Post, In Search of Jefferson's Moose: Notes on the State of Cyberspace, New York 2009

POSTMAN, 1993. Neil Postman, Technopoly: The surrender of culture to technology, New York 1993

Q

R

RAUSTIALA, 2002. Kal R. Raustiala, The Architecture of International Cooperation: Transgovernmental Networks and the Future of International Law, Virginia Journal of International Law 43 (2002), 1–92.

RAWLS, 1971. John Rawls, Theory of Justice, Cambridge 1971

RAZ, 2004. Joseph Raz, Incorporation by Law, Legal Theory 10 (2004), 1–17

RAZ, 1994. Joseph Raz, Ethics and the Public Domain, Oxford 1994

RAZ, 1986. Joseph Raz, The Morality of Freedom, Oxford 1986

REED, 2012. Chris Reed, Making Laws for Cyberspace, Oxford 2012

REED, 2010, Chris Reed, Online and Offline Equivalence: Aspiration and Achievement, International Journal of Law and Information Technology 18 (2010), 248–273

REIDENBERG, 1998. Joel R. Reidenberg, Lex Informatica: The Formulation of Information Policy Rules Through Technology, Texas Law Review 76 (1998), 553–593

ROUSSEAU, 1754/62. Jean-Jacques Rousseau, The Social Contract and Discourses by Jean-Jacques Rousseau, translated with an Introduction by GEORGE D. H. COLE, London/Toronto 1923, available at: http://olll.libertyfund.org

S

SAND, 2009. Inger Johanne Sand, Law in a Global Society of Differentiation and Change, in: GRALF-PETER CALLIES/ANDREAS FISCHER-LESCANO/DAN WIELSCH/PEER ZUMBANSEN (eds.), Soziologische Jurisprudenz, Festschrift für Gunther Teubner zum 65. Geburtstag, Berlin 2009, 871–886

SASSEN, 2008. Saskia Sassen, Territory, Authority, Rights: From Medieval to Global Assemblages, 2nd ed. Princeton 2008

SCHMIDT/COHEN, 2013. Eric Schmidt/Jared Cohen, The New Digital Age, London 2013

SENN, 2011. Myriam Senn, Non-State Regulatory Regimes. Understanding Institutional Transformation, Heidelberg et al. 2011

SHAFFER, 2010. Gregory Shaffer, Transnational Legal Process and State Change: Opportunities and Constraints, University of Minnesota Law School, Research Paper No.10 28, 2010

SHAPIRO, 1999. Andrew Shapiro, The Control Revolution, New York 1999

SHAPIRO, 1998. Andrew Shapiro, The Disappearance of Cyberspace and the Rise of Code, Seton Hall Constitutional Law Journal (1997–1998), 703–723

SIMMA, 1994. Bruno Simma, From bilateralism to community interest in international law, Receuil des Cours 250 (1994), VI, 221–384

SLAUGHTER, 2004. Anne-Marie Slaughter, A New World Order, Princeton/Oxford 2004

SLAUGHTER/ZARING, 2006. Anne-Marie Slaughter/David Zaring, Networking Goes International: An Update, Annual Review of Law and Social Science 2 (2006), 211–229

SOMMER, 2000. Joseph H. Sommer, Against Cyberlaw, Berkeley Technology Law Journal 15 (2000), 1145–1232

SUNSTEIN, 2006. Cass R. Sunstein: Infotopia, How Many Minds Produce Knowledge, Oxford 2006

SUSSKIND, 1996. Richard Susskind, The Future of Law, Oxford 1996

T

TAMBINI/LEONARDI/MARSDEN, 2008. Damian Tambini/Danilo Leonardi/Chris Marsden, Codifying Cyberspace: Communications self-regulation in the age of Internet convergence, London 2008

TAMM HALLSTRÖM/BOSTRÖM, 2010. Kristina Tamm Hallström/Magnus Boström, Transnational Multi-Stakeholder Standardization: Organizing Fragile Non-State Authority, Cheltenham/Northampton MA 2010

TEUBNER, 2012. Gunther Teubner, Constitutional Fragments: Societal Constitutionalism and Globalisation, Oxford 2012

TEUBNER, 1989. Gunther Teubner, Recht als autopoietisches System, Frankfurt 1989

THOMPSON, 2013. Marcelo Thompson, Evaluating Neutrality in the Information Age – On the Value of Persons and Access, Oxford (Bodleian) 2013

THOMPSON, 2011. Marcelo Thompson, In Search of Alterity: On Google, Neutrality, and Otherness, Tulane Journal of Technology and Intellectual Property 14 (2011), 137–190

TRACHTMAN, 2010. Joel P. Trachtman, The International Law of Financial Crisis: Spillovers, Subsidiarity, Fragmentation and Cooperation, Journal of International Economic Law 13 (2010) 719–742

U

UERPMANN-WITTZACK, 2010. Robert Uerpmann-Wittzack, Principles of International Internet Law, German Law Journal 11 (2010), 1245–1263

V

W

WATERS, 2009. Timothy William Waters, The Momentous Gravity of the State of Things Now Obtaining: Annoying Westphalian Objections to the Idea of Global Governance, Indiana Journal of Global Studies 16 (2009), 25–58

WAZ/WEISER, 2012. Joe Waz/Philip J. Weiser, Internet Governance: The Role of Multistakeholder Organizations, Journal of Telecommunications & High Technological Law 10 (2012), 331–350

WEBER, 2013. Rolf H. Weber, Visions of Political Power: Treaty Making and Multistakeholder Understanding, in: ROXANA RADU/JEAN-MARIE CHENOU/ROLF H. WEBER (eds.), The Evolution of Global Internet Governance, Principles in the Making, Zurich 2013, 95–113

WEBER, 2012a. Rolf H. Weber, Overcoming the Hard Law/Soft Law Dichotomy in Times of (Financial) Crises, Journal of Governance and Regulation 1 (2012), 8–14

WEBER, 2012b. Rolf H. Weber, Future Design of Cyberspace Law, Journal of Politics and Law 5 (2012), 1–14

WEBER, 2012c. Rolf H. Weber, How Does Privacy Change in the Age of the Internet?, in: CHRISTIAN FUCHS/KEES BOERSMA/ANDERS ALBRECHTSLUND/MARISOL SANDOVAL (eds.), Internet and Surveillance: The Challenges of Web 2.0 and Social Media, New York/London 2012, 253–273

WEBER, 2011a. Rolf H. Weber, Shift of legislative powers and multistakeholder governance, International Journal of Publics Law and Policy 1 (2011), 4–22

WEBER, 2011b. Rolf H. Weber, Accountability in the Internet of Things, Computer Law & Security Review 27 (2011), 133–138

WEBER, 2010a. Rolf H. Weber, New Sovereignty Concepts in the Age of Internet?, Journal of Internet Law 14 (2010), 12–20

WEBER, 2010b. Rolf H. Weber, New Rule-Making Elements for Financial Architecture's Reform, Journal of International Banking Law and Regulation 25 (2010), 512–521

WEBER. 2010c. Rolf H. Weber, Multilayered Governance in International Financial Regulation and Supervision, Journal of International Economic Law 13 (2010), 683–704

WEBER, 2009. Rolf H. Weber, Shaping Internet Governance: Regulatory Challenges, Zürich 2009

WEBER, 2003. Rolf H. Weber, Towards a Legal Framework for the Information Society, Zürich 2003

WEBER, 2002. Rolf H. Weber, Regulatory Models for the Online World, Zürich 2002

WEBER, 1986. Rolf H. Weber, Wirtschaftsregulierung in wettbewerbspolitischen Ausnahmebereichen, Baden-Baden 1986

WEBER/GUNNARSON, 2012. Rolf H. Weber/ R. Shawn Gunnarson, A Constitutional Solution for Internet Governance, The Columbia Science and Technology Law Review XIV (2012), 1–71

WEBER/MENOUD, 2008. Rolf H. Weber/Valérie Menoud, The Information Society and the Digital Divide. Legal Strategies to Finance Global Access, Zürich 2008

WEBER/WEBER, 2009. Rolf H. Weber/Romana Weber, Social Contract for the Internet Community? Historical and Philosophical Theories as Basis for the Inclusion of Civil Society in Internet Governance?, SCRIPT-ed 6 (2009), 90–105

WEISER, 2009. Philip J. Weiser, The Future of Internet Regulation, University of California, Davis 43 (2009), 529–590

WEISS/THAKUR, 2006. Thomas G. Weiss/Ramesh Thakur, The UN and Global Governance: An Idea and Its Prospects, Bloomington 2006

WEITZENBOECK, 2014. Emily M. Weitzenboëck, Hybrid net: the regulatory framework of ICANN and the DNS, International Journal of Law and Information Technology 22 (2014), 49–73

WINCHESTER, 2009. N. Brian Winchester, Emerging Global Environmental Governance, Indiana Journal of Global Legal Studies 16 (2009), 7–23

WOUTERS/RAMOPOULOS, 2012. Jan Wouters/Thomas Ramopoulos, The G20 and Global Economic Governance: Lessons from Multilevel European Governance?, Journal of International Economic Law 15 (2012), 751–775

WU, 1997. Timothy S. Wu, Cyberspace Sovereignty? The Internet and the International System, Harvard Journal of Law & Technology 10 (1997), 647–666

X

Y

YU, 2002. Peter K. Yu, Bridging the Digital Divide: Equality in the Information Age, Cardozo Arts & Entertainment Law Journal 20 (2002), 1–52

Z

ZITTRAIN, 2008. Jonathan Zittrain, The Regulation of the Internet and How to Stop It, New York 2008

ZITTRAIN, 2006. The generative Internet, Harvard Law Review 119 (2006), 1974–2014

ZITTRAIN, 2000. Jonathan Zittrain, What the Publisher can Teach the Patient: Intellectual Property and Privacy in an Era of Trusted Privication, Stanford Law Review 52 (2000), 1201–1

Abbreviations

ACTA	Anti-Counterfeiting Trade Agreement
APC	Association for Progressive Communications
APEC	Asia-Pacific Economic Cooperation
ARPANET	Advanced Research Projects Agency Network
BIT	Binary Digit
CA	Certificate Authority
ccTLD	Country Code Top-Level Domain
CERT	Computer Emergency Response Team
CESCR	Committee on Social, Economic and Cultural Rights
CIR	Critical Internet Resource
COM	(European) Commission Document
CSIRT	Computer Security Incident Response Team
DBMS	Database Management System
DDoS	Distributed Denial of Service
DNS	Domain Name System
DNSSEC	Domain Name System Security Extensions
Doc.	Document
DoC	Department of Commerce (United States)
DPI	Deep Packet Inspection
DRM	Digital Rights Management
DSL	Digital Subscriber Line
ed./eds.	Editor/editors
EFF	Electronic Frontier Foundation
e.g.	For example
ETNO	European Telecommunications Network Operators' Association
EU	European Union
EuroDig	European Dialogue on Internet Governance
FCC	Federal Communications Commission
Fn.	Footnote
FTP	File Transfer Protocol
GATS	General Agreement on Trade in Services
GATT	General Agreement on Tariffs and Trade
GCF	Global Cyberspace Framework
GNI	Global Network Initiative
gTLD	Generic Top-Level Domain
HTML	Hypertext Markup Language
HTTP	Hypertext Transfer Protocol
IAB	Internet Architecture Board
IANA	Internet Assigned Numbers Authority
ICANN	Internet Corporation for Assigned Names and Numbers
ICC	International Chamber of Commerce
ICCPR	International Covenant on Civil and Political Rights

ICESCR	International Covenant on Economic, Social, and Cultural Rights
ICJS	Statue of the International Court of Justice
ICT	Information and Communication Technologies
i.e.	That is ("id est" in Latin)
IEEE	Institute of Electrical and Electronics Engineers
IESG	Internet Engineering Steering Group
IETF	Internet Engineering Task Force
IGF	Internet Governance Forum
IGO	Inter-Governmental Organization
IP	Internet Protocol
IPR	Intellectual Property Rights
IPsec	Internet Protocol Security
IPv4	Internet Protocol Version 4
IPv6	Internet Protocol Version 6
IOSCO	International Organization of Securities Commissions
ISO	International Organization for Standardization
ISOC	Internet Society
ISP	Internet Service Provider
IT	Information Technology
ITR	International Telecommunication Regulations
ITU	International Telecommunication Union
IXP	Internet Exchange Point
JPEG	Joint Photographic Experts Group
LAN	Local Area Network
LIR	Local Internet Registries
MA	Massachusetts
MPEG	Motion Pictures Expert Group
NGO	Nongovernmental Organization
NIR	National Internet Registries
No.	Number
NSI	Network Solution Inc.
NTIA	National Telecommunications and Information Administration
OECD	Organization for Economic Cooperation and Development
OSI	Open Systems Interconnection
p./pp.	Page/pages
P2P	Peer-to-Peer
P3P	Platform for Privacy Preferences
Para./paras.	Paragraph/paragraphs
PET	Privacy Enhancing Technologies
QoS	Quality of Service
RFC	Request for Comments
RFID	Radio-Frequency Identification
RIPE NCC	Réseaux IP Européens-Network Coordination Centre
RIR	Regional Internet Registries
SMTP	Simple Mail Transfer Protocol

SNA	Systems Network Architecture
TBT	Technical Barriers to Trade
TCP	Transmission Control Protocol
TCP/IP	Transmission Control Protocol/Internet Protocol
TLD	Top-Level Domain
TLS	Transport Layer Security
TRIPS	Trade Related Aspects of Intellectual Property Rights
TTP	Trusted Third Party
UDHR	Universal Declaration of Human Rights
UDRP	Uniform Domain-Name Dispute-Resolution Policy
UN	United Nations
UNCITRAL	United Nations Commission on International Trade Law
UNESCO	United Nations Educational, Scientific and Cultural Organizations
UNTS	United Nations Treaty Series
URL	Uniform Resource Locator
US	United States
VoIP	Voice over Internet Protocol
Vol.	Volume
W3C	World Wide Web Consortium
WCIT	World Conference on International Telecommunications
WGEC	Working Group on Enhanced Cooperation
WGIG	Working Group on Internet Governance
WIPO	World Intellectual Property Organization
WSIS	World Summit on the Information Society
WTO	World Trade Organization
WWW	World Wide Web

I. Introduction

A. Objectives of the book

In many respects cyberspace has created a new world. The online phenomena encompass social, cultural, economic, and legal facets. Notwithstanding intensive discussions about the foundations and the guiding principles of a global cyberspace framework the theoretical grounds still seem partly shaky.

Therefore, this book attempts to address the problems caused by the existing normative order of cyberspace, i.e. the traditional legal instruments, and developed for the "real" world when applied to the online world, thereby being exposed to the challenges of coping with fast growing information technologies. In fact, the existing framework composed of national laws and a few multilateral treaties does not offer appropriate "tools" for the prevailing relations in cyberspace. A major problem for overcoming the present tensions in "using" the available legal norms in cyberspace consists in the fact that even new theoretical approaches do not sufficiently try to embed technological developments into the international "system".[1]

The concept of this book consists in the assessment of the viability of different legal concepts for the rule-making processes in cyberspace. Indeed, legal concepts have a central function for the communication of legal rules.[2] The timing for such a normative study now appears to be appropriate since a good amount of experience is available about past rule-making attempts. Brown/Marsden are distinguishing three periods, namely as follows:[3] The first decade (1993–2002) encompasses the proclamations of the so-called cyberlibertarians[4], the second decade (2003–2012) reflects the re-regulatory phase following the dot-com bust and the States' security imperatives driven by the US 9/11 and the European follow-up attacks, and the third decade (since 2013) is based on new sophisticated regulatory perspectives.[5]

This book is structured as follows: Chapter II looks at the confrontation of traditional legal concepts with the ongoing globalization and the challenges caused thereby; in particular, the territoriality principle as consequence of the understanding of States as sovereign bodies and the escape movement to soft law are

1 See WEBER, 2012b, 2.
2 MAHLER, 2014, 32.
3 BROWN/MARSDEN, 2013, ix/x.
4 See below II.B.2.
5 BROWN/MARSDEN, 2013, xix, rely on a code solution regime supporting competition and efficiency, which does not fully coincide with the approach of this study.

Co-Publication with Schulthess Juristische Medien AG

Published by Springer-Verlag GmbH Berlin Heidelberg 2015
R.H. Weber, *Realizing a New Global Cyberspace Framework*,
DOI 10.1007/978-3-662-44677-5_1

discussed. Chapter III addresses the specific challenges for regulatory approaches in cyberspace; traditional theories are not apt to be applied to the online world since social/environmental developments need to be taken into account to a greater degree. Chapter IV discusses new rule-making approaches in cyberspace, based on philosophical and sociological concepts; noteworthy theories are the code-based regulation, the regulation through formalized standards and networks, different forms of informal law-making (incl. the Internet-ional customary law) and the regulation based on normative expectations. The final Chapter V attempts to develop a "Global Cyberspace Framework" (GCF) by outlining some basic guiding principles and parameters to be observed in online rule-making processes.

The core idea of the "Global Cyberspace Framework" lies in the objective of having a basic legal structure as theoretical foundation of cyberspace regulation; such structure should accommodate the technological and social environment in the online world and provide for rule-making standards, which to a great extent reflect the perceptions of a global civil society.

B. Notion and meaning of cyberspace

Cyberspace is based on new technologies developed during the last fifty years. The fact that technology affects society is not a novelty only shown by the recent vast expansion of the Internet. Already more than twenty years ago, Postman introduced his famous book "Technopoly"[6] with a reference to Plato who in his work referred "Phaedrus" to Thamus, King of Egypt, having assessed the new technology of writing as means to entrust people to external characters causing them to learn nothing and forget of themselves.[7]

As mentioned, in many respects cyberspace has created a new world, however, the "virtual world will not overtake or overhaul the existing world order, but it will complicate almost every behavior".[8] This clear assessment can be seen as acknowledgment of the perception that the existing body of law will survive but needs to be adapted and complemented by new rules.

The term "cyberspace", first used by Gibson in a specific, slightly different way[9], gained substantial importance and became common in everyday and legal lan-

6 Postman, 1993.

7 Plato, Phaedrus, ca. 370 BC.

8 Schmidt/Cohen, 2013, 255.

9 Gibson, 1984, 51; for further details on Gibson's "Neuromancer" see Sherry Turkle, Life on the Screen – Identity in the Age of Internet, London 1995, 42 et seq.

guage within a few years. Correspondingly, the question arose whether cyberspace would be a place governed by its own (new) laws.[10]

Gibson, as the originator of the term "cyberspace", did not view this space as an autonomous place, but as a "consensual hallucination" in this world.[11] Etymologically, cyberspace is derived from cybernetics, the science of communication and control theory, particularly the study of automatic control systems.[12] Considering that the ancient Greek word "Kybernetes" means steersman (of a ship) or governor, there is no linguistic justification for interpreting "cyberspace" as a place without governance.[13]

In general terms, cyberspace can be defined as the invisible, intangible world of electronic information and processes stored at multiple interconnected sites with controlled access and manifold possibilities for interaction.[14] Cyberspace thus includes the interaction of people, businesses and other entities over computer networks.[15] Consequently, the new phenomena of cyberspace cannot be reduced to the control of communication channels. The digital revolution that is influencing the whole "organization" of informational relationships requires policymakers to take into account many particularities of the online regimes (including a minimal legal framework).[16]

C. Internet governance as part of cyberspace regulation

An important discussion field within the cyberspace framework concerns Internet governance; according to a well-known description, Internet governance "is the simplest, most direct, and inclusive label for the ongoing set of disputes and deliberations over how the Internet is coordinated, managed, and shaped to reflect policies".[17] In other words, Internet governance encompasses (i) the design and administration of the technologies necessary to keep the Internet operational as well as (ii) the enactment of substantive policies around these technologies.[18]

10 Weber, 2002, 26/27.
11 Gibson, 1984, 51.
12 Weber, 2002, 27; for more details see Norbert Wiener, Cybernetics and Society, New York 1950.
13 Weber, 2002, 27.
14 Grewlich, 1999, 1.
15 Grewlich, 1999, 19.
16 See also Weber, 2002, 29.
17 Mueller, 2010, 9.
18 DeNardis, 2014, 6.

Looking from a conceptual perspective (not mainly addressing the relations between infrastructure and institutions[19]) five major features of global Internet governance can be distinguished:[20]

- Arrangements of technical architecture as an allocation of power based on large-scale technological systems;
- Internet governance infrastructure as a proxy for content control, particularly by enabling the infrastructure intermediaries to exercise content control in the context of larger global vicissitudes of political and economic power;
- Privatization of Internet governance by having manifold actors involved in an exercise in bricolage (often called multistakeholderism);
- Internet control points as sites of global conflict over competing values including aspects of the problem whose voices are allowed to participate and whose voices are able to participate in light of cultural barriers of social norms, access, and language.
- Regional initiatives addressing geopolitical strategies versus collective action problems as influencing factors of Internet globalization.

As the five features show, Internet governance, which originally mainly addressed technical standardization and domain name allocation in the Internet, is now also confronted with the exercise of power in the enactment of certain public interest goals related to the use of the Internet; in other words, due to the increasing importance of online activities in daily life, the Internet governance's scope was extended over the last decade. A particular issue concerns the problem of the appropriate power allocation between sovereign States and non-territorial and privatized regimes.[21] In this context, Internet governance has to tackle similar issues as the broader concept of cyberspace regulation.

As mentioned, this book looks at the wider perspective of a cyberspace framework, particularly at its normative foundations, and does not limit the discussions to the specific Internet governance topics. This focus is justified since extensive literature is available on Internet governance describing the fifteen years' debate about Internet policies.[22]

---

19 To infrastructure and institutions in more detail see Bygrave/Michaelsen, 2009, 92 et seq.

20 DeNardis, 2014, 7–18.

21 DeNardis, 2014, 23; see also Eric Brousseau/Meryem Marzouki, Internet governance: old issues, new framings, uncertain implications, in: Brousseau/Marzouki/Méadel, 2012, 368, 371–384.

22 For a detailed overview see Chenou/Radu, 2013, 3–11; Kurbalija, 2012, 31 et seq.; see also Wolfgang Kleinwächter, Internet Governance Outlook 2014: Good News, Bad News, No News?, available at http://www.circleid.com/posts/20131231_internet_governance_outlook_2014_good_news_bad_news_no_news/.

II. Confrontation of traditional legal concepts with globalization

A. Development of international public law concepts

For decades, scholars have attempted to define and describe international public law as well as establish its key characteristics. However, the growing globalization, the increasing power of non-state organizations and the expanded existence of epistemic and fragmented communities make this task more and more difficult.[23] After considering the historical developments from the Roman law to the problems caused by the Westphalian sovereignty concept the challenges to which the present legal framework is exposed must be addressed.

1. Insights from Roman law

Already Roman law was confronted with the situation that its genuine scope implemented for a restricted geographical area had to be extended to new regions and particularly to people outside the Roman society. In order to overcome the respective difficulties, Roman law developed different categories of legal regimes.

a) Res nullius and res communis

The law of international spaces such as cyberspace does have some roots in the legal system of Roman law, namely:[24]

- *Res nullius* applies in respect of objects without an owner; as a result, each State may take over the territory if requirements traditionally imposed on State independence are met. In line with this Roman law approach based on the concept of legal "attribution", John Locke developed the notion of natural law.[25]
- *Res communis* means that objects are freely available in the public domain and do not belong to a specific person; consequently, everybody has access to the respective available "objects", for example access to shipping on the high sea.

Already prior to the Internet age, States debated the question whether, for example, the international water space, Antarctica, or the moon and the celestial bodies

23 See below II.B.

24 This section follows KULESZA, 2012, 20.

25 LOCKE, 1689, Book II, Chapter II: Of the State of Nature.

Co-Publication with Schulthess Juristische Medien AG

Published by Springer-Verlag GmbH Berlin Heidelberg 2015
R.H. Weber, *Realizing a New Global Cyberspace Framework*,
DOI 10.1007/978-3-662-44677-5_2

would have to be considered as *res nullius* or *res communis*.[26] More and more voices are of the opinion that international resources cannot be subject to State sovereign ownership; less developed countries would identify such an ownership approach with the imperial dominance of colonial powers.[27] As a result, the approach of *res communis* corresponds to the concept of common heritage of mankind and is now also reflected in such documents as the Convention on the Law of the Sea or the Treaty on Principles governing the Activities of States in the Exploration and Use of Outer Space, including the Moon and other Celestial Bodies.[28]

b) Jus naturale and jus gentium

The two normative systems of Roman law consisted in the *jus naturale* (composed of rules and values recognized throughout all communities) and religious law. These normative systems were the foundations of the *jus gentium,* which was initially operated as common custom and eventually evolved into binding customary law. The legal framework referred to values common to the whole humanity.[29] In a broader sense the *jus gentium* can be understood as a common good for the international legal order based on moral and political considerations.[30]

The principles of *jus gentium* were based on two pillars, namely trust (*fides*) and equity (*aequitas*); its content was to reflect the features of human nature as well as the human sense of justice and fairness as the basic common grounds for human interactions among and between individuals from diverse provinces of the Roman Empire.[31] The *jus gentium* served as a set of basic references settling disputes arising out of such interactions.[32]

The term *jus gentium* was used in Roman law to describe customary regulations on relations between foreigners (non-citizens) and Roman citizens. The general character of its norms and its versatile application established its authority among various cultures and social systems.[33] Therefore, the *jus gentium* principle builds an early feature of public international law, or – in other words – public international law originated from *jus gentium* institutions.[34]

---

26 See also below II.B.3.

27 Kulesza, 2012, 20.

28 For more details see below II.B.3.

29 Kulesza, 2012, 151.

30 See Juliane Kokott/Frank Hoffmeister, International Public Order, in: Max Planck Encyclopedia of Public International Law, Heidelberg/Oxford 2013, para. 2.

31 Kulesza, 2012, 151.

32 Kulesza/Balleste, 2013, 1338.

33 See also Kulesza/Balleste, 2013, 1338 with further references.

34 For further details to the *jus gentium* see Joanna Kulesza, Jus Internet – New Legal Regime for Cyberspace, in: Erich Schweighofer/Franz Kummer/Walter Hötzendorfer

In identifying ethical standards common to all communities the objective should be to arrive at a consensus satisfying all concerned individuals and entities.[35] In light of this objective, the *jus gentium* can be seen as model for regulating the heterogeneous cyberspace, based on the identification of principles recognized as common to all the governed.[36]

2. Nation States: sovereignty principle

The sovereignty notion is a basic principle of international public law as interpreted by the States. The principle assumes that every State has the right to monopolize certain exercises of power in view of its territory and citizens.[37]

a) Concept of Westphalian Peace Treaty

(i) The traditional concept of sovereignty goes back to its theoretical "invention" by Jean Bodin (1576) and particularly to its consolidation as reality in the Westphalian Peace Treaty of 1648. The approach chosen more than 350 years ago paved the way for later perceptions of international regulations. Usually, sovereignty is now understood as a concept composed of four principles,[38] namely (i) the power monopoly principle enabling each State to exclusively exercise certain powers, (ii) the equality of nations principle, meaning, for example, the realization of the (partly contested) "one nation, one vote" approach related to the decision-making processes in international institutions, (iii) the immunity principle attributing certain privileges to officials acting in another State, and (iv) the right against interference or intervention by any foreign (or international) power in domestic affairs.[39]

The scope of this Westphalian notion of sovereignty has been limited by the Charter of the United Nations restricting the traditional concept by prohibiting the use of force as formal element of sovereignty and excluding some substantial areas from the "domain reservé" (for example human rights). Additionally, under cer-

(eds.), Transformation juristischer Sprachen, IRIS 2012, Wien 2012, 461, 465/66.

35 Kulesza, 2012, 151.

36 Kulesza/Balleste, 2013, 1338/39.

37 Article 2 of the Charter of the United Nations (June 26, 1945); for a general overview to the meaning of sovereignty see Koskenniemi, 2005, 240–245 and 576–583.

38 Jackson, 2003, 782.

39 Weber, 2010a, 12; to the principles of the Westphalian peace regime see also Leo Gross, The Piece of Westphalia, 1648–1948, American Journal of International Law 42 (1948), 20, 21/22, 40; for a detailed overview of the sovereignty discussions in the traditional legal theory see Koskenniemi, 2005, 226–238.

tain circumstances individuals and international organizations were acknowledged as partial subjects of international law.[40]

Another (hereinafter less relevant) use of the term "sovereignty" is applied in relation to the distinction of powers in a State: In this context sovereignty can be understood in the sense that organized power must be subservient to the power of individual citizens[41], or parliamentary sovereignty ought to be subservient to the sovereignty of people, respectively.[42]

(ii) For obvious practical reasons, legal doctrine has discredited the traditional sovereignty notion in many ways during the last few years.[43] The main reason has to be seen in the fact that the need for cross-border and international cooperation in a globalized world is growing. In particular, sovereign borders are becoming less significant in light of global communication possibilities that lower barriers to social and commercial intercourse,[44] meaning that the logic of geographically defined and confined legal rules and systems, based on the logic of territoriality, is losing importance or is eroding, respectively.[45] Consequently, the competence of States to regulate cross-border issues must be redefined.

For the last twenty years, a shift toward a "post-Westphalian mode of frame-setting" has been discussed, namely one that generates and emanates from the emergence of "other structures, both extra- and non-territorial".[46] This type of frame-setting should bear in mind that internationalization is a political concept but globalization is a sociological concept and should have an impact on the efforts to achieve socio-economic equity, to combat all forms of injustice, and to sustain democratic ideals and probity in real life.[47]

(iii) The legal challenges are associated with some weaknesses of international politics, which are (at least partly) responsible for the disarray in global society. Some scholars mention three phenomena: (i) In view of globalization, States can become partly de-constitutionalized by the transfer of governmental functions either to the transnational level or to non-state actors; (ii) the extraterritorial effects of certain national legislations create a law without sufficient democratic

40 See Preamble of the Charter of the United Nations (June 26, 1945).

41 BRAITHWAITE/DRAHOS, 2000, 604.

42 BRAITHWAITE/DRAHOS, 2000, 606.

43 See for example JACKSON, 2003, 785/86; KOSKENNIEMI, 2005, 225/26 using terms such as "ambiguity" and "paradox".

44 CHIK, 2010, 7.

45 WEBER, 2010a, 12; BERMAN, 2007, 1774/75; to the dilemma of interpretation see also KOSKENNIEMI, 2005, 246–254.

46 FRASER, 2005, 82 and 83.

47 FRANKLIN, 2013, 45.

legitimation; (iii) a democratic mandate for transnational governance is widely missing.[48]

Even if these developments merit particular attention it should not be underestimated that the concept of sovereignty (and the contrasting concept of global constitutionalism) is deeply interwoven into the fabric of international law, and to abandon the concept of sovereignty wholesale requires very serious thoughts about the substitute that could efficiently fill the gaps left by its absence.[49] Furthermore, valid aspects raised in the sovereignty debates may be analyzed for their future impact on policy.[50] This assessment, however, does not mean that a "cybered Westphalian age"[51] could remediate the threats in the Internet. Moreover, such a concept could lead to a "fenced cyberspace" and potentially do more harm than good.[52] In principle, no territorially-based regime can successfully be applied to the a-territorial cyberspace.[53] Therefore, doubts relating to the recognition of a "digital territory" as an element of a State's national territory are justified.[54]

According to the Westphalian concept sovereign State interests rather than religious or personal motives have been the guiding principle of international relations; in order to allow for peaceful coexistence, the States seemed to be the ideal "protectors".[55] Social/environmental changes are questioning this perception in the 21st century; in fact, no frontier lasts forever, and no freely occupied global commons extend endlessly when human societies are involved.[56] Even if this statement underestimates the value of the "global commons" recognized by certain communities and protected for the enjoyment of the concerned individuals,[57] it reflects the need for new laws promoting greater opportunities for humanity and supporting the development of global public commons.

48 See TEUBNER, 2012, 5; PETERS, 2006, 591.

49 JACKSON, 2003, 790.

50 WEBER, 2010a, 12.

51 See DEMCHAK/DOMBROWSKI, 2011, 36–39.

52 KULESZA/BALLESTE, 2013, 1313/14, 1322/23 and 1332; see also DEMCHAK/DOMBROWSKI, 2011, 32–35 to the "fencing" in light of cybercrime.

53 JOHNSON/POST, 1996, 1367–1376; see also BRAITHWAITE/DRAHOS, 2000, 511/12 and 602–611.

54 KULESZA/BALLESTE, 2013, 1316.

55 See JULIANE KOKOTT, States, Sovereign Equality, in: Max Planck Encyclopedia of Public International Law, Heiderlberg/Oxford 2013, para. 6; KULESZA/BALLESTE, 2013, 1317/18.

56 DEMCHAK/DOMBROWSKI, 2011, 32.

57 See also KULESZA/BALLESTE, 2013, 1320/21.

b) Challenges of borderless cyberspace

(i) The limitation of the traditional sovereignty concept is particularly obvious in the online world. For example, as far as the changes in the Internet world are concerned, intermediaries have a strong power to shape norms, even legal norms, for example, towards a stake in Internet-nation building, giving such types of customary norms sufficient legitimacy.[58] In 1999, the then UN-Secretary General Kofi Annan referred to the fact that a global era would require global engagement and that necessary actions in favor of humanity could not embark on such recourse of action in expectation of sovereignty.[59]

Moreover, experience has shown that national legislation cannot appropriately cope with the challenges posed by the globalized cyberspace.[60] Several disadvantages, apart from the weakness of the sovereignty principle in the online world[61], have been identified in legal doctrine:[62] State legislators often do not have sufficient "technical" knowledge for the preparation and enactment of the respective legal provisions, governmental laws might not be accepted by market participants if the practical needs are not sufficiently taken into account, and the democratic process is long and cumbersome in many countries. Furthermore, the effect of national rules must be measured in view of the political and legal externalities caused by them in the online world.[63] Externalities, which have already been recognized in connection with satellite technology when people talked about "information wars"[64], can also occur as a result of the threat that a powerful country would have an inappropriate influence on the online world.[65]

(ii) Therefore, debates about sovereignty must address (alternative) values involved in a power allocation analysis that could become a new social construct for civil society. In this context, the discussion about global public goods and global commons merits special attention.[66] The issues surrounding public goods have long been the focus of economic and legal theories, which endeavored to identify and classify public goods as well as to define the role of the State in allocating resources to their production and distribution (allocation of power, competence

58 Wu, 1997, 666.

59 Kofi Annan, quoted in Jackson, 2003, 787.

60 See also Brown/Marsden, 2013, 2 and 16.

61 See below II.B.1.

62 Weber, 2002, 59.

63 See also Gibbons, 1997, 483; Weber, 2002, 61.

64 See Anne W. Branscomb, Global Governance of Global Networks: A Survey of Transborder Data Flow in Transition, Vanderbilt Law Review 36 (1983), 985, 987/88.

65 Biegel, 2001, 125/26 refers to the widely discussed risk of „American hegemony" and „Yankee imperialism".

66 Weber/Menoud, 2008, 21–27; see also Brown/Marsden, 2013, xv.

and responsibility).[67] Nevertheless, a clear definition does not yet exist; public goods are manifold and framing them with an abstract notion might lead to undue limitations.[68]

Public goods can either be constituted by law or contribute to general benefits independently from any norm. They ideally have two qualities stemming from their public nature:[69] At least in principle, everybody should be in a position to derive benefits from the provision of such goods, i.e. they are non-rivalrous in consumption and non-excludable. Public goods are usually classified according to different criteria:[70] (i) For instance, there are norm-dependent and norm-independent as well as pure and impure global public goods. (ii) They can also be categorized according to their scope of effect, being local, national, regional, and global.

Ideally, global public goods are those that benefit humanity as a whole, meaning that they have to fulfill three criteria (a geographical, a social-economic, and a generational criterion).[71] Consequently, global public goods should provide benefits to (i) more than one group of countries or geographic regions, to (ii) a broad spectrum of the global population, crossing population segments, and to (iii) the present generations without jeopardizing the ability of future generations to meet their own needs.

The concept of "communality" also lies in the core of concepts such as *jus cogens*, norms *erga omnes*, or "public interest".[72] Communality calls for a community-related approach to rule-making, i.e. the various online communities should have the right and possibility to actively participate in open discourses and decision-making processes.[73]

(iii) As a result, sovereignty needs to be understood as an approach containing cooperative elements and entailing an understanding of meaningful coordination of different levels of governance, from local to global. A pluralism-based reconstruction of the actual relations among sovereign States could give rise to a reflex-

---

67 For a general overview see KAUL/GRUNBERG/STERN, 1999, particularly p. xxiii to the history and the economic literature.

68 The first rigorous definition was provided by PAUL A SAMUELSON, The Pure Theory of Public Expenditure, Review of Economics and Statistics 36 (1954), 387, 389.

69 See PETER DRAHOS, The Regulation of Public Goods, Journal of International Economic Law 7 (2004), 321.

70 WEBER/MENOUD, 2008, 24.

71 KAUL/GRUNBERG/STERN, 1999, 10–12.

72 WEBER, 2010a, 13.

73 See also below V.C.3.

ive concept of cooperation.[74] In view of these considerations related to a new globalized concept of sovereignty, several questions arise:[75]

- Do States have a shared responsibility based on shared sovereignty to promote and encourage the development of policies that observe human rights?
- Do States have a shared responsibility based on shared sovereignty to ensure a fair and equitable allocation of resources?
- Do States have a shared responsibility based on shared sovereignty to refrain from influencing the transnational policies of trans-boundary information flows?

There are no easy and quick answers to these questions; the ongoing debate about sovereignty, however, should reflect the mentioned problematic elements, particularly in connection with the territoriality principle, and better reflect polycentric regulatory concepts.

(iv) Theoretically, the weaknesses of national legislation based on the sovereignty principle could be overcome by a "world government" or by a compact network of international agreements. A world government (as consequence of the demise of national sovereignty) becoming the solution to the inevitable globalization of phenomena (such as cyberspace) is a utopianism.[76]

International agreements – whether bilateral or multilateral in nature – have a contractual character since the legally binding relations are entered into voluntarily ("*pacta sunt servanda*"). Sovereign States have the authority to account for the mandatory force of agreements, and such agreements are legally binding because they have been concluded by sovereign States consenting to be bound.[77] However, the difficulties of establishing and actually implementing international agreements are substantial; recent experience, for instance the WCIT 2012 in Dubai, has shown that the willingness of States to agree to joint solutions is not always very high. Nevertheless, in cyberspace a transnational approach is inevitable; national rules, based on sovereign thinking, will not overcome pending problems nor offer viable solutions.[78]

---

74 For more details see Besson, 2005, 534/35.

75 Weber, 2010a, 16; to the aspect of interstate cooperation see also Uerpmann-Wittzack, 2011, 1259/60.

76 Braithwaite/Drahos, 2000, 607.

77 Weber, 2002, 64 with further references.

78 Weber, 2002, 77.

B. Present international public law in transition

Some challenges for the current international public law framework have already been mentioned and are mainly related to the concept of sovereignty. Other problems caused by the new cyberspace structures also merit further elaboration. In fact, international public law appears to be in a transitional stage making it necessary to reconsider its fundamental principles.

1. Relativization of territoriality principle

a) Scope of territoriality principle

From a legal perspective, the sovereign State is an original entity; its legal and international subjectivity originates from the fact of its sole existence.[79] The most general definition describes the sovereign State as a conglomerate of three features, namely territory, operation and authority.[80]

This concept encompasses the right to exercise jurisdiction in respects of a territorial, a personal and an effective scope. The respective principles are:[81]

- the territoriality principle (the principle of territorial jurisdiction);
- the effects principle (the principle of effective jurisdiction);
- the personality principle (the principle of personal jurisdiction);
- the protective principle (the principle of protective jurisdiction).

Hereinafter, the territoriality principle, i.e. any activity of a State related to prescribing laws within its territory and enforcing them internally, will be shortly analyzed. The issues of the applicable law and the jurisdiction are indeed causing major problems in the "border-less" cyberspace.

b) Applicable law

As far as the legal environment is concerned, the sovereignty principle enables a State to establish the norms necessary for the nation-wide organization of civil society or a social sphere (in a material dimension) as well as to safeguard the application of the relevant norms and the execution of jurisdiction (in a formal dimension).[82] Thereby, law does not evolve completely unrelated to the given so-

79 Kelsen, 1952, 207 et seq.
80 Kulesza, 2012, 1.
81 Kulesza, 2012, 6.
82 Kelsen, 1952, 191 et seq.

cial environment; a two-way influence between civil society and rule-making bodies is an obvious characteristic of the ongoing developments.[83] Generally, the governed person might feel more bound by a law if the rule-maker is nearby rather than remote;[84] the understanding of responsiveness corresponds to the territorial application range of norms.[85]

As mentioned, this inter-relation between rule-maker and governed is based on the given understanding of the involved persons/entities. Depending on their appreciation a strictly nation-centered approach or a more open perspective is chosen. If the rule-making activity mainly translates national values, cross-border harmonization of norms will not be achieved. However, physical location is usually not relevant in cyberspace, i.e. traditional geographical boundaries are losing importance.[86] As a consequence, in case of differing national laws, the assessment of an international issue can yield completely deviating results for some countries with a disparate legal framework, which in the global cyberspace is an undesirable solution.

Another aspect concerns the decision as to which (national) law is applicable. In case of cross-border relations the so-called "conflict of law" rules are relevant for assessing the question whether national or foreign law is to be applied in a given dispute. The respective rules are pursuing the objective of making the "closest" law applicable in a concrete situation; often this is the law of the party offering a typical performance under a contract or the law of the country, where the effect of a harmful action occurs.

A specific issue is the extraterritoriality effect ("spillover effect") which can be subject to two strategies of national legislators: A rule-making authority interested in "exporting" national law might have the intention of making its law applicable abroad, at least if a (certain) link can be established to its country; if such an approach is chosen by several States, disputes between States or national legal systems cannot be excluded[87] and the inappropriate application of a foreign law could diminish the respect of cyberspace users for that country's law.[88] Another strategy would consist in avoiding unintended extraterritorial effects of national law.[89]

---

83 See below III.C.1.

84 See Biegel, 2001, 111–113.

85 Weber, 2002, 48.

86 See also Weber, 2002, 48.

87 European Commission, COM(2014) 72 final, 10; see also the inventory of examples from the Internet and Jurisdiction project, http://www.internetjursidiction.net.

88 See Reed, 2012, 30–34.

89 For further details see Reed, 2012, 36–44.

c) Jurisdiction

Based on the sovereignty principle, the execution of jurisdictional competence is a territorial phenomenon since State competence, as a rule, refers to a particular physical space.[90] The jurisdiction to adjudicate is based on the capacity to enforce law by way of court proceedings. Therefore, State competence is principally executed within the State territory and unlimited in scope of powers with the exception of specific rules that can be applied in a cross-border context (for example based on binding international obligations or acknowledged extraterritorial effects of certain norms).[91] The foundation of this concept has been laid down by the Permanent Court of International Justice (PCIJ) in the famous Lotus case[92] arguing that the first and foremost restriction by international law upon a State is that it may not exercise its power in any form in the territory of another State and that jurisdiction cannot be executed by a State outside its territory except by virtue of a permissible rule derived from international custom or from a convention.

The increasing globalization, mainly in the context of worldwide information and communication networks, confronts this traditional concept with the challenges of inherent cross-border activities. The existing rules on jurisdiction and the recognition and enforcement of judgments only exist in some areas (for example contractual relations); on an international level, however, the respective rules are insufficiently developed.[93] Since this uncertainty can be harmful in cyberspace matters jurisdictional issues merit particular attention and issues such as the question whether State authority may also be exercised abroad or whether certain powers are limited due to the protected interests of other States should become subject to a harmonized understanding.[94]

2. Provocation by the "autonomy of cyberspace" concept

(i) In February 1996, John Perry Barlow issued a manifesto called "A Declaration of the Independence of Cyberspace," containing the following emphatic pronouncements:[95]

> "Governments of the Industrial World, you weary giants of flesh and steel, I come from Cyberspace, the new home of Mind. On behalf of the future, I ask you of the

[90] See also Uerpmann-Wittzack, 2011, 1253–1256; Kulesza, 2012, 2.

[91] Kulesza, 2012, 3.

[92] France v. Turkey, PCIJ 1927, Ser. A No. 10 (the Lotus case); to this seminal case see Koskenniemi, 2005, 255 et seq.

[93] European Commission, COM(2014) 72 final, 11.

[94] As a reaction to these questions, informal law-making gains importance (see below IV.C.).

[95] http://www.eff.org/pub/Publications/John_Perry_Barlow/barlow0296.declaration.

> past to leave us alone. You are not welcome among us. You have no sovereignty where we gather....
>
> I declare the global social space we are building to be naturally independent of the tyrannies you seek to impose on us. You have no moral right to rule us nor do you possess any methods of enforcement we have true reason to fear.
>
> Governments derive their just powers from the consent of the governed. You have neither solicited nor received ours. We did not invite you. You do not know us, nor do you know our world. Cyberspace does not lie within your borders...
>
> Where there are real conflicts, where there are wrongs, we will identify them and address them by our means. We are forming our own Social Contract. This governance will arise according to the conditions of our world, not yours. Our world is different."

Barlow, a brilliant engineer and open mind who laid the foundation for the concept of free software, wrote a first manifesto already in July 1990, together with Mitchell Kapor, entitled "Across the Electronic Frontier" with the simultaneous launch of the Electronic Frontier Foundation:[96]

> "Over the last 50 years, the people of the developed world have begun to cross into a landscape unlike any which humanity has experienced before. It is a region without physical shape or form. It exists, like a standing wave, in the vast web of our electronic communication systems. It consists of electron States, microwaves, magnetic fields, light pulses and thought itself....
>
> Whatever it is eventually called, it is the homeland of the Information Age, the place where the future is destined to dwell."

This approach has led to the assumption that the participants in cyberspace are creating a „net nation", in contrast to civil society in the real world that would be governed by laws, which were conceived in and for a world of atoms rather than bits.[97] Following Barlow, the seminal article of Johnson/Post on "Law and Borders" (1996) has translated the cyberlibertarian approach into a legal concept: Expressing some doubts, that the enforcement of national law would be possible in the practice of cyberspace at all[98], Johnson/Post recognized the following legitimacy issues:[99] (i) Rule-making is only effective to the extent that the exercise of power over the concerned persons is given (control by State through a law-enforcing mechanism).[100] (ii) Legitimacy cannot be based on the argument that national law has specific effects (since the effects are similar all over the world in

96 http://www.eff.org/pub/Publications/John_Perry_Barlow/html/eff.html.
97 Weber, 2002, 26.
98 Johnson/Post, 1996, 1367 et seq.
99 See also Reed, 2012, 6.
100 Johnson/Post, 1996, 1369.

cyberspace).[101] (iii) Legitimacy of rule-making power derives from the consent of the governed.[102] (iv) National borders do not exist in cyberspace so that no notice can be given on whether an individual enters into the space of a specific national legal order.[103] As a consequence, Johnson/Post conclude that cyberspace must be seen as area with a-territorial nature.[104]

(ii) In the meantime, however, hectic legislative activities have shown that governments are indeed concerned about the "legalization" of cyberspace. During the last two decades, more and more national legislators have tried to regain control over the Internet making it again a national space (for example by censoring information or by establishing a separated root zone system); scholars refer to the terms of fragmentation[105] or even Balkanization[106] of the Internet. Therefore, it can hardly be said anymore that the Internet is the "world's largest ungoverned space".[107] Similarly, even Barlow admitted in the preface of his "Internet Commons Treaty" (2004) that (while continuing to proclaim the non-governmental libertarian ideal) cyberspace "seems to have lost the special status that led most governments to 'hands off' policies during the 90s".[108]

Nevertheless, some basic assessments that were made at the rise of the Internet age still remain valid. Generally, the fundamental question, who should regulate[109], has to be asked afresh; thereby, order in cyberspace cannot completely evade the order based on national law[110], even if the impact of national law should not be understood as new form of cyberpaternalism.[111] In addition, the traditional principles of territorial jurisdiction are not fit for cyberspace since this virtual space requires different, tailor-made solutions.[112] Identifying specific principles and recognizing the legal and practical meaning of electronic boundaries can constitute the foundation for an efficient and coherent Internet governance system.[113]

---

101 Johnson/Post, 1996, 1369, 1375.

102 Johnson/Post, 1996, 1369; for more details see below V.B.4.

103 Johnson/Post, 1996, 1370.

104 Johnson/Post, 1996, 1376 and 1390.

105 Lanier, 2013, 192; see also the statements made by the two Internet pioneers Vint Cerf and Robert Kahn in an interview with the New York Times (The New York Times Internationally Weekly of January 27, 2014); for further quotes of Vint Cerf see Kulesza/Balleste, 2013, 1311 and 1312.

106 See Kulesza/Balleste, 2013, 1332; Schmidt/Cohen, 2013, 83–85.

107 As recently expressed by Schmidt/Cohen, 2013, 3.

108 See Treaty on Principles Governing the Activities of States in the Exploration, Development and Use of The Internet Commons (2004), http://www.internationalunity.org.

109 Reed, 2012, 7.

110 Goldsmith/Wu, 2006, 142.

111 See also Reed, 2012, 8/9.

112 See already Johnson/Post, 1996, 1367 et seq.

113 See also Kulesza, 2012, 147.

According to Johnson/Post the basic set of common principles, shared by all netizens, should be seen in the so-called "civic virtue" reflecting the decentralized, diverse and complex nature of the Internet.[114]

(iii) From a more theoretical legal perspective, the cyberlibertarian approach of the early promoters of a "rule-free" Internet was also questioned by those scholars who argued that something like the "law of cyberspace" would anyhow not exist.[115] Insofar, the most powerful stand was taken by Easterbrook who expressed the opinion that there was no more a "law of cyberspace" than there was a "law of the horse".[116] Reacting to this statement, a compelling challenge to this denial was presented by Lessig, stating that it is necessary to think about how law and cyberspace connect.[117] Lessig illustrates the regulatory tensions that arise when real space meets cyberspace; based on this assessment, his famous concept of regulatory modalities and their effects both within and without cyberspace was developed.[118] By arguing that the cyber-regulatory community can give back something to the legal debate and that cyberspace cannot "function" without a minimal legal framework, Lessig demonstrated that cyber-lawyers may make a contribution to the law.[119]

Sommer, arguing that social phenomena, not technologies, define laws and subjects of legal studies, raised another critical approach.[120] The appreciation that technology lacks longevity is certainly correct; the same is true for the statement that the development of railroads did not lead to a law of steam engines notwithstanding the huge social impacts caused by railroads, however, technological changes, for example the possibility to encrypt a message, can also not be fully neglected by law since normative decisions might have to be taken into account if the application of a certain technology leads to undesired social results.[121]

(iv) In view of the described developments, recently Barlow's famous manifesto has been converted into a "Declaration of the Interdependence" (instead of "Independence") with the following wording:[122]

---

114 Johnson/Post, 1998, Congruence, Cyberspace, and Civic Virtue.

115 See to this discussion also Weber, 2002, 27–29; Murray, 2007, 5–12; Reed, 2012, 5/6.

116 Easterbrook, 1996, 207.

117 Lessig, 1999b, 501.

118 See below IV.A.1.

119 See Weber, 2002, 29; Murray, 2007, 10.

120 Sommer, 2000, 1145.

121 Murray, 2007, 11/12.

122 Daniel Castro, A Declaration of the Interdependence of Cyberspace, Computerworld, February 8, 2013, http://www.computerworld.com/s/article/9236603/A_Declaration_of_the_Interdependence_of_Cyberspace.

> "Libertarians of the Virtual World… we too come from Cyberspace…The Internet… is ruled, as are all technologies, not only by the norms and beliefs of its users, but also by the laws and values of the societies in which they live. You allege that government has had no role in the Internet, and for this reason it has no claim to the Internet today, Government labs and government-funded research programs gave birth to the Internet's essential technologies, and government policies continue to guide the development of important Internet innovations today."

(v) Even if cyberspace may preserve some "autonomy", the need for a legal framework governing the online world seems obvious. In addition, as mentioned, States keep "an enormous amount of power over the *mechanics* of the Internet".[123] National filtering and other restrictions tend to transform the global Internet into a (connected) series of national networks.[124] States' interventions into (functioning) global networks can be blatant, sheepish or politically and culturally acceptable;[125] the larger the extent of the interventions, the more likely a fragmentation of the Internet will occur. From civil society's point of view, such developments are not desirable; therefore, efforts to find adequate foundations for a globally acceptable legal framework governing cyberspace must be strengthened.

3. Adequacy of analogies to other legal fields

The regulations related to certain global spaces are necessarily of an international nature. This assessment goes back to Hugo Grotius in the seventeenth century,[126] mainly looking at the Law of the Sea. Grotius explained the law of all nations (and its innate characteristic) as the law "derived from nature, the common mother of us all, and whose sway extends over those who rule nations, and which is held most sacred by those who are most scrupulously just".[127]

In the meantime many other spaces, constituting a "law of international spaces"[128], have turned out to be relevant, as a result, State authority was restricted not to extend over some spaces.[129] From a substantive perspective it can be said that a feature common to the international spaces consists in the obligation of peaceful use and in the principle of equal rights of all States, international organizations and other international legal bodies.

---

123 Schmidt/Cohen, 2013, 82.

124 For a detailed analysis see Goldsmith/Wu, 2006.

125 These three approaches are discussed, with country-specific examples, by Schmidt/Cohen, 2013, 85–89.

126 Grotius, 1916, 7–10.

127 Grotius, 1916, 5.

128 This term was introduced by John F. Kish, The Law of International Spaces, Leiden 1973.

129 See also Weber, 2002, 75/76; Kulesza, 2012, 19 et seq.

(i) *High Sea:* The most important rules for the maritime area (i.e. the oceans) are contained in the Convention on the High Seas of 1958[130] and the Convention on the Law of the Sea of 1982.[131] The main objective of these Conventions, constituting a good example of a wide multifaceted cooperation,[132] consists in the establishment of the freedom of seas' principle meaning that seas might not be subject to sovereignty claims. This principle encompasses the freedom of research, the freedom of navigation, the freedom to fly over the high seas, the freedom of fishing, the freedom to lay submarine cables and pipelines, the freedom to construct artificial islands and other installations permitted under international law.[133] Special rules apply regarding a continental shelf, a contiguous zone and an (legally acceptable) exclusive economic/fishing zone.

The freedom of the high seas applies to all States including those who are landlocked.[134] The legal provisions of the two Conventions specify the jurisdiction of the States over the high seas to a large extent, particularly by granting them the jurisdiction over ships flying their flags; thereby, each State can implement its own conditions for granting its nationality to ships in its territory, with the exception that a genuine link must exist between the State and the ship.[135] Consequently, each State has exclusive jurisdiction in respect of ships on the seas sailing under its flag.[136]

Nevertheless, some limitations apply, similarly as in the case of territorial jurisdiction, particularly the right to visit, search and seize a ship if there is reasonable suspicion that illegal activities are at stake (for example piracy, slave trade, unauthorized broadcasting, threat of environmental damages, etc.).[137]

The treaties and guidelines being applicable and the organizations involved in the maritime area constitute a very complex network structure; the density of the relations is similar to a possible matrix in the area of cyberspace. In order to gain an adequate understanding of the given complexity a chart designing the network structure must be developed.[138]

130 450 UNTS 11.

131 1833 UNTS 397.

132 See also Kulesza/Balleste, 2013, 1346.

133 Kulesza, 2012, 25.

134 Kulesza, 2012, 25.

135 Article 91 of the Convention on the Law of the Sea.

136 Article 92 of the Convention on the Law of the Sea.

137 For further details see Kulesza, 2012, 26.

138 A good chart for the maritime area can be found in The Economist, February 22–28, 2014, 48.

(ii) *Antarctica:* The Antarctic Treaty of 1959[139] became effective in 1961 and evolved into a multilateral regional system. The Antarctic Treaty System (ATS) consists of the Antarctic Treaty, the Convention for the Conservation of Antarctic Seals (CCAS) of 1972, the Convention for the Conservation of Antarctic Marine Living Resources (CCAMLR) of 1980 and the Protocol on Environmental Protection of the Antarctic Treaty (the Madrid Protocol) of 1991. For many decades the ATS was applied without its own permanent body; the Antarctic Treaty Secretariat was only established recently. The decision-making processes are based on negotiations and exchanges of comments within the framework of the "Consultative Parties".[140]

The main objective of the Antarctic Treaty consists in Antarctica's use for peaceful purposes only (without measures of military nature); furthermore, scientific investigations and observations as well as the exchange of information allowing co-operative work should be facilitated.[141] The Antarctic Treaty refrained from establishing any jurisdictional regime. Moreover, contested issues should be dealt with during the consultative meetings, with the exception of the partial jurisdictional rule of Article VIII providing that the observers designated under the Treaty, scientific personnel, and members of their staff conducting inspections and research are subject to the jurisdiction of their home States.[142] The other mentioned Treaties of the ATS are more specific in respect of jurisdiction.[143] The ATS does not have *erga omnes* effect; nevertheless, generally the chosen regime appears to be broadly accepted, i.e. the Antarctic Treaty System (constituting *res communis*) has developed into a customary rule of international law.[144]

(iii) *Celestial bodies:* The legal regime of outer space was basically established by the Treaty of Principles Governing the Activities of States in the Exploration and Use of Outer Space, Including the Moon and Other Celestial Bodies of 1967.[145] Many provisions are quite similar to the norms of the Antarctic Treaty.

The main purpose of this Treaty consists in the opening of outer space for inspection and exploration by all States without discrimination (Article I), in the submission of all activities in outer space to international law (Article III), and in the principle of non-appropriation by any claim of sovereignty (Article II). Other provisions attempt to establish a prohibition in respect of the stationing or use of

139 402 UNTS 71.

140 For more details see Article IX of the Antarctic Treaty.

141 See Articles III and IV of the Antarctic Treaty.

142 Kulesza, 2012, 22.

143 For further details see Kulesza, 2012, 22/23.

144 See Bruno Simma, The Antarctic Treaty as Treaty Providing for an „Objective Regime", Cornell International Law Journal 19 (1986), 189–198.

145 610 UNTS 205.

weapons of all kinds (Article VI) and the realization of the peaceful purposes' principle (Article IV); the legal foundation for these regulatory objectives lies in customary law.[146] Furthermore, a liability regime has been introduced (Article VII), later codified in the Convention on International Liability for Damage Caused by Space Objects of 1992.[147]

(iv) *Assessment:* The laws of other international spaces[148] cannot be copied in a way that the respective rules could suitably be applied in cyberspace.[149] However, the chosen models show how a legal framework can be designed in order to serve global needs. The online world, that establishes a new supranational space of interactions, similarly requires the introduction of new legal solutions and a thorough reconsideration of those already in existence.[150] Traditional principles of sovereignty and jurisdiction are to be reinterpreted along the lines of the legal frameworks governing other international spaces.

C. Escape movement: soft law

As outlined[151], traditional legal instruments (for example traditional governmental regulations, international agreements) can hardly cope with the regulatory needs of modern times anymore. Therefore, in many fields the need for alternative rules emerged; cyberspace is a particularly important area that calls for respective norms. As a result, so-called "soft law" has gained importance and is complementing or even replacing traditional (hard) law; the most well-known form of "soft law" is self-regulation.

1. Notion and forms of self-regulation

Early promoters of cyberspace believed that governments do not have any place in the online world, but that cyberspace would constitute an autonomous regula-

146 Kulesza, 2012, 24.
147 961 UNTS 187.
148 Apart from the discussed examples (High Sea, Antarctica, Moon and Other Celestial Bodies) other legal areas with strong transnational impact could also be studied, amongst others the aviation regulations (see Weber, 2002, 75/76), the environmental legal framework containing many neighborhood rules related to water, environmental protection, climate change, etc. (see Weber, 2010a, 16/17; Kulesza, 2012, 144/45), as well as the ecclesial Canon Law [see below V.D.3.a) and V.D.3.b)].
149 See also Brown/Marsden, 2013, 5.
150 See also Kulesza, 2012, 29.
151 See above II.A.2.b).

tory environment.[152] In the meantime, activities of national legislators showed that such understanding does not correspond to reality; nevertheless, autonomous regulation can play a role in the online world.[153]

Originally, self-regulation was not seen to happen in any recognized and established form, but rather as "spontaneous" regulation; such regulatory autonomy means independence from any structured form of rule-making.[154] Looking from this angle and taking into account the motions of the cyberlibertarians, self-regulation can become the laboratory of law and regulation for cyberspace.[155]

Usually, self-regulation is based on the principle of subsidiarity, meaning that governmental intervention should only take place if participants of a specific community are not able to find suitable solutions themselves. To a certain extent, public law can thereby define the contours of self-regulatory mechanisms.[156]

Self-regulation refers to rules that are considered to be adequate guidelines by the persons "governed". Consequently, the legitimacy of self-regulation is based on the fact that private incentives lead to a need-driven rule-setting process.[157] From the perspective of legal sociology self-regulation is justified (i) if its application leads to a higher efficiency than provided by State law and (ii) if compliance with the rules of the community is less likely than compliance with private rules.[158]

Generally speaking, self-regulation is a "law" which is responsive to changes in the environment and which develops/establishes rules independent of the principle of territoriality. Two different notions of self-regulation are usually distinguished:[159]

- Self-regulation can be a concept of private groups which – on their own initiatives – make decisions that limit behavior, bound only by broad laws of general application.
- Self-regulation can be a concept occurring within a framework that is set by the government; depending on the degree of governmental involvement, scholars call these forms of co-operative rule-making (i) co-regulation, (ii)

152 Most typically the manifesto "A Declaration of Independence of Cyberspace" of John Perry Barlow (1996); see above I.B.2.

153 Weber, 2002, 79.

154 Johnson/Post, 1996, 1367, 1370 et seq.

155 Tambini/Leonardi/Marsden, 2008, 4.

156 Weber, 2002, 79, with further references.

157 Black, 1996, 32 et seq.; Campbell, 1999, 758 et seq.; see also Tamm Hallström/Boström, 2010, 14–26, to the authority, power, and legitimacy of self-regulatory standardization organizations.

158 Gibbons, 1997, 509.

159 Weber, 2002. 80.

regulated self-regulation, (iii) directed self-regulation or (iv) audited self-regulation.[160]

The scope and framework of self-regulation depends on the given practical circumstances in real life. Among others, the following factors can play a role:[161]

- The self-regulatory approach requires a specific design depending on the number of participants and the nature of the problem concerned.
- Self-regulation can contain either procedural rules or material rules dealing with substantive topics or both kinds of rules.
- Different self-regulatory approaches need to be established (i) in case participants in the same societal segment agree on "private rules" and (ii) in case participants from not identical segments are interested in adopting "private rules" in order to balance conflicting interests.

Self-regulation already exists in many fields, particularly in the media environment and the banking markets. Well-known research has also been conducted in these fields, for example in view (i) of the changed roles of media enterprises in times of convergence[162], (ii) of media models encompassing compliance with new technological developments in a competitive situation (e.g. vertical layer control of the media industries, vertical layer control potential of the press, telecom and Internet industries)[163], and of methodologically designed codes of conduct for media.[164] Self-regulation is also known and common in the electronic gaming industry[165], in the film industry[166], and in the mobile telephony industry.[167]

2. Legal "quality" of self-regulation

The legal doctrine has not yet formulated a universally accepted theory related to the qualification of self-regulation as legal instrument. Several alternatives may be considered:[168]

(i) Laws are the main legal source. Since provisions of a self-regulatory nature are not enforceable through public action and are usually not addressed to an unlim-

160 See also Tambini/Leonardi/Marsden, 2008, 43/44, outlining a specific typology of co-operative rule-making, mainly in the media sector.
161 Weber, 2002, 81.
162 Tambini/Leonardi/Marsden, 2008, 28 et seq.
163 Tambini/Leonardi/Marsden, 2008, 41/42.
164 Tambini/Leonardi/Marsden, 2008, 50–62.
165 Tambini/Leonardi/Marsden, 2008, 190–198.
166 Tambini/Leonardi/Marsden, 2008, 210–214.
167 Tambini/Leonardi/Marsden, 2008, 216–228.
168 For more details see Weber, 2002, 81–83.

ited number of persons in a general and abstract way, such rules do not have the quality of law in the traditional sense but only similar effects in case of persuasion or moral pressure.

(ii) Contracts and joint undertakings constitute private laws or norms enforceable in accordance with their terms. Certain forms of self-regulation are close to the understanding of contracts, in particular gentlemen's agreements. However, notwithstanding the word "agreement", such arrangements do not fully comply with the term "contract"; if the participants of a gentlemen's agreement consider the reached understanding as non-binding, legal obligations do not accrue.[169] This assessment usually applies in case of codes of conduct.

(iii) In order to overcome dogmatic problems relating to the traditional notion of the contract, modern legal doctrine has taken up the old concept of "social contract" as developed by Rousseau.[170] A social contract is an understanding that the participants of an arrangement morally undertake to follow the agreed provisions notwithstanding their lack of legal force.[171] In theory, the social contract is an agreement between persons by which each member undertakes to comply with duties in consideration of the benefits gained under the condition that all members fulfill similar duties, the objective being to preserve social order and property.

(iv) Self-regulation can also be understood as a social control model.[172] Such a system of control consists of rules defining normatively appropriate human behavior. Socially accepted rules are enforced through reputational sanctions. The social control model uses the social constraints of a cohesive community; sanctions range from truthful negative gossip causing moral pressure to ostracism from the community.

The mentioned approaches trying to describe the legal quality of self-regulation show the challenges of new forms of rule-making in a more and more complex global society. Generally applicable principles do not exist; therefore, the legal quality of self-regulation mainly depends on the chosen form of self-regulation as adopted by the concerned participants:[173]

- A traditional form of self-regulation are the so-called collective arrangements within the same market segment or between enterprises of two different mar-

---

169 Already more than eighty years ago HERSCH LAUTERPACHT, The Function of Law in the International Community, Oxford 1933, 189, argued that a binding obligation cannot be assumed if the scope of it is left to the free appreciation of the obligee.

170 For further details see below IV.C.1 and WEBER/WEBER, 2009, 90 et seq.

171 BIEGEL, 2001, 101/02.

172 See GIBBONS, 1997, 519 et seq.; ELLICKSON, 1991, 124 et seq.

173 WEBER, 2002, 81.

ket segments; in this case, a contractual arrangement prevails and the enforceability depends on the agreed terms.

- A less strict form of self-regulation is the gentlemen's agreement. Similarly, rules of conduct or behavior aim at inducing participants to voluntarily observe certain specified provisions. A type of code of conduct particularly applicable in the online world is called "netiquette".[174]

During the last three decades, legal doctrine has developed and refined the general notion of "soft law" consisting in self-regulation for something between State law and no law.[175] Not having a clear scope and reliable content, soft law is confronted with the situation that as far as it concerns enforceability of rules, law is either in force or not in force, meaning that it is difficult to distinguish between various degrees of legal force.[176] Insofar, soft law can be considered as a social notion close to law covering certain forms of expected and acceptable codes of conduct.[177]

More recently, several scholars observed that it would be important to build bridges in order to overcome the dichotomy between hard law and soft law as well as to attach hard sanctions to "soft law" non-compliance.[178] In theory[179], hard law is rule-oriented and focuses on the importance of predictability and stability of the provisions for all participants in the concerned social arrangement. However, with this perspective, the traditional hard law regime cannot satisfy the uncertainties of technological developments.[180] A further problem with international hard law consists in a certain lack of sufficiently involved international organizations and in the fact that the multilateral treaty negotiation processes are usually slow tending to a low common denominator in the achieved results.[181]

Nevertheless, "soft law" as a term has gained widespread acceptance over the last years; therefore, it will be used hereinafter, notwithstanding the fact that this term is partly problematic. Apart from terminology, it is uncontested that other forms besides traditional law-making must gain importance, particularly an approach which can adapt the necessary rules to the actual reality.[182] Such an approach is

174 See below II.C.5.

175 The term "soft law" was introduced by René Jean Dupuy, Declaratory Law and Programmatory Law: From Revolutionary Custom to "Soft Law", in: Robert A. Akkerman/Peter J. Krieken/Charles O. Pannenborg (eds.), Declaration on Principles, Leyden 1977, 252.

176 Weber, 2002, 83.

177 A good overview can be found in the detailed study of Brummer, 2012.

178 See Weber, 2012a, 8 et seq.

179 See Gadbaw, 2010, 568–572.

180 Weber, 2012b, 3.

181 See Weber, 2012b, 3 with further references.

182 See also Guzman/Meyer, 2010, 179–183.

even more justified in view of the assessment that hard law is qualitatively not necessarily better than other normative orders; the notion that legalization entails a specific form of discourse, requiring persuasion in terms of applicable rules, is not only an element of a specific normative structure.[183]

Since self-regulation plays a considerable role in cyberspace and is usually seen as part of "soft law", its strengths and weaknesses as well as its concrete importance in the online world need to be shortly addressed.

3. Strengths of self-regulation

The participants of a specific community often use self-regulation to enhance the image of the market segment and to improve marketing possibilities. The general benefits of self-regulation include the following elements:[184]

- Rules created by the participants of a specific community are efficient since they respond to real needs and mirror the technology.
- Meaningful self-regulation provides the opportunity to adapt the regulatory framework to changing technology in a flexible way.
- Self-regulation can usually be implemented at reduced cost (saving effect).
- In view of the fact that self-regulation is developed by the actors themselves and not imposed by the State, chances are good that the rules contain incentives for compliance.
- Effective self-regulation induces the concerned persons to be open to a permanent consultation process in respect of the development and implementation of the rules; their involvement is necessary to ensure that the self-regulatory mechanism accurately reflects real needs.

Apart from a self-regulatory stand-alone scheme, it is also possible that private rules can help to interpret general legislative norms, which allow broad discretion in their scope of application.

183 See Abbott/Snidal, 2000, 429.

184 Weber, 2002, 83/84 with further references; see also Johnson/Post, 1996, 1370; Campbell, 1999, 715/16; Grewlich, 1999, 324/325; Hüpkes, 2009, 429.

4. Weaknesses of self-regulation

Nevertheless, certain weaknesses of self-regulation mechanisms cannot be overlooked; in particular, the following aspects should be taken into account:[185]

- Uncertainties exist in respect of the quality of the "legislative" process. Often, self-regulation is introduced quickly in order to avoid the enactment of State laws. In addition, the process is not always transparent and not every relevant group is necessarily involved. The participants that are not involved in the development, monitoring, and implementation of self-regulation can benefit from the solutions found free of charge ("free rider-problem").
- Self-regulation tends to be based on a case-driven approach rather than general rules.
- Self-regulation is not generally binding in legal terms; the private rules are only applicable to those persons that have accepted the regulatory regime; in addition, accountability is not always ensured to a satisfactory degree.[186]
- If the number of "outsiders" or "dark sheep" not acknowledging the validity of self-regulation is large, the respective rules lose their legitimacy.
- Since self-regulation very much depends on the agreement of the concerned participants, standards could differ from segment to segment depending upon the willingness to agree on the scope of the self-regulation.
- Self-regulatory mechanisms are not always stable; participants can decide at any time to abolish the rules without being forced to follow a specific procedure. Therefore, the risk arises that rules that turn out to be too burdensome for key players will be weakened.
- The main problem of self-regulation lies in the lack of enforcement procedures; non-compliance with private rules does not necessarily lead to sanctions. In contrast to government regulations, real enforcement is not possible.
- Apart from the mentioned formal and procedural issues, self-regulation can also have negative substantive effects; for example in the field of freedom of expression, self-regulation leads to a privatization of censorship.[187]

Even considering the weaknesses of self-regulation, the advantages of having efficient and flexible rules in an area, which can only be regulated by State laws with great difficulty, should not be underestimated.

[185] Weber, 2002, 84/85 with further references; see also Hüpkes, 2009, 429/30; Teubner, 2012, 46–48; Brown/Marsden, 2013, 2.

[186] See also Tambini/Leonardi/Marsden, 2008, 282–284.

[187] For more details see Tambini/Leonardi/Marsden, 2008, 269–286.

5. Importance of self-regulation in the online world

Beyond the discussion in the legal doctrine, self-regulation indeed plays an important role in the online world. Numerous codes of conduct are available and addressed mainly to Internet service providers and search engine businesses.[188] The original form of such "undertakings" was the "netiquette", the moral adherence to certain rules that gained general acceptance in civil society.[189] Two examples can illustrate this approach.

Already some years ago, the Computer Ethics Institute issued a special form of "netiquette", the Ten Commandments of Computer Ethics reading as follows *(Table 1)*:[190]

(i)	Thou shalt not use a computer to harm other people.
(ii)	Thou shalt not interfere with other people's computer work.
(iii)	Thou shalt not snoop around in other people's computer files.
(iv)	Thou shalt not use a computer to steal.
(v)	Thou shalt not use a computer to bear false witness.
(vi)	Thou shalt not copy or use proprietary software for which you have not paid.
(vii)	Thou shalt not use other people's computer resources without authorization or proper compensation.
(viii)	Thou shalt not appropriate other people's intellectual output.
(ix)	Thou shalt think about the social consequences of the program you are writing or the system you are designing.
(x)	Thou shalt always use a computer in ways that insure consideration and respect for your fellow humans.

In 2003, "The Online News Association" published a very detailed "Bloggers' Code of Ethics" looking at moral duties of bloggers with the following wording *(Table 2)*:[191]

188 For more details see TAMBINI/LEONARDI/MARSDEN, 2008, 112–128.

189 WEBER, 2002, 86; MURRAY, 2007, 141–144; SASSEN, 2008, 242–247 and 265–268.

190 See http://www.cprs.org/program/ethics/cei.html.

191 Taken from: http://www.deliberation.info/a-bloggers-code-of-ethics-cyberjournalist-net/.

(i)	**Be Honest and Fair.**
(ii)	**Bloggers should be honest and fair in gathering, reporting and interpreting information.**
Bloggers should:	
(i)	Never plagiarize.
(ii)	Identify and link to sources whenever feasible. The public is entitled to as much information as possible on sources' reliability.
(iii)	Make certain that Weblog entries, quotations, headlines, photos and all other content do not misrepresent. They should not oversimplify or highlight incidents out of context.
(iv)	Never distort the content of photos without disclosing what has been changed. Image enhancement is only acceptable for technical clarity. Label montages and photo illustrations.
(v)	Never publish information they know is inaccurate — and if publishing questionable information, make it clear it's in doubt.
(vi)	Distinguish between advocacy, commentary and factual information. Even advocacy writing and commentary should not misrepresent fact or context.
(vii)	Distinguish factual information and commentary from advertising and shun hybrids that blur the lines between the two.
(viii)	Minimize Harm.
(ix)	Ethical bloggers treat sources and subjects as human beings deserving of respect.
Bloggers should:	
(x)	Show compassion for those who may be affected adversely by Weblog content. Use special sensitivity when dealing with children and inexperienced sources or subjects.
(xi)	Be sensitive when seeking or using interviews or photographs of those affected by tragedy or grief.
(xii)	Recognize that gathering and reporting information may cause harm or discomfort. Pursuit of information is not a license for arrogance.
(xiii)	Recognize that private people have a greater right to control information about themselves than do public officials and others who seek power, influence or attention. Only an overriding public need can justify intrusion into anyone's privacy.
(xiv)	Show good taste. Avoid pandering to lurid curiosity.
(xv)	Be cautious about identifying juvenile suspects, victims of sex crimes and criminal suspects before the formal filing of charges.
(xvi)	Be Accountable.

Bloggers should:	
(xvii)	Admit mistakes and correct them promptly.
(xviii)	Explain each Weblog's mission and invite dialogue with the public over its content and the bloggers' conduct.
(xix)	Disclose conflicts of interest, affiliations, activities and personal agendas.
(xx)	Deny favored treatment to advertisers and special interests and resist their pressure to influence content. When exceptions are made, disclose them fully to readers.
(xxi)	Be wary of sources offering information for favors. When accepting such information, disclose the favors.
(xxii)	Expose unethical practices of other bloggers.
(xxiii)	Abide by the same high standards to which they hold others.

Such rules of conduct are generally accepted in the online community; therefore, it can be said that the self-regulatory approach has gained widespread application in the cyberspace environment, from the implementation of technical standards to the protection of individuals against spam, data intrusion or pornography.[192] Possible elements are organizational rules of the Internet industry (hotlines, self-rating, awareness promotion), the implementation of self-rating/filtering measures (international and national standards), the installation of hotlines (information about illegal and harmful content), and the law enforcement activities (cooperation with other Internet service providers, cooperation with police).[193] The last aspect, namely law enforcement, requires the introduction of a basic set of rules, outlining the way the joint efforts should be executed; this task can be fulfilled in form of co-regulation or directed self-regulation.

However, the most important example of self-regulation obviously concerns the allocation of domain names. ICANN, a private organization domiciled in California, established the structure for the registration of domain names and released special procedural rules for their enforcement.[194] But looking at the reality, even in times of relaxation of the contractual ties between ICANN and the United States, the domain name allocation rules cannot be qualified as "pure" self-regulation since ICANN has to take into account input factors from other stakeholders (for example from the governments through the Governmental Advisory Commit-

192 Gibbons, 1997, 511 et seq.

193 See Tambini/Leonardi/Marsden, 2008, 121.

194 The description of ICANN and the domain name system is not a topic of this book, dealing with the theoretical framework of cyberspace regulation; vast literature exists on these issues (see for example the early ground-breaking study of Mueller, 2002; see also Weber, 2009, 51–56 and DeNardis, 2014, 33–62 to the root and the domain name system).

tee or from civil society through propositions on the basis of the Internet Governance Forum declaration). This development was clearly evidenced at the occasion of the NetMundial in Sao Paolo (April 2014) when State representatives acknowledged the multistakeholder participation approach.

III. Challenges for regulatory approaches in cyberspace

Before addressing new rule-making approaches for cyberspace, a deeper analysis of the prevailing regulatory challenges may be fruitful. A first topic concerns the understanding of law and regulation, mainly the question what expectations these two tools can fulfill in the societal environment. The subsequent discussion of the traditional rationales and concepts of regulation attempts to clarify whether the available approaches can contribute to a better understanding of cyberspace rule-making.

The most important analytical part of this chapter looks at the social change as a challenge for regulation. Rule-making cannot be achieved in an isolated manner anywhere without considering the conditions in which it will play a role. This assessment is particularly relevant for cyberspace: The developments in the technological field have a direct impact on the societal and environmental embedment of law and regulation; in addition, these developments require a high degree of flexibility in the rule-making processes and cannot remain irrelevant to the establishment of a legal framework or another structured normative order.

A. Understanding of law and regulation

1. Law as a system

Legal theory considers law as a structural system.[195] Law contains information issued by the legislator/regulator and addressed to a specific, concerned part of the society. Usually legal norms are expressed in a linguistic form giving guidance about the desired behavior, thereby stabilizing normative expectations; information related to law is a type of communication since the addressees are asked to take note of its contents.[196] In addition, (intermediate) legal concepts help to support adequate normative reasoning.[197]

The functions of law crystallize in a system of rules and institutions that underpin civil society, facilitate orderly interaction and resolve disputes and conflicts arising in spite of such rules.[198] Law can be created by way of negotiation, imposition

195 Frankel, 1998, 1322/23.
196 Weber, 2002, 32; see also Amstutz, 2011, 402.
197 See also Mahler, 2014, 33.
198 Chik, 2010, 6.

Co-Publication with Schulthess Juristische Medien AG

Published by Springer-Verlag GmbH Berlin Heidelberg 2015
R.H. Weber, *Realizing a New Global Cyberspace Framework*,
DOI 10.1007/978-3-662-44677-5_3

and/or evolution.[199] In cyberspace, the evolutionary aspect is of major importance since new concepts are developing, for example through the creation of new legal rules or the implementation of "rules" derived from codes of conduct, corporate social responsibility and other similar initiatives.[200]

Generally, but in cyberspace with special emphasis, norms are only perceived as legally binding if their addressees acknowledge the authority of the rule-making body or bodies. Such authority is given if the addressees are likely to, or at least ought to, comply with the rules; this, however, is not at all obvious in cyberspace. Reed identifies five factors corresponding to the internal state of mind of the cyberspace actors which can lead to the situation that an authority is not accepted:[201] (i) The mere applicability of law according to the rules of a specific State does not necessarily make it binding as long as the addressees are not convinced of its justification in the given environment. (ii) Compliance with enacted rules is unlikely if addressees have doubts about the State's willingness or ability to enforce them. (iii) Certain members of civil society might not be aware of the existence of certain rules (for example ignorance of foreign law). (iv) Depending on the circumstances the addressees of rules can simply not be in a position to comply with them (impossibility due to the theoretical applicability of contradicting norms in a specific territory if addressees are members of multiple communities or due to substantial technological changes making the rules outdated). (v) The addressees perceive an insufficient connection between their activities and the space over which the rule-making body has authority or an insufficient connection with achieving the rules' aims.

Law as a structural system is able to regulate behavior and it allows people in a community to determine the limits of what can and cannot be done in their collective interest.[202] If law is properly implemented, its provisions can be enforced against the will of individuals. Insofar, law has a different legal quality than self-regulation or soft law.[203] Enforcement does not only play a crucial role in making law applicable with respect to all individuals to which the rules are addressed,[204] but also holds a function on a macro-level: If members of civil society know that certain rules will be enforced compliance with them might increase since the ad-

199 N. Hughes Lynn, Contracts, Custom and Courts in Cyberspace, Northwestern University Law Review 96 (2002), 1599, 1601/02.

200 Amstutz, 2011, 403; for a detailed analysis of the evolutionary theory see Amstutz, 2011, 395 et seq.

201 Reed, 2012, 70–73; later in the book, Reed, 105/06, coins the term of "meaningful law" describing the authority of the rule-making bodies similarly.

202 Hart, 1997, 55–57.

203 See above II.C.2.

204 See Reed, 2012, 50–54.

dressees consider these rules as expression of commonly accepted principles or guidelines.[205]

However, irrespective of its quality, the legal system is embedded in other socially relevant systems; "cyber-norms" especially depend on social norms.[206] Developments in technology and/or society, expressed in informal standards, can and should give input to legislative bodies; the acceptability of legal norms increases if they are based on informal social standards.[207] Notwithstanding the linkages between different sub-systems in society, however, the system of law retains a certain autonomy.[208]

If the authority of the law- or rule-making body is missing, societal order will be based on other notions: Alternatives can be (i) power if accepted by the individuals subject to it, (ii) legitimacy through substantive or procedural mechanisms acknowledged by their addressees, (iii) community membership leading to an interaction between the individuals and the organized group to which they belong, or (iv) individualized authority looking at the acceptance of rules on a specific person-related basis.[209] Irrespective of the way norms actually influence behavior, the rule-making bodies have to understand the different processes in which authority can work; this assessment is particularly important in cyberspace since the development and enactment of norms often does not happen very close to the addressed individuals, i.e. a natural and direct conviction based on the given circumstances is relatively unlikely to occur.

2. Regulation as a tool of the State

Linguistically, regulation refers to an activity with the objective of controlling, governing, or directing by rule.[210] This quite narrow definition has been challenged by some scholars emphasizing different ways of describing regulation and referring to the manifold roles and functions of regulations. Obviously, regulation does indeed have a connection to the public interest criterion and represents a specific set of commands.

Regulation determines human behavior in a number of different situations; it reflects the understanding of economic and societal phenomena and the application

205 Reed, 2012, 54–66 exemplifies this assessment by discussing phenomena such as child sexual-abuse images, copyright infringement by file sharing, and indirect enforcement.

206 Major, 2000, 60, 86.

207 Major, 2000, 70/71; Weber, 2002, 32.

208 See below II.C.3.

209 For more details see Reed, 2012, 74–83.

210 See also Senn, 2011, 5 and 44; Ogus, 2004, 2.

of public policy.[211] Therefore, in view of this reality it is advisable to use a wide definition of regulation encompassing all forms of social control, State and non-State, intended and unintended.[212]

A broad approach to the term regulation allows a wide range of actions and modes of influence to be taken into account.[213] In this sense, one feature of regulation is its expression of morality within society affecting behavioral mechanisms.[214] Consequently, regulation can be understood to represent an activity of attempting to influence, determine, or control the behavior of others.[215]

Furthermore, an adequate understanding of regulation includes the notion and understanding of how regulatory conflicts arise and how they can be resolved.[216] This perception encompasses the element of the evolving processes, which can be influenced at different stages of their life-cycle.

B. Traditional rationales and concepts of regulation

Scholars around the globe have developed many rationales for regulations over the centuries. Regulatory intervention is mainly justified in case of structural problems and it also plays a role as means of coordination. Since, however, the traditional rationales for regulatory intervention hardly meet the needs and requirements of a normative cyberspace framework as outlined in this book, only a few theoretical approaches will shortly be addressed hereinafter.[217]

1. Public interest theory

The oldest rationale for regulation is the implementation of a public interest regime; from a functionalist perspective, a State implements norms as means to correct failures in social developments.[218] This approach is often qualified as a paternalistic rationale.[219] Several links can be drawn from the public interest

211 Senn, 2011, 7.
212 See Baldwin/Scott/Hood, 1998, 4.
213 See also Murray, 2007, 22; Senn, 2011, 45.
214 Baldwin/Cave/Lodge, 2012, 3 et seq.
215 Senn, 2011, 45.
216 Murray, 2007, 23.
217 From the extensive literature see, each with further references, Breyer, 1982, 15 et seq.; Weber, 1986, 79 et seq.; Murray, 2007, 35 et seq.; Senn, 2011, 8 et seq.; Baldwin/Cave/Lodge, 2012, 15 et seq., 105 et seq.
218 Murray, 2007, 35; Baldwin/Cave/Lodge, 2012, 67.
219 Baldwin/Cave/Lodge, 2012, 19.

theory to general concepts of political and economic theory (for example theocracy, principle of invisible hand) or to concepts of political scientists (for example Malthus, Rousseau, Marx, Wells).[220]

The most well-known objectives of public interest regulation are the overcoming of monopolistic situations (or managing natural monopolies), the dissolution of information asymmetries (assuming that information is a public good[221]), the avoidance of negative externalities (e.g. limits on pollution) and the realization of public goods (e.g. defense, police).[222] Furthermore, the continuity and availability of public services (e.g. transport or communication services) are further objectives of regulation.[223] In a nutshell, regulations attempt to achieve public policy objectives since policy is supposed to govern the conduct in the public sphere or in the public interest

2. Welfare economics theory

Often economic theory is seen as the basis of interactions between rent-seeking interest groups demanding regulation and politicians satisfying this demand. This approach is associated with the so-called Chicago School (law & economics) arguing that all forms of regulation actually disadvantage consumers, as producers and powerful users are the most relevant interest groups pursuing their own objectives.[224] Similarly, the neo-classical theory is based on the idea of non-intervention by the State and opposes regulatory measures as inefficient.[225] These concepts are criticized as being too narrow as they only focus on the material self-interest and fail to consider other possible interests.[226]

Another economy-oriented approach originally goes back to Adam Smith[227] arguing (i) that the principal human motive is self-interest, (ii) that the invisible hand of competition automatically transforms the self-interest of many into the common good, and (iii) that the best government policy corresponds to the lowest interventional level.[228] Even if the goal of this approach is the maximization of so-

220 For further details and specific references see LANIER, 2013, 116–119.
221 See for example TAMBINI/LEONARDI/MARSDEN, 2008, 10.
222 For further details see BREYER, 1982, 23–26; BALDWIN/CAVE/LODGE, 2012, 18; SENN, 2011, 8/9.
223 BALDWIN/CAVE/LODGE, 2012, 19.
224 MURRAY, 2007, 36.
225 SENN, 2011, 23.
226 HOOD, 1994, 24; OGUS, 2004, 29–54.
227 ADAM SMITH, 1776, Book I, Chapter II: Of the principles which gives occasion to the division of labour.
228 See also SENN, 2011, 22.

cial welfare, non-economic elements seem to have been underestimated and were only taken up by Jeremy Bentham who designed the concept of utilitarianism, based on the assumption that the right action or policy is the one that leads to the realization of the greatest happiness for the greatest number of individuals.[229]

A critical assessment of the approaches pursuing economic efficiency as an end in itself is also expressed by John Rawls for reasons of justice: His procedural theory is based on a collective perception of welfare and attempts to promote a policy orientation that turns out to be beneficial to the individuals in general.[230]

3. Public choice theory

The public choice theory tries to distinguish between the different actors involved in the regulatory discourse. Each group of interested actors has its own set of objectives; politicians, bureaucrats, regulators, and regulated entities often try to pursue their own motivations behind a given regulatory regime.[231]

The problem with the public choice theory consists in the fact that the reasons for regulatory change can hardly be explained.[232] Furthermore, adequate governance should overcome different interests' streams and be the expression of the values or the moral criteria according to which regulatory choices and institutions are properly assessed.[233]

4. Institutionalism theory

The theory of (historic) institutionalism looks at the involved institutions, with their history, actors, and powers. Institutions determine the applicable rules and assume the responsibility for their implementation. The theory attempts to explain why different States develop different interests and in turn different regulations.

In the cyberspace context, both State institutions and private institutions play an important role:[234] (i) The State, constituted as community of individuals and exer-

229 See Jeremy Bentham, An Introduction to the Principles of Morals and Legislation, originally published in 1780.
230 Rawls, 1971, 3, 15 et seq.; Senn, 2011, 22.
231 Murray, 2007, 36.
232 See also Brown/Marsden, 2013, 17, for the weaknesses of the public choice theory.
233 Braithwaite, 2008, 198 et seq.; Senn, 2011, 20.
234 Senn, 2011, 25–27.

cising sovereign competences in a delimited territory,[235] is the primary regulator (for example traditionally in the field of telecommunications law), however, the delegation of regulatory power to private organizations and individuals is possible (for example in view of the development of technical standards). (ii) Private institutions may exercise delegated competences (in form of cooperation) or operate independently, based on their own initiative (for example domain name system of ICANN).[236]

The approach of the institutionalism theory assesses that interests emerge from a context, rather than something to be assumed.[237] However, such an approach can hardly explain regulatory trends and changes which are based on socially mediated developments (incl. regulatory disturbances); in addition, even if any alteration to the regulatory regime appears to be a policy decision, this is not necessarily the case if the change is driven by social/environmental modalities.[238]

5. Capturel cyclical theory

The so-called "capturel cyclical theory" is based on research of political scientists noting that in some cases the regulators and the regulated entities try to achieve a level of consensus often based on a capture of agencies by the interested regulated subjects.[239] This approach qualifies regulations as means of protecting the interests of the concerned industries rather than as means of protecting the interests of consumers and new entrants into a market.[240]

The merits of this theory are challenged since interests often are not monolithic and the approach is assessed as being too simplistic;[241] it does also not pay sufficient attention to the interests and activities of other actors (such as members of civil society, consumers, courts). However, the valuable part of this approach lies in the fact that it considers the politics of regulating and the translation of interests.[242]

In reality, the politics of regulating activities often lead to the situation that a regulatory cycle can be observed; public policy issues emerging and causing the

235 See above II.B.1.
236 See above II.C.2.
237 Murray, 2007, 37.
238 See below III.C.1.
239 Murray, 2007, 35/36.
240 Baldwin/Cave/Lodge, 2012, 107.
241 Hood, 1994, 22.
242 Murray, 2007, 36.

implementation of regulatory solutions can encompass the following scenarios *(Table 3)*:[243]

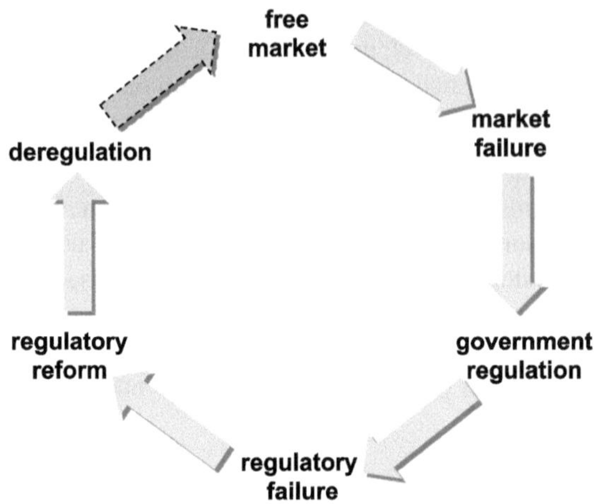

As shown in the above diagram, the last step of the regulatory cycle, namely deregulation, comes very close to the free market again and experience shows (for example in the field of energy) that a new cycle starts as soon as the previous cycle is closed.

The regulatory cycle generally questions the appropriateness and the viability of regulatory intervention. In addition, particularly in the cyberspace environment, it is not easy to find an obvious justification for regulatory intervention; therefore, the traditional rationales for regulation are of little help in cyberspace debates.

C. Social change as challenge for regulation

Obviously some laws of nature do exist,[244] such as (i) the force of gravity (as shown by Isaac Newton in his study "Principia", 1686), even if this force must now be seen through Albert Einstein's theory of general relativity, as well as (ii) the electromagnetic force and (iii) the nuclear force, both governed by quantum theory and its uncertainty principle which assesses that it is impossible to know for certain the location of any atom. Rule-makers do not have any other choice than to take into account these laws of nature while establishing a legal framework.

243 SENN, 2011, 11–17; to the regulatory failure in particular see BALDWIN/CAVE/LODGE, 2012, 77.

244 See also WEBER, 2012b, 2.

A further important aspect concerns the question whether an additional potential of societal influence through technology needs to be considered. Indeed, already more than twenty years ago Postman in "Technopoly" pointed to the fact that technologies have major effects on society.[245] This assessment is particularly true and not contestable in times of fast changing technologies, for example the vast expansion of the Internet. In such circumstances, social change occurs and does have a direct impact on regulation. Thereby, the principle must be kept in mind that laws regulating behavior do not transpose easily to cyberspace in case an activity is moved online.[246]

1. Social/environmental developments and dynamic concepts

Technological developments, in the information and communication field particularly the process of digitization, have caused advances that lead to widespread social change.[247] These advances need to comply with at least three social expectations:[248] (i) Applications for the public have to be available from a technical point of view; (ii) applications and projects leading to them must be socially and commercially acceptable; (iii) the implementation and usage of the systems should be done in a way that they are achievable from a cultural perspective.

Correspondingly, the technological developments require an adaptation of the regulatory design and its modalities, which can be differentiated into socially-mediated and environmental modalities.[249] Since mediated modalities are related to competition, the regulatory authority called upon to settle a regulatory disruption might choose to "utilize any of the socially mediated modalities either alone or in a hybrid regulatory model".[250] Therefore, modern socio-legal theory has tried to develop models, which ideally overcome legal instability.[251] As a consequence, the legal framework should become manageable, available, realistic, workable, and easily interwoven with all aspects of social life.[252]

These types of rule-making processes make the legal framework more dynamic. This dynamism is necessary in the cyberspace field since the online communities transcend geographic boundaries and tend to overlap and interact with each other

245 See above I.B.
246 REED, 2012, 111.
247 MURRAY, 2007, 30–35 (addressing the example of radio communications); SENN, 2011, 10.
248 See SUSSKIND, 1996, 240.
249 For further details see below IV.B.3.
250 MURRAY, 2007, 40.
251 See TRACHTMAN, 2010, 719 et seq. regarding international finance law.
252 SUSSKIND, 1996, 12.

in complex ways.[253] Cyberspace participants can have completely different (active or passive) roles and multiple memberships in various communities are common.

For cyberspace communities certain fundamental rules also need to be developed as a basis for living together, similarly to the concept of a "social contract";[254] at the very least these rules should define how the members participate in the community and whether breaches are sanctioned, for example by disapproval and ostracism.[255] As soon as an online community moves ahead to a commercial sphere, the implementation of such rules is unavoidable.[256]

Furthermore, many examples show that internal norms of cyberspace participants can be more efficient than actual law. This situation occurs if a change of law does not directly affect the underlying norms of conduct. The most prominent substantive case concerns file sharing in the online world evidencing an obvious gap between the widely accepted social norms in cyberspace and the legal norms, which the (national, partly even international) legislator wishes to implement.[257] Although copyright law holds the infringer liable for unauthorized copying, new technology has changed the context in which the unchanged legal provision against unauthorized copying operates; therefore, the rule-making bodies should try to decouple the *is* of the positive law from the *ought* of its normative contents.[258] Looking at this discrepancy, it seems unavoidable that legislators attempt to narrow or even close the gap since the reform of social norms is quite likely to fail. In view of the prevailing cyberspace culture[259] rule-making bodies cannot bypass the task of drawing the law nearer to the social norms.[260]

The best way forward in this situation would be to design a framework which embraces different layers comprising the underlying reality as foundation, followed by the social norms, and the legal principles at the top: The crucial starting point of the design lies in the distinction between facts and values of the underlying reality; this assessment leads to a differentiation between the descriptive and the evaluative elements on the layer of the social norms and finally also on the layer of the legal norms as shown in the following overview *(Table 4)*:[261]

253 Reed, 2012, 121.

254 See below IV.C.1.

255 Reed, 2012, 121.

256 A good example is eBay; for further details see Goldsmith/Wu, 2006, 130–145; Reed, 2012, 121–123.

257 Benkler, 2011b, 145–148, refers to the "power of combining fairness with conformity".

258 See Christopher Jensen, The More Things Change, the More They Stay the Same: Copyright, Digital Technology, and Social Norms, Stanford Law Review 56 (2003), 531, 562.

259 See also below V.C.4.a).

260 Reed, 2012, 127.

261 Thompson, 2013, 39.

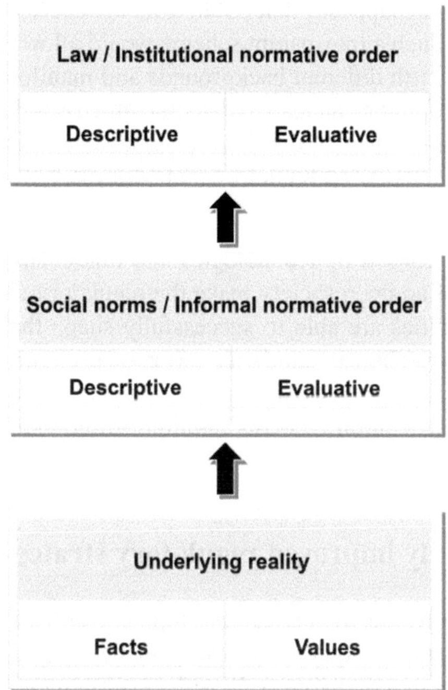

This fundamental layer model[262] has been (partly unconsciously) taken up by the scholars who developed theories based on informal law-making, thereby taking into account the elements of an informal normative order.[263]

For the sake of completeness it should be added that the mentioned technological developments and the design of an informal normative order also contribute to the establishment of an "open society" as already postulated by Karl Popper in 1945. The aims of this openness that evolve from a perpetual process of attempting to ameliorate and "correct errors" (in the sense of "falsification" by the majority opinion) are the preservation of individual freedom as well as the ideal of political-ideological pluralism.[264] In other words: Openness and acceptance of other approaches and solutions for problems should lead to a comparative environment and allow the best alternative to establish itself.[265] Cyberspace is particularly apt for an "open society" since new possibilities for participation may be discovered and previous involvement processes can be ameliorated.

262 See to the multi-layer governance approach in more detail below V.B.3.
263 See below IV.C.2.
264 Karl Popper, The Open Society and Its Enemies, London 1945.
265 Weber/Weber, 2009, 96 with further references.

The "openness" also presupposes that public fora are accessible and allow an exchange of opinions. Such a transparent scheme would allow wide-spread involvement of participants with different backgrounds and manifold ideas; taking note of other individuals' opinion can lead to dynamic processes directed to new social and environmental horizons.[266] Such kind of involvement is particularly important since behind every new technology lurks someone's desire to exert control over it.[267]

These developments caused by technologies and influencing the social/environmental parameters of an open society make the regulatory systems more dynamic.[268] Cyber-communities are able to successfully shape their internal relations with non-legal tools (technical standards, terms of use, and codes of ethics).[269] Therefore, the regulators have to take into account the assessments of network engineers and communication theorists pointing to the vital function played by environmental layers in communication networks.[270]

2. Qualitatively improved regulatory strategies

In view of the mentioned technological developments it becomes imperative that the conditions for regulatory quality and performance should also be designed in a way that the socially-mediated as well as the environmental modalities can be adequately taken into account. Furthermore, regulatory prudence in light of the fast changing technologies must become an important pillar of rule-making.[271]

The traditional regulatory discourse was mainly based on the different spheres of law and on specific issues of society. As outlined, the need to consider the discussed dynamic social and environmental elements is widely acknowledged by now. Consequently, the need for a re-design of the regulatory approaches appears to be obvious; in addition, the quality of the regulatory processes and the substantive regulatory outcome merit higher attention.

Several criteria that can improve the quality of regulation should be taken into account:[272]

- Is the regulatory action supported by legislative authority?

---

266 See also Weber/Weber, 2009, 96.
267 Kulesza/Balleste, 2013, 1313.
268 See also Reed, 2012, 121.
269 Kulesza/Balleste, 2013, 1346.
270 Murray, 2007, 43.
271 See also Brownsword, 2012, 255/56.
272 See Baldwin/Cave/Lodge, 2012, 27–33.

- Does the regime implement an appropriate scheme of accountability?
- Are procedures fair, accessible and open?
- Is the regulator acting with sufficient expertise?
- Can the regulatory regime be assessed as efficient system?

In order to comply with the requirement of improving regulatory quality, the OECD Council has issued the "Guiding Principles for Regulatory Quality and Performance" (2005), which encompass an extended scope of relevant aspects that reflect the social and environmental developments:[273]

- Adoption of broad programs of regulatory reform that establish clear objectives and frameworks for implementation at the political level;
- Systematic assessment of impacts and review regulations in order to ensure that the intended objectives are efficiently and effectively reached in a changing and complex economic and social environment;
- Assurance that regulations, regulatory institutions charged with their implementation, and regulatory processes are transparent and non-discriminatory;
- Strengthening and review of scope, effectiveness and enforcement of competition policy;
- Design of economic regulations in all sectors in order to stimulate competition and efficiency as well as to serve broad public interests;
- Elimination of unnecessary regulatory barriers to trade and investment through continued liberalization and enhancement of market openness throughout the regulatory processes;
- Identification of important linkages with other policy objectives and development of policies to achieve those objectives in ways that support reform.

By releasing these "Guiding Principles" the OECD intended to establish a check list for regulatory decision-making to ensure that regulators carry out, early in the regulatory process, an informal comparison of a variety of regulatory and non-regulatory policy instruments, considering relevant issues such as costs, benefits, distributional effects and administrative requirements, i.e. dynamic social/environmental elements. This approach would also allow a subsequent regulatory impact analysis.

An important element related to the improvement of regulatory quality is its continuous measuring, i.e. the *ex post* evaluations of regulatory tools and institutions.[274] The methods to be used for the measurement depend on the circum-

273 OECD Guiding Principles for Regulatory Quality and Performance, Paris 2005.

274 OECD, Regulatory Performance: Ex Post Evaluation of Regulatory Tools and Institutions, Working Party on Regulatory Management and Reform, GOV/PGC/Reg, Paris 2004.

stances; relevant elements can consist in benchmarks and policy objectives. Furthermore, the regulatory performance should be assessed.

In view of the mentioned developments and societal practices, eight (alternative) regulatory strategies were outlined in relation to traditional market segments such as finance or media *(Table 5)*:[275]

- Command and control;
- Self-regulation;
- Incentives;
- Market-harnessing controls;
- Disclosure;
- Direct action;
- Rights and liabilities;
- Public compensation.

The eight strategies describe forms of application of the basic capacities or resources available to governments that can be used to influence economic and social activity:[276] Regulators may (i) use legal authority and the command of law to promote policy objectives, or they may (ii) deploy wealth through contracts, loans, grants, subsidies or other incentives to influence conduct, or (iii) harness markets by channeling competitive forces into a specific direction, or (iv) deploy information strategically, or (v) act directly by taking physical action, or (vi) confer protection to create incentives.[277]

In the cyberspace age, the appropriateness of these strategies remains unchanged, but the approach needs to be widened. Regulatory design and interpretation cannot only be based (i) on classical economics and (ii) on political economy, but also (iii) on the principles of political science and law as well as (iv) on the impact of sociological inputs.[278] In considering the different interpretation modes, regulators will have to design hybrid regulatory models incorporating a variety of regulatory strategies, thus choosing the best mix among the different approaches. In designing hybrid models, four different modalities of regulation should be taken into account, namely (i) hierarchical control, (ii) competition-based control, (iii) community-based control and (iv) design-based control.[279] An appropriate combination of the approaches dependent on the actual social/environmental conditions at stake leads to the most promising and effective regulatory design.

[275] Baldwin/Cave/Lodge, 2012, 106–130.
[276] Baldwin/Cave/Lodge, 2012, 106.
[277] Murray, 2007, 28.
[278] Murray, 2007, 28.
[279] Murray/Scott, 2002, 491.

3. Flexibility of law: relative autonomy

In view of the described rapid technological developments that cause social changes and lead to an open society[280] as well as in consideration of the partly changed understanding of law as a system and of potentially improved regulatory strategies,[281] it becomes imperative to have a flexible legal framework in an open systems' design.

a) Theory of open systems

As developed by cybernetics and information theory, the complexity of any system depends on the inclusion of other organized systems; since modern societies are differentiated into a plurality of several sub-systems, sociological "functionalism" becomes important.[282] The most influential and ambitious attempt to describe an "interchange paradigm" goes back to Talcott Parsons, who distinguished four social sub-systems, composed of the functions of adaptation, goal attainment, integration and pattern-maintenance/latent tension management (AGIL).[283] The problem in this interchange conception consists in the fact that there are unlimited numbers of interrelations between sub-systems and the reconciliation with the premise of social differentiation becomes difficult.[284] Nevertheless, since, at least to a certain extent, the legal system uses its own standards and criteria, it remains selectively attentive to processes of other social systems.[285]

Systems theory also looks at the aspect of behavior's moral impact; individuals need recognition related to the specific particularities of their personality and social reputation.[286] Moral values govern interpersonal relations, the integrity of individuals, and the actual execution of willingly conducted activities which in turn lead to the need for a certain openness in the social sub-systems for the interchange of communication.[287]

b) Autopoiesis approach

With the aim of overcoming the borderless application range of open systems, Niklas Luhmann developed his theory of autopoiesis assuming that a system's

280 See above II.C.1.

281 See above II.C.2.

282 Baxter, 1998, 1999.

283 Talcott Parsons, The Social System, New York 1991.

284 Baxter, 1998, 2001/02.

285 Weber, 2002, 33.

286 Habermas, 1992, 399 et seq.

287 Habermas, 1992, 119 et seq.

operative closure is a condition of its inherent openness.[288] In view of such "closure" of any social system the legal system in particular must be "construed" as a recursive, self-referential, self-producing, self-reproducing, self-observing, and self-describing system.[289]

The function of defining relevant boundaries is exercised by a system-specific "code",[290] i.e. a binary opposition between a positive and a negative value has to be found.[291] In theory, the closure of the legal system is coextensive with its coded communicative operation; the code of the legal system is the opposition between "Recht" (legal) and "Unrecht" (illegal).[292] As a result, control is the fundamental premise of regulation.[293]

For Luhmann, a system must be self-referential even though the difference between the system and its environment requires the establishment of a special connection.[294] Sub-systems evolve and develop through the internalization of information communicated from other sub-systems.[295] A system outfitted only with the legal code would be incapable of operation.[296] Consequently, the coding/programming difference must be connected to the distinction between operative closure and competitive openness.[297] Luhmann suggests new strategies for legal regulation, based on the improvement of the law's responsiveness to circumstantial needs.[298]

The legal system should be linked to coded communications of other social subsystems and executed through a framework of structural couplings.[299] Luhmann identifies two sets of structural couplings as essential for the legal system, namely the connection of law and politics through constitutions and the connection of law and economy through property and contract.[300] Even if law and politics have different codes, the place of transformation of politics into law is legislation, as it is the key to the respective structural coupling.[301] Between law and economy the

[288] LUHMANN, 1993, 38 et seq.
[289] LUHMANN, 1993, 54 et seq.
[290] To the code theory see below IV.A.1.
[291] LUHMANN, 1993, 60, 69/70.
[292] LUHMANN, 1993, 67, 131, 165–213.
[293] MURRAY, 2007, 245.
[294] LUHMANN, 1993, 23, 76, 92, 440
[295] See MURRAY, 2007, 245.
[296] LUHMANN, 1993, 187–191.
[297] LUHMANN, 1993, 93; see also WEBER, 2002, 35.
[298] See also BAXTER, 1998, 2033/34.
[299] LUHMANN, 1993, 441.
[300] For more details see BAXTER, 1998, 2039–2062.
[301] LUHMANN, 1993, 283.

structural code is based on property as final primary code, and contract providing the exchange mechanism as secondary code.[302]

Notwithstanding the fact that Luhmann's theory of autopoiesis is subject to different lines of critical assessment and evaluation,[303] the approach does have some value in the context of regulating cyberspace, in particular:[304]

- The theory of autopoiesis is directly linked to the relative autonomy of rule-making as an important element of the cyberspace order.
- The concept of incorporating the norms of the regulated sphere by direct "conversion" into legally enforceable rules or by reference to social norms lays the foundation for Lessig's code theory.[305]
- An effective legal regulation has to take the attentiveness of the addressees in the already discussed social context into consideration.

Apart from offering a foundation to the code theory of Lessig (which has not been fully "exploited" by Lessig in his conceptual design of code regulation) the main merits of Luhmann's theory can be seen in the fact that it underlines the importance of social norms and that law only attains a relative autonomy in view of the informal rule-making developments of cyberspace communities as they are reflected in the obvious difficulties to control (or order or influence) the behavior of cyberspace participants.[306]

c) Relative autonomy and change of law

The use of the term "relative" shows that exchanges between the law and other social spheres take place in both directions. Furthermore, the structural coupling between the legal system and other social systems substantially corresponds to the boundaries' discussion of the legal norms' applicability.[307] In addition, the law as a standard[308] may draw on insights in some other fields of discourse while retaining its separate identity to the extent necessary.[309]

As mentioned, a legal system must provide for mechanisms allowing a change of law according to social needs and circumstances; this assessment corresponds to the cited falsification concept of Popper enabling the majority opinion to correct

302 LUHMANN, 1993, 456.
303 See BAXTER, 1998, 2064–2071.
304 See WEBER, 2002, 36.
305 See below IV.A.1.
306 To the last aspect see also REED, 2012, 13/14.
307 WEBER, 2002, 37.
308 See BURK, 2006, 71–74.
309 BAXTER, 1998, 1995, 2036, 2064.

an "error". Only if such mechanisms are institutionalized the continuous existence of the legal system can be secured over time; notwithstanding the fact that the predictability of law requires a stable structure, the adaptability of legal rules and resilience to change keep the law intact in case of social variation.[310] Furthermore, it can reasonably be expected that most norms viewed over time become more rational and coherent.

The relativity of norms is also reflected in the fact that norms can come in a variety of shapes with different effects as is shown in the following diagram *(Table 6)*:[311]

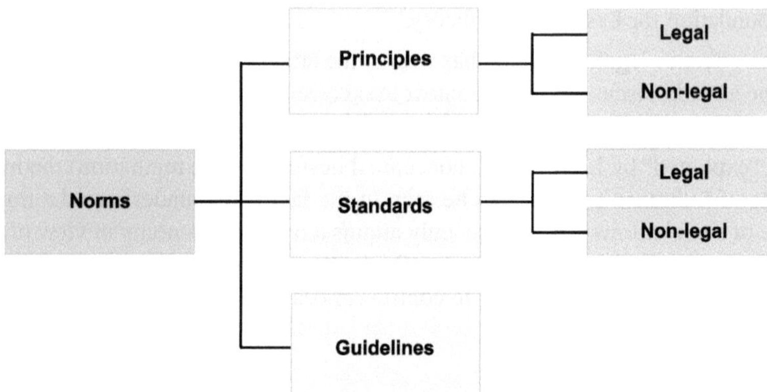

The relative autonomy approach allows the amendment of the legal system if required by social changes. However, the problem consists in the fact that different adaptation initiatives do not necessarily proceed in the same ways. Furthermore, when changing existing laws the fact that a legal change might have a social impact has to be considered, since laws are not created in a vacuum; new legal rules can be risky as well as costly and individuals and organizations may not devote the necessary attention to the new legal rules.[312]

In the cyberspace environment particular attention must be paid to the layers in networks as developed by engineers and communication theorists. In his seminal book "Weaving the Web" the architect of the World Wide Web, Tim Berners-Lee, identified four layers within the architecture of the web, namely the transmission layer, the computer layer, the software layer, and the content layer.[313] Almost si-

310 Weber, 2002, 38.

311 Braithwaite/Drahos, 2000, 20; similarly Senn, 2011, 241, who further differentiates between efficacy and non-efficacy.

312 See also Weber, 2002, 39.

313 Berners-Lee, 2000, 128/29.

multaneously, Benkler developed a three-layer structure, encompassing the physical infrastructure layer, the logical infrastructure layer, and the content layer; this structure recognizes the particularity that vertical regulation does not flow from the higher layers to the lower layers, but – in order to be effective – from the supporting layers to the higher layers.[314] Finally, Lessig rebranded Benkler's structure of layers in his book "The Future of Ideas" (2001)[315] by using the notion of the physical layer, the code layer, and the content layer, allowing him to further develop and increase the effectiveness of his theory of code regulation contained in his book "Code and Other Laws of Cyberspace" (1999).[316] The details of the design of possible layers are less relevant for the understanding of law as a system than the fact that social changes based on technological developments (such as network communications) do have a direct impact on the regulatory environment.

314 See the illustrative chart in MURRAY, 2007, 45; for the details see YOCHAI BENKLER, From Consumers to Users: Shifting the Deeper Structures of Regulation Toward Sustainable Commons and User Access, Federal Communications Law Journal 52 (2000), 561 et seq.

315 LESSIG, 2001.

316 See below IV.A.1.

IV. In search for new rule-making approaches in cyberspace

As mentioned[317], in the early days of the Internet the concept of cyberspace law was partly criticized by scholars; Easterbrook questioned the viability of a special legal discipline for cyberspace and Sommer maintained that cyberlaw or Internet law would not be useful concepts.[318] Terms like "cyberia", used for a place without governmental control[319], or like *lex cyberteria* and *lex digitalis*[320] did not survive. In the meantime it seems to be commonly accepted that cyberspace is not only a technological and social phenomenon but also a legal reality. Therefore, legal theory has been attempting to structure the legal framework of cyberspace. However, the difficulties of introducing a legal framework in cyberspace through traditional law-making by States are obvious and have led to a variety of approaches and concepts that tried to establish a legal framework that corresponds to the needs of the online world.

Hereinafter in this chapter the most important advances developing theoretical foundations for cyberspace regulation are discussed. In this context, the model of the code-based regulation is highly relevant. A partly parallel approach looks at formalized standards and networks. Quite influential is the concept of informal law-making, addressing parameters like the social contract, informality features and customary law. Apart from these more procedural theories the different approaches enshrining aspects of normative expectations (thus being of a substantive nature) merit attention. This chapter will be concluded with some thoughts regarding the complexity of the various models and the need to better emphasize structural elements.

A. Code-based regulation

The most prominent approach to designing legal rules in the new technological world refers to the importance of the "code" as technically applied in the Internet.

317 See above II.B.2.

318 For a more detailed historical overview see Weber, 2002, 27–29; Murray, 2007, 5–12.

319 Gibbons, 1997, 485, 499; see also Weber, 2002, 17 to the respective discussion.

320 These terms were still used in 2011 by Senn, 2011, 166.

Co-Publication with Schulthess Juristische Medien AG

Published by Springer-Verlag GmbH Berlin Heidelberg 2015
R.H. Weber, *Realizing a New Global Cyberspace Framework*,
DOI 10.1007/978-3-662-44677-5_4

1. Concept of Lessig

a) Architecture as key element

The theory of code-based regulation was mainly developed by Lawrence Lessig.[321] Conceptually, for Lessig, code has a technical meaning, looking at the basic structure of the Internet, thereby deviating from the use of the term "code" as applied by social scientists such as Niklas Luhmann.[322]

In a social scientists theory, the operative closure of a system requires the organization of its communication and the definition of the relevant boundaries. According to Luhmann, this function is assumed by a system-specific "code", a binary opposition between a positive and a negative value. Thereby, the closure of the legal system is co-extensive with its coded communicative operations; as mentioned, the code of the legal system is the opposition between "Recht" (legal) and "Unrecht" (illegal).[323]

In Luhmann's perception a system only outfitted with the legal code would be incapable of operating.[324] Therefore, Luhmann introduced a system-internal distinction between coding and programming (leading to an allocation of the code values in particular situations); the coding/programming difference is connected to the distinction between operative closure and competitive openness.[325]

Without specific reference to Luhmann, the concept of code-based regulation introduced by Lessig is based on a complex interrelation between four forces, namely law, markets, social norms and architecture *(Table 7)*.[326]

321 LESSIG, 1999a.
322 LUHMANN, 1993, 60, 69/70; see also above III.B.3.c).
323 LUHMANN, 1993, 67, 131, 165–213.
324 LUHMANN, 1993, 187–191.
325 LUHMANN, 1993, 93, 189.
326 LESSIG, 1999a, 88.

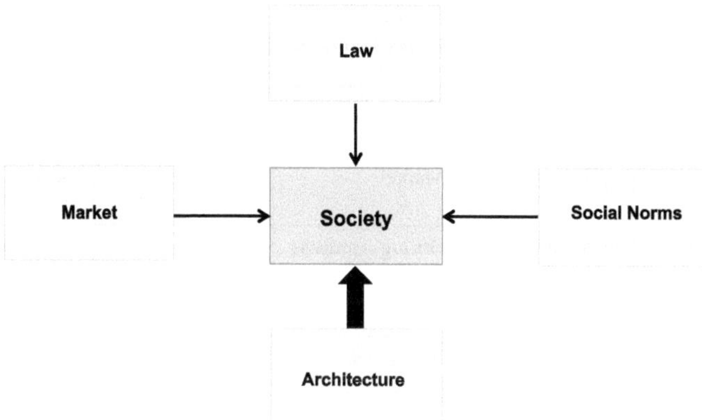

Lessig's approach relates "information" to "code solutions", primarily founded on the economic model developed by scholars of the Chicago-School, acknowledging property and liability rules as entitlements.[327] Property rules allow market participants to change the initial entitlement allocation through contracts according to their own preferences. Liability rules do not allow parties to transfer entitlements without paying State-mandated amounts. As a result, the cyberspace world with its low costs is better designed for property rules allowing for bargaining between participants in order to optimize their preference levels.[328]

The terms "law", "markets", and "social norms" are well-known concepts applicable in all societies. Lessig adds "architecture" as the fourth "regulator", combining constraints of physics, nature, and technology.[329] The architecture determines what the foundation of cyberspace will be in the life of individuals. In Lessig's concept architecture is based on the code being described as the design of the hardware and the software elements constituting any kind of network (particularly the Internet) and of the communication protocols allowing these elements to interact with each other. The constraints of the code are self-executing and apply without specific intervention from the participants.[330]

327 Lessig, 1999a, 25 et seq.
328 See also Weber, 2002, 94.
329 Lessig, 1999a, 87; see also Mayer-Schönberger, 2008, 719/20.
330 Lessig, 1999a, 236/37.

The four factors in Lessig's concept can be translated into the realms of a social order exemplifying their relative importance as follows *(Table 8)*:[331]

	Architecture – 'code'	*Economics*	*Social norms*	*Law*
Enforcement agent	Designers	Market	Peer group	Police courts
Prior or post facto constraint	Prior – design	During – process	Prior / Post – reputational	Post – sanction
Constraint type	Physical	Economic	Opprobrium	Sanction
Basis of interaction	Structural design	Production and exchange	Social / group	Power
Basis of participation	User	Buyer / seller	Group member	Citizen / subject
Primary institutions	Protocols Engineering institutes	Corporation Enterprise Market	Family Community Church / faith	State Public information

The Lessig's key message is that the design of the code materially influences human behavior because architecture is one of the four regulators. Depending on the particular architectures certain activities will be possible, others difficult and others even impossible to carry out.[332] Since according to Lessig the code can achieve a nearly perfect control of cyberspace, architecture becomes the most powerful regulator *(Table 9)*:

Practical examples:[333]
- Filtering measures and censorship introduced by governments
- Trusted systems and digital rights management introduced by private enterprises

Consequently, Lessig arrives at a framework in which code can do much of "the work that the law used to do far more effectively than the law did".[334] Moreover, code "can, and increasingly will, displace law", leading to a world in which "effective regulatory power [shifts] from law to code, from severance to software".[335] Architectural regulation is effective since it causes an immediate, final, and complete change.

331 This chart has been developed by Tambini/Leonardi/Marsden, 2008, 12.

332 See also Weber, 2002, 95; Mayer-Schönberger, 2008, 721 et seq. to the „choice"-element.

333 See also Lessig, 1999a, 129; Mayer-Schönberger, 2008, 726/27.

334 Lessig, 1999a, 130.

335 Lessig, 1999a, 126.

b) Influence of law and policy

Historically (at least partially) building on Bentham's and Foucault's Panopticum, Lessig shows how structures regulate.[336] Thereby, he does not overlook that code-based regulation is also influenced by legal rules, at least to a certain extent, even if this influence is considered to be relatively weak in cyberspace. This influence can come from State legislators (on a national or international level) or from private "rule-makers" (mainly enterprises).[337] However, looking at the developments over the last decade, the respective influence might be more substantial than anticipated by Lessig in 1999.

In this context, the second element of the code theory becomes relevant, namely the question of who is in control of and responsible for the code.[338] According to Lessig the States should prevent cyberspace from turning into a place perfectly controlled by commercial entities;[339] furthermore, governments should take steps to alter or supplement the architecture in order to reflect public policy.[340] Lessig does not assume the existence of checks and balances in the business environment, in contrast to the ones that exist in civil community.[341]

At this point, Lessig turns from an analytical and theoretical approach to a political (in his opinion constitutional) judgment that has caused criticism from various angles.[342] In a nutshell, Lessig's approach can be visually translated as follows: The most competent political body should be on top of the pyramid of code/architecture,[343] since deciding code structures involves political values rather than market values *(Table 10):*

336 Lessig, 1999a, 91–93; see also Murray, 2007, 42.
337 Lessig, 1999a, 93.
338 Lessig, 1999a, 25.
339 Lessig, 1999a, 109.
340 Lessig, 1999a, 98.
341 Lessig, 1999a, 207.
342 See Nunziato, 2000, 758 et seq.; Mayer-Schönberger, 2008, 728 et seq.
343 Lessig, 1999a, 59.

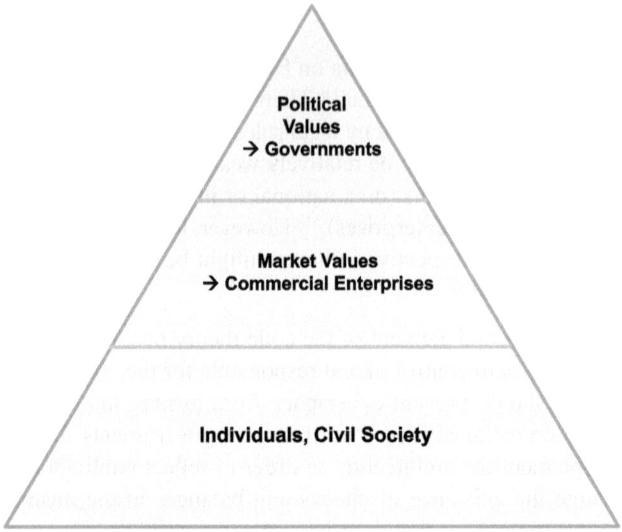

As this pyramid makes clear, Lessig calls for collective action, i.e. for more, not less, governmental intervention in cyberspace.[344]

c) Problems of the code-based approach

The theory of code/architecture developed by Lessig is neither as new nor as technical (i.e. "neutral") as it may seem at first glance.[345] Since the description of the technical framework, particularly in respect of the importance of the TCP/IP and the value of infrastructure, corresponds to the given reality, the discussion mainly concerns those facets of Lessig's approach that relate the code/architecture to the control paradigm. Obviously, the issue of the control structure has a political impact.[346] Relevant questions are:[347]

- Will important collective values be endangered if the architecture merely aggregates individual preferences?
- How much State regulation is necessary to secure collective values in the given technical architecture?
- Are choices among architectures necessarily political, making it imperative that these choices are subject to "collective" decision-making?

[344] Lessig, 1999a, 220.
[345] Weber, 2002, 98.
[346] Biegel, 2001, 195; Benkler, 2000, 1236/37; Shapiro, 1999, 15 et seq.
[347] Weber, 2002, 99.

- Would it be appropriate to establish code or architecture as a semi-autonomous, semi-distinct social domain?
- Would full disintermediation and private rule-making indeed balkanize public discourse and leave citizens without any real possibility to assess the reliability and importance of the manifold opinions swirling around cyberspace?

There are no quick answers to these questions. Obviously, the understanding of how governments function in cyberspace and how the choice between centralized and distributed control over communities is made depends upon the societal circumstances.[348] Lessig's approach is of limited influence, in so far as even in his own opinion there are different architectures in a code structure. Furthermore, as Lessig notes, code can overcome law, but law can also overcome code (mainly in case of "generativity").[349]

In particular, if many different architectural elements are applicable, then markets will reflect the aggregate of the performances and the users of the infrastructure will have a choice.[350] Furthermore, courts can impose checks on the powers of private regulators if private rule-making threatens important collective values.[351] In addition, different parts of the online world might not change at the same speed or in the same direction. If code-based regulation is derived from independent decision-making by private or quasi-private entities at different stages of the technical structure and hierarchy, then the occurrence of uniformity is not very probable.[352]

Furthermore, exit is a "normal" regulator in many markets; individuals that are not satisfied with the performance of certain activities or the conditions of certain developments can leave the (market) environment. In contrast to Lessig's assessment that such an exit is an inappropriate preference-expressing mechanism in cyberspace,[353] the general understanding considers exit as an indirect, impersonal and non-participatory mechanism for expressing dissatisfaction with a specific situation. Exit is a traditional tool in the economic realm,[354] just as voice is typical for the political realm. The ease of exiting one "organization" and entering another makes exit a reliable mechanism for expressing preferences in cyberspace.[355]

348 Weber, 2002, 99.
349 Brown/Marsden, 2013, 29 with reference to Zittrain, 2006.
350 Weber, 2002, 97; Mayer-Schönberger, 2008, 721 et seq.
351 Nunziato, 2000, 772.
352 Weber, 2002, 97.
353 Lessig, 1999a, 203, 219.
354 Albert Hirschmann, Exit, Voice, and Loyality: Responses to Decline in Firms, Organizations, and States, Cambridge MA 1970, 15/16.
355 Nunziato, 2000, 766, 770/771.

Additional critical voices have elaborated on the following issues, thereby questioning the viability of Lessig's code-based model:

- Mayer-Schönberger[356] expressed the opinion that Lessig's conceptualization based on market and choice might not comply with individual rights and social values being based on participation and process.[357] Similarly, the emphasis on transparency overlooks the problem of information asymmetries. Furthermore, Lessig's concept does not adequately distinguish between the actual status and the desired outcome and seems to rely too much on a technological determinism,[358] thereby underestimating the power of social developments.
- Reed[359] arguing along the lines of Mayer-Schönberger points to the fact that perfection of control may be unachievable since at least in theory any code control may be circumvented by another code. In addition, code fails to achieve perfect control over user behavior since it does not operate in a regulatory vacuum.[360]

Consequently, Lessig's masterful analysis is challenged by several objections based on theoretical and practical grounds. Even if a regulator will have to understand the technical infrastructure of cyberspace and if the notion of code and architecture helps to drive the rule-making processes, the code-based regulatory approach does not offer an easy tool for solving current and future problems in the online world. Nevertheless, many known scholars have taken up and further developed Lessig's concept, for example by elaborating how code can control and how code can be controlled[361], how the adaptability and regulability of code concepts can be improved[362], and how the interdependence between code and law can be assessed.[363]

2. Lex informatica as alternative

An alternative, developed in parallel to Lessig's code-based theory, is the concept of a "*lex informatica*", namely the approach of forming information policy rules through technology.[364] The need for a *lex informatica* as established by Joel Reidenberg can be compared to the need for a *lex mercatoria*, a legal body independ-

356 For more details see MAYER-SCHÖNBERGER, 2008, 713, 728 et seq.
357 MAYER-SCHÖNBERGER, 2008, 734.
358 MAYER-SCHÖNBERGER, 2008, 736–739.
359 For more details see REED, 2012, 207 et seq.
360 REED, 2012, 213.
361 See the detailed analysis given by MURRAY, 2007, 74–125.
362 See BROWN/MARSDEN, 2013, 29–31.
363 BROWN/MARSDEN, 2013, 165.
364 REIDENBERG, 1998, 553 et seq.

ent of local sovereign rules ensuring basic fairness to commercial participants in their relationships.[365] According to Reidenberg, the *lex informatica* is composed of a set of rules for information flows imposed by technology and communication networks that policy-makers must understand.[366]

From a theoretical point of view, the *lex infomatica* concept can be seen as a system of rules analogous to a legal regime.[367] Consequently, Reidenberg described the *lex informatica* as a "parallel rule system"[368], i.e. a system of technological architectures capable of achieving similar regulatory settlements to that of legal regulation.[369] Therefore, in essence, Reidenberg outlined the choice of alternative regulatory tools (design and legal tools) available to a hierarchical regulator.[370]

In contrast to Lessig, Reidenberg not only looked at technical features, but he also analyzed three substantive topics in detail, namely content, personal information, and ownership rights related to intellectual property as examples for the elaboration of the *lex informatica* approach:[371]

- *Content:* The regulation of information content covers fundamental political issues for democratic societies, since governmental intervention usually touches on human rights (for example in case of racism, pornography, libel).
- *Personal information:* The application of privacy standards to information circulating in cyberspace is imperative in order to protect confidential data.
- *Ownership rights:* The traditional intellectual property regime only provides for limited protection for information owners; trusted systems might offer a tool enabling the owner to control its use.

As outlined, certain similarities between a governmental regulatory regime and the concept of the *lex informatica* cannot be overlooked,[372] particularly as far as the features of the substantive topics are concerned. However, the *lex informatica* is insofar more open as system configurations allow two types of substantive rules, namely immutable policies embedded in technology standards and flexible policies embedded in the technical architecture.[373] Consequently, the *lex informatica* offers easy customization of rules with a variety of technical mechanisms.[374]

365 Reidenberg, 1998, 553.
366 Reidenberg, 1998, 555; see also Weber, 2002, 90.
367 See Murray, 2007, 8.
368 Reidenberg, 1998, 565.
369 Murray, 2007, 86.
370 Murray, 2007, 86.
371 Reidenberg, 1998, 558 et seq.
372 Weber, 2002, 91.
373 Reidenberg, 1998, 568, 587/88.
374 Reidenberg, 1998, 577–580.

In essence, Reidenberg's approach (similar to Lessig's approach) makes policy choices available through technology and regulation. However, the differences between legal regulations and the *lex informatica* can be illustrated as follows *(Table 11)*:[375]

	Legal Regulation	***Lex Informatica***
Framework	Law	Architectural Standards
Jurisdiction	Physical Territory	Networks
Content	Statutory/Court Expression	Technical Capabilities Customary Practice
Source	State	Technologists
Customized Rules	Contract	Configuration
Customization Process	Low Cost Moderate Cost Standard Form High Cost Negotiation	Off-the-Shelf Configuration Installable Configuration User Choice
Primary Enforcement	Court	Automated, Self-execution

In a nutshell, the *lex informatica* has the advantage of embedding non-derogable, public-order rules in network systems allowing the framework to customize the rules to the needs of the participants.[376] Furthermore, the existence of flexible standards, based on the technological environment, can offer incentives to adjust the technological framework. As a positive consequence, rule-makers might more often be directed to possible approaches that may affect the development of the technical design.[377]

A weakness of the *lex informatica*, thus the flip side of showing flexibility and openness consists in the fact that in respect of the assessment of reliable relations between persons predictability could be weakened. If the regulatory architecture is based solely on technological developments, the governed persons may regret the lack of predictable rules.[378] In addition, the question arises as to who would be in charge of setting the framework for technical solutions; in particular, the democratic legitimacy of the technological "policy-makers" becomes debatable.

375 Reidenberg, 1998, 569.
376 Reidenberg, 1998, 582.
377 Reidenberg, 1998, 588–590.
378 Weber, 2002, 93.

The concept of the *lex informatica* as described by Reidenberg should be kept in mind. The fact that this concept is partly overlapped by the similar approach of code-based regulation as developed by Lessig and has remained in the shadow of the related controversies seems unfortunate.[379] The same assessment applies to attempts in the German legal doctrine to develop a so-called "information law" that was designed in the eighties of the last century, but not further pursued in the age of the Internet.[380] Therefore, in light of the inherent value of the *lex informatica* concept, its foundation should be further elaborated.

B. Regulation through formalized standards and networks

The Internet as completely new communication infrastructure also moved the deliberations about rule-making concepts to the aspects of networks characteristics. Therefore, these theoretical approaches need to be discussed in more detail.

1. Socio-legal background

As experience in cyberspace has shown, the notion that legalization entails a specific form of discourse, requiring certain justification and persuasion elements in terms of applicable rules, is not a decisive aspect of appropriate rule-making (anymore). Different forms of rules and standards can fulfill similar functions as the ones previously tied to legal norms in the sense of hard law, for example the notion of coordinating devices or realizing interoperability between different networks.[381]

This appreciation is not a new result derived from "legislative" reactions to the actual, potential and perceived needs in cyberspace, but corresponds to manifold ideas developed in legal philosophy: Several authors expressed the opinion that the quality of informal rule-making reaches at least the same level of "compliance" as the traditional "legalistic" rule-making.[382] By way of example, the concepts of three known scholars, namely Herbert L.A. Hart, Michel Foucault, and Gunther Teubner, will shortly be discussed hereinafter.

379 WEBER, 2002, 93.

380 For further details see ROLF H. WEBER, Strukturations- und Steuerungstheorie als "Ordnungshilfen" im Informationsrecht, Rechtstheorie 40 (2009), 516–532.

381 WEBER, 2012a, 11.

382 See below IV.C.1 and 2.

(i) The legal philosopher Hart described the process of formalization and institutionalization or codification of general standards as "secondary norms". In contrast to primary legal rules imposing duties or obligations on individuals, secondary norms regulate how these primary rules are adopted, changed or enforced;[383] Hart regarded these norm characteristics as the "minimum conditions necessary and sufficient for the existence of a legal system".[384]

Following this perception, secondary norms are based on standards that have been experienced in a positive way by the concerned (market) participants. Civil society actors can monitor the rules of formalization by applying different instruments depending on their degree of specification.[385] Therefore, secondary norms in the form of widely accepted standards in cyberspace can play a major role in the legal framework.

(ii) With the objective of strengthening the influence of civil society in rule-making processes, Foucault in his collection of taught courses "Naissance de la Biopolitique" (1978/79) proclaimed the need for an "*art de gouverner*" which would allow mirroring the epistemic networks and autonomous self-regulation regimes in the public interest activities better.[386] Foucault critically analyzed the concept of neo-liberalism in different countries since the 18th century[387] and assessed the problem of enlarging the model of the *homo oeconomicus* by including elements of societal policies.[388]

In looking at policies Foucault developed the concept of civil society constituting "*le moteur de l'histoire*"[389] and opening the door to the acknowledgment that the individuals are shaped by the social environment.[390] Based on that, Foucault emphasized the importance of a new political thinking.[391] Consequently it can be said that the involvement of civil society allows expressing the relevant priorities; this approach lays the foundation for the widely discussed multistakeholder concept of Internet governance.[392]

383 Secondary norms include rules of recognition, rules of change, and rules of adjudication (HART 1997, 94–99).
384 HART, 1997 116.
385 HART, 1997, 79–81.
386 FOUCAULT, 2004, 4.
387 FOUCAULT, 2004, 29 et seq., 105 et seq. and 221 et seq.
388 FOUCAULT, 2004, 165 et seq. and 271 et seq.
389 FOUCAULT, 2004, 308; to the power element in Foucault's work see FRANKLIN, 2013, 20/21.
390 „Le bonheur des individus est le grand objet de la société civile" (FOUCAULT, 2004, 304).
391 FOUCAULT, 2004, 312 et seq.; to the "governmentality paradox" in Foucault's thinking see also FRANKLIN, 2013, 11 and 176.
392 See below V.C.3.

(iii) According to Teubner the idea that the unity of regulatory regimes is significant for the perception of phenomena at the supra-, infra-, and trans-state levels should become prevalent.[393] Thus, a new evolutionary stage can be forecasted in which the law establishes a system for the coordination of actions within and between semi-autonomous and societal subsystems.[394] As a consequence, members of civil society will be able to express the priorities for further coordination, particularly if the legal framework is based on networks established by the concerned communities and linked together through interconnection mechanisms.

Teubner assesses the weaknesses of international politics and societal constitutionalism[395] in light of three phenomena, namely (i) the fact that sovereign States are de-constitutionalized by the transfer of government functions to the transnational level and, at the same time, the partial assumption of these functions by non-state actors, (ii) the fact that extraterritorial effects of sovereign States actions create a law without democratic legitimation, and (iii) the fact that a lack of democratic mandate for transnational governance exists.[396]

(iv) Summarizing the general theories based on network concepts it can be said that the foundational frameworks developed in legal philosophy (Hart, Teubner) tend to have exchangeable rule-makers from different communities since a number of agencies, entities and individuals can assume legislative functions.[397] This assessment leads to the necessity of including different stakeholders into the regulatory processes. Partly it is argued that epistemic communities are emerging, namely networks of persons with expertise and competence in a particular domain[398] composed of audiences who sporadically meet and share a common discourse based on a shared set of normative and principled beliefs and shared notions of validity (for example in respect of technical standards).[399] Looking from the substantive angle, the outcome of such processes can lead to legal pluralism.

2. Interlinked networks approach

Some ten years ago legal doctrine started developing conceptual thoughts about the establishment of network structures. This theoretical approach should help to overcome the weaknesses of the traditional concepts based on sovereign law-making.

393 Teubner, 1989, 81 et seq.
394 Teubner, 1989, 118 et seq.
395 See also below IV.D.3.c).
396 Teubner, 2012, 5.
397 Weber, 2012b, 4.
398 See Senn, 2011, 101 with further references; see also below IV.E.2.
399 Braithwaite/Drahos, 2000, 24, 29 and 501 et seq.

Kal Raustiala assessed the viability of trans-governmental networks and evaluated their relationship to liberal internationalism.[400] He exemplified the trans-governmental cooperation by addressing the fields of securities regulation, competition policy, and environmental regulation and emphasized the informal information exchanges among the competent authorities for sector-specific legal rules through the development of a set of direct interactions among sub-units of different governments that are not controlled by the decision-making bodies of the respective States. Even if the examples do not concern the rule-making needs in the online world, the consequences drawn by Raustiala, namely the acknowledgment of a disaggregation of States in favor of the established networks, also applies to cyberspace, i.e. actual cooperation and solution achievement are based on a framework of "disaggregated sovereignty".[401]

Correspondingly, the assessment of network structures leads to the result that even treaty compliance might gain better attention in a system of trans-governmentalism.[402] However, the weakness of this approach consists in the lack of political control and in the potential democratic deficit, as well as in the normative concerns regarding the failure to come to a (formal) legal framework.[403]

The most prominent theoretical concept in the network discussion has been developed by Anne-Marie Slaughter in her well-known book "A New World Order", offering a solution for the "governance dilemma" by referring to "governmental networks". These networks are set out as "relatively loose, cooperative arrangements across borders between and among like agencies that seek to respond to global issues".[404] Governmental networks manage to close gaps through coordination among governments from different States, thereby creating a new sort of power, authority, and legitimacy.[405]

The model developed by Slaughter presupposes disaggregated States, i.e. the concept sees governments as a decomposed collection of disparate institutions, each with its own powers, mandates, incentives, motivations, abilities, etc.[406] This approach contrasts with the perception of unitary States in the sense of traditional international law.[407] According to Slaughter, national governments cannot effec-

400 Raustiala, 2002, 17.
401 Raustiala, 2002, 10, 23/24, 55/56.
402 Raustiala, 2002, 76.
403 Weber, 2010b, 13.
404 Kenneth Anderson, Book Review: Squaring the Circle? Reconciling Sovereignty and Global Governance Through Global Government Network, Harvard Law Review 118 (2005), 1255, 1257.
405 Slaughter, 2004, 14.
406 Slaughter, 2004, 12/13.
407 Weber, 2010a, 14; see also Weber, 2010b, 515.

tively address every problem in a networked world and should therefore delegate their responsibilities and "actual sovereign power to a limited number of supranational government officials".[408] The mandated officials would have to engage in intensive interactions and in the elaboration and adoption of codes of best practice and agreements on coordinated solutions to common problems.[409]

The establishment of government networks as advocated by Slaughter has been further refined by Slaughter/Zaring, who propose the establishment of a network structure that permits the realization of coordination on a global level and allows the creation of a new authority responsible and accountable for the development of international rules.[410] In this sense, networks are understood as being (i) linked to a transformation process involving the communities' specifications as experts' groups and decision-takers within the public sphere, (ii) directed towards concretization of the agreed rules, and (iii) focused on the interests represented.[411]

Looking at the theoretical foundation of these approaches it seems that scholars see networks as an institutional answer that allows the rationalization of potential conflicts resulting from the differentiation and autonomization of systems.[412] In principle, law has the tendency to support this autonomization since it enables the medium "power" to materialize, for example by allocating power to individuals (subjective rights and human rights) or to different governmental authorities (split of competence among several agencies).[413] As a consequence, the structural conditions of the networks' (sub-systems') capacity become important, and, correspondingly, the element of structural primacy gains importance.[414] However, for a transnational regulatory network to function properly, a number of conditions must be met, namely the proper definition of common rules and communication channels, a widely-shared regulatory philosophy, a high level of professionalism, and a sufficient amount of mutual trust. Though the fulfillment of these conditions is difficult, the very existence of the concerned network should provide an environment that is favorable to the development of the requisite processes.[415]

408 Slaughter, 2004, 263.
409 Slaughter, 2004, 263.
410 Slaughter/Zaring, 2006, 215.
411 See also Senn, 2011, 101.
412 Teubner, 2012, 159.
413 Teubner, 2012, 133.
414 Luhmann, 1975, 63.
415 Senn, 2011, 103.

3. Complexity structures in networks

Looking from a socio-economic perspective, officials in networks may compete for recognition by offering corresponding incentives or by appealing directly to the public to safeguard their regulatory role; this regulatory competition can lead to webs of regulation as a further development of network structures.[416] The regulatory environment is embedded in a structural complexity matrix (for example designed as systems on the national and the international level or as networks relying on regional or cultural communities)[417] dealing with issues such as how regulatory conflicts can arise and how they might be resolved. Legal theory labels these types of complexity structures as "polycentric regulation".[418] Since regulatory models in these situations may be converted into a hybrid nature, the best mix to obtain the desired outcome has to be selected.[419]

Since socio-legal and socio-technological elements play a major role in cyberspace, they must be considered as key components of regulatory design and regulatory theory.[420] Taking up the concept of Lessig, specific families of modalities have been developed by Andrew Murray as shown in the following diagram *(Table 12)*:[421]

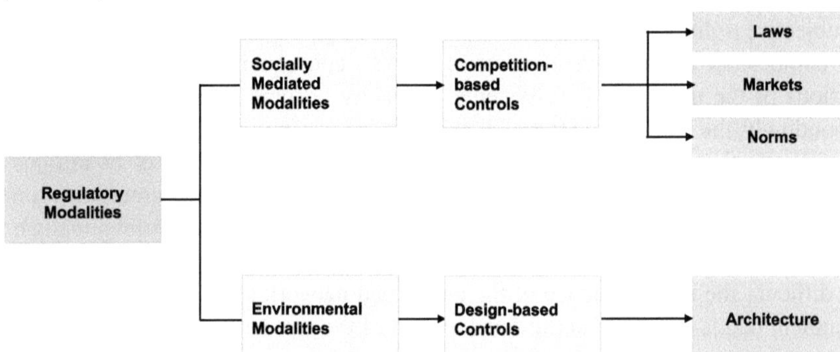

The regulation of technology-based platforms and environmental layers (network architecture) allows to observe how structures evolve.[422] This assessment should be the foundation for further research on layer designs.[423]

416 MURRAY, 2007, 22 et seq.
417 TEUBNER, 2012, 14.
418 For further details see below IV.E.2.
419 LESSIG, 1999a, 87/88.
420 MURRAY, 2007, 35.
421 MURRAY, 2007, 37.
422 See also LESSIG, 1999a, 91–93.
423 See below V.B.3.

Such kind of polycentric regulation mirrors the complexity in regulatory design. Depending on the regulatory needs, a three-dimensional regulatory matrix can be developed that allows showing a regulatory intervention potentially occurring at each point in the matrix. Mostly, the complexity of the matrix means that it is impossible to predict the response of any other point in the matrix. For example, the three-dimensional map of the ICANN regulatory matrix could have the following design *(Table 13)*:[424]

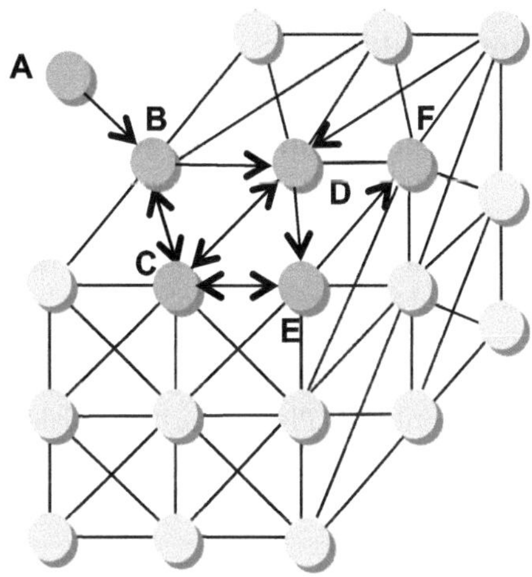

The letters have the following meaning:

- **A** is an external regulatory intervention (for example the US government);
- **B** represents the UN acting through its institutions;
- **C** refers to the domain name owners; as stakeholders in the ICANN regulatory matrix the European Union (EU) (D) and the World Summit on the Information Society (WSIS) (E) do also play a role;
- a further important institution is the Internet Governance Forum (IGF) (F).

The design of the matrix shows that complexity is increasing and that, consequently, policymakers and regulators have to extend the scope of their perspectives. More actors have to be heard and their opinions and perceptions must be taken into account.

As a consequence, a dynamic model of regulation will evolve in which several participants of the concerned environment continually and simultaneously act as "regulator" and "regulatee". Such kind of "order" has to take into account the fol-

424 Murray, 2007, 53/54, 236.

lowing issues:[425] (i) The complex model requires the mapping of the communication dynamic within a certain regulatory matrix. (ii) Regulatory tensions likely to arise, when participants of the environment communicate, should be appropriately anticipated. (iii) A constant monitoring of (both positive and negative) feedback from regulatory nodes is advisable. Obviously, such a model or matrix tends to produce a high degree of complexity, which may become problematic.[426]

C. Informal law-making

1. Law-making through (informal) social contract

Human evolution and history show that individuals transformed from their natural state into members of society. With the emergence of personal property social structures develop and a need for regulation evolves. This assessment is the foundation for the "social contract" theory already used by Socrates to explain to Crito why he (Socrates) must remain in prison and accept the death penalty; Socrates presented the argument, described by Plato in the "Five Dialogues", that he should not flee Athens since he had entered into an agreement with the State that in return for many benefits he would consent to abide by the rules and the principles of the State.[427]

The aspect of bargain as explained by Socrates was taken up by Thomas Hobbes in his classic text "Leviathan", where he argued that without government civil society would live in the state of nature causing violence and fear, thus in conditions that would not offer any place for industry, culture, knowledge, art, society, etc.[428] Therefore, Hobbes pleaded for the formation of the commonwealth (being a rudimentary form of social contract) which could create "a new artificial person (the Leviathan) to whom all responsibility for social order and public welfare is entrusted".[429] The social contract could secure the benefits of orderly government by obeying the dictates of the sovereign authority.[430]

Thereafter, John Locke refined and partly changed Hobbes' theory by putting more emphasis on the merits of natural law; according to Locke, the government has the role to preserve and enhance natural law as a state of equality and free-

---

425 Murray, 2007, 250.

426 See below IV.E.1.

427 Plato, Five Dialogues, 77/78; see also Murray, 2007, 131/32.

428 Hobbes, 1651, no. 1.13.

429 Murray, 2007, 134.

430 Hobbes, 1651, no. 2.18.

dom.[431] Social constructs such as family and community as natural orders are the foundation for the propagation of the human species through successive generations.[432] The formation of any government can secure social order but such order invariably requires the consent of those who are to be governed.[433]

However, Jean-Jacques Rousseau was the one who mainly conceptualized the social contract theory.[434] Rousseau's approach follows Locke's specific idea that inequalities begin to exist with the emergence of personal properties creating the risk of disagreements or even actual war. If this situation should arise, individuals will join together in order to interrupt the process and protect their properties. From a theoretical point of view Rousseau distinguished between two concepts of "contract", namely (i) the account of the moral and political evolution of humans from a state of nature to a modern society and (ii) the normative, or idealized approach of the social contract.[435]

According to Rousseau, a "social contract"[436] amongst all members of society must be concluded because individuals by themselves are unable to originate new forces; therefore, they have no other choice than to unify.[437] The purpose of this social contract is the accumulation of forces in a community to protect each individual;[438] although each member of society stays as free as before and only obeys to him-/herself, the individual merges completely and utterly with the collective.[439] Similarly, Immanuel Kant argues that individuals do not naturally live in communities and create laws; they do it for rational reasons.[440] Consequently, individuals weigh the advantages of living as a society against its disadvantages and draw the conclusion that they profit more from the establishment of a community.[441]

Even though the social contract has never been pronounced aloud, its validity is implicitly accepted and approved on the whole territory of a community, as it constitutes everyone's personal will.[442] Each individual is transformed from a solitary

431 Locke, 1689, no. 2.4 and no. 9.123.
432 Locke, 1689, no. 5.78.
433 Locke, 1689, no. 8.95; for further details see Murray, 2007, 135–137.
434 Rousseau, 1754/62.
435 See also Murray, 2007, 137/38.
436 An established definition of social contract, going further than the understanding according to which the members of society agree to a certain forum of collectivity, does not yet exist (see the description in Wikipedia, available at http://en.wikipedia.org/wiki/social_contract).
437 To this topic see Weber/Weber, 2009, 92.
438 Rousseau, 1754/62, Book 1, Chapter 6, para. 2.
439 Rousseau, 1754/62, Book 1, Chapter 6, para. 5.
440 Immanuel Kant, Metaphysics of Morals, Riga 1797, XIX 99/100.
441 Weber/Weber, 2009, 92.
442 Rousseau, 1754/62, Book 1, Chapter 6, para. 5.

human being into a part of a greater communitarian whole.[443] Since every person knows of the advantage a community gives to the individuals, the merging into society is not questioned, i.e. the decision to form a community is based on conviction.[444]

The general will ("volonté générale") of all individuals in a society is the core of the social contract. Finding a consensus amongst the entirety of civil society and merging its members into a moral and political collective is a major issue; the better the consensus that is found, the less "regulation" becomes necessary as all members of society agree on the appropriate rules of behavior.[445] Ideally, the will of the entire civil society and the will of the governing persons should be identical; in case of divergent opinions related to an important issue, the social reunion with the political bodies would have to be dissolved.[446]

Applying Rousseau's concept to the Internet, the establishment of open communication structures is of utmost importance. In this sense, Lawrence Lessig described the Internet as "commons of knowledge" and compared it to an "Allmend", a medieval collective pasture land.[447] On the one hand, this "openness" should not be withdrawn from civil society, i.e. be privatized,[448] on the other hand, individuals should use the Internet in a manner that is considerate of all other users. The "openness" should also be preserved in the ruling of the Internet framework, thus letting all members of civil society participate in its regulation.[449]

The social contract does not award authority to some individuals to govern others. Based on Rousseau's theoretical concept the individuals responsible for the leadership of the community are actually appointed by the entire community after the social contract has been established. Consequently, the sovereign of the State has to be seen in the population; contrary to Thomas Hobbes[450], in Rousseau's perception the government is only established to carry out the will of the sovereign and act as an arbitrator.[451]

According to Rousseau, the social contract includes single members of the community. If somebody does not agree to the terms stated in the social contract, such

443 Rousseau, 1754/62, Book 1, Chapter 6, para. 6.
444 Weber/Weber, 2009, 92.
445 Rousseau, 1754/62, Book 4, Chapter 1, para. 3.
446 Rousseau, 1754/62, Book 3, Chapter 1, para. 17.
447 Lessig, 2001, 22.
448 Lessig, 2001, 17 et seq.
449 Weber/Weber, 2009, 98.
450 Hobbes, 1651, argues that the individuals confer their right to self-determination and self-protection to the State as the sovereign; in response, the sovereign protects all the parties to the (social) contract.
451 Rousseau, 1754/62, Book 3, Chapter 1, para. 18.

a person is considered a foreigner.[452] In Rousseau's opinion the reason for the necessity of a consensus of all in the social contract lies in the fact that the civic membership is the most voluntary action of all; only the free will of all members justifies the institution of a common society.[453] Insofar, and similar to the original understanding of the community in the Internet, the social contract is perceived as a moral arrangement between participants who agree to follow the jointly accepted social norms notwithstanding their lack of legal force.[454]

Concerning other decisions than the social contract itself, two basic principles apply: (i) The more important a decision is, the higher ratio of approval needs to be reached; Rousseau proposes a proportional majority rule depending on the importance of the particular matter.[455] In fact, with a society as large as the cyberspace community, a proportional majority is necessary in order for the decision to be supported and effectively carried out. Since only a minority of stakeholders controls the functioning of the Internet at present, more members of civil society need to be included in these processes in order to improve awareness and inclusion as well as to achieve legitimacy of the decisions taken.[456] (ii) According to Rousseau, the faster a decision has to be taken, the less agreeing voices are necessary.[457] In case of urgency it may not be possible to consult the entire community; therefore, a smaller number of agreeing voices should be sufficient to take the necessary actions.[458] With respect to the Internet, such an incident might, for example, be the emergence of an aggressive virus threatening the functioning of the network.[459]

The problem of Rousseau's social contract theory consists in the fact that the cyberspace community is not a society being built afresh based on a spontaneous gathering. Moreover, pre-existing structures must be observed and a certain degree of proceduralization is unavoidable. These elements cannot be adequately dealt with by the social contract concept.

More than 200 years after Rousseau, John Rawls advanced the theoretical approach of the social contract to a higher level of abstraction, departing from the

452 Rousseau, 1754/62, Book 4, Chapter 2, para. 6.

453 Rousseau, 1754/62, Book 4, Chapter 2, para. 5.

454 See above II.B.2 to the early cyberspace proclamations; see also Weber/Weber, 2009, 93; Biegel, 2001, 101/02; Gibbons, 1997, 518–523.

455 See also Paul Weirich, Rousseau on Proportional Majority Rule, Philosophy and Phenomenological Research 47 (1986), 111–126.

456 See Weber/Weber, 2009, 94.

457 Rousseau, 1754/62, Book 4, Chapter 2, para. 11.

458 See also Ethan Putterman, Rousseau on Agenda-Setting and Majority Rule, American Political Science Rule 97 (2005), 459–469.

459 Weber/Weber, 2009, 94.

hypothetical situation that people live in an original position of equality (which corresponds to the state of nature in the traditional theory of the social contract) and assuming that individuals do not know their place in society (veil of ignorance), their class position or social status, fortune and abilities, intelligence, strengths and the like. Therefore, choices are made by individuals based on the principles of justice and are the result of a fair agreement or bargain.[460] According to Rawls, if decisions need to be taken, individuals have to consider the positions of all persons affected by the respective decision and to opt for the solution they deem most favorable for everyone; thereby the common interests of society are implemented.[461]

For the sake of completeness it must be added that contracts are to be generally seen as legal source since an agreement between two individuals or entities establishes a bilateral normative order that can be enforced. In practice, contracts, particularly in the form of Terms of Service (ToS), play an important role in cyberspace, which should not be underestimated. However, the contract model does not ensure compliance with public policy considerations, mainly if the parties do not have the same bargaining power (which is quite often the case in reality). Therefore, the classic contract model between two parties will not be treated as viable regulatory regime hereinafter.

2. Informality features in law-making

Since law with its traditional formal character does not easily comply with the needs of cyberspace regulation, informal norm-development gains importance.[462] In order to cope with this finding, Joost Pauwelyn distinguished three specific features of informal law-making:[463]

- *Process-informality:* This feature encompasses norms developed not in treaty-based international organizations but in networks, fora and other groups often not being vested with international legal personality;
- *Actor-informality:* This feature does not look at formal State representatives or diplomats but assesses regulators, agencies, sub-federal entities or other elements including private actors, industry associations, civil society and similar networks not belonging to the traditional State powers, thereby causing a certain "disaggregation" of States.

[460] For further details see Rawls, 1971, 10 et seq.

[461] See Weber/Weber, 2009, 93.

[462] See above III.C.1.

[463] Pauwelyn, 2011, 126.

- *Output-informality*: This feature addresses those norms that are not formal treaties or traditional sources of international law but standards, non-binding guidelines or indicators that do not belong to the usual remit of public international law.

Consequently, informal law-making crosses the boundaries between the traditional lines of law as applied in a sovereign State environment. Informal law-making does not mean that international cooperation will no longer be of relevance, but different forms of cooperation are leading to a greater variety of law-making features, particularly through less formal and less traditional channels.[464] The output based on flexible coordination will often have a soft law character.[465]

During the last few years, informal cooperation has moved beyond cooperation between like-minded States to also cover broader networks traditionally reserved for regulation by treaty. Informal rules can set standards that can be procedurally and substantially superior to formal law-making practices.[466]

Nevertheless, informal law-making has to overcome some challenges: (i) The informality approach must maintain the law's neutrality and protective force (particularly in favor of the weak) as well as the rule of law being the only justification for any form of coercion or limitation on freedom. (ii) Measures are to be developed that allow balancing informality, which may be needed to enable effective cooperation or to avoid traditional strictures, with the layers of control and accountability required to sustain this cooperation in democratic societies.[467]

The formal law is confronted with a basic decision on which way to go: In the face of the obvious move toward informality, "law can adjust and reduce its formal requirements, both in terms of subjects of law and the sources of law, so as to remain sociologically relevant in a very dynamic reality. Or law can insist on its formalities, risking it will be increasingly marginalized, but hoping that the tides will turn again and the actors will realize that formal cooperation under law is more sustainable and power-neutral".[468]

---

464 PAUWELYN, 2011, 127.
465 See above II.C.
466 PAUWELYN, 2011, 129.
467 PAUWELYN, 2011, 137/38.
468 PAUWELYN, 2011, 138.

3. Customary Internet-ional law

The disjuncture between the law and the practices in cyberspace caused by the information technologies' developments including the socio-economic problems can also be tackled by a framework of "Internet-ional" legal principles based on the history of customs as a source of law. Such kind of approach was developed by Warren Chik who argued that customary law would constitute the most suitable common denominator of cyberspace law-making since the nature of custom makes it the ideal default device that will fill in the gaps in the law applicable to the Internet.[469] The two main benefits of customary rules consist in the recognition of legal legitimacy of existing and established practices as well as in the implementation of informal norms for newly emerging practices, thereby supplementing existing applicable laws (with a gap-filling function in respect of new practices and technologies).[470]

The foundations of customary rules can be seen in the Middle Ages' law of the merchants and in the generally accepted "netiquette". According to Article 38 of the Statute of the International Court of Justice (ICJS) three recognized core sources of international law can be identified, namely law by treaty or convention, customary international law, general principles, and universal law (*"jus cogens"*). Therefore, customs are recognized as a source of international law (Article 38 (1) (b) ICJS). In legal doctrine it is even said that customary law is not only a *source* of international law, but that it *is* international law.[471] In principle, customary rules are created by two essential elements, namely (i) the widespread and uniform persistence and repetition of the conducted behavior over time (*"usus"*) representing almost universal consensus (objective element) and the fact that the conduct is done out of a sense of obligation and accompanied by a conviction of the concerned person/entity (subjective element, *"opinio juris"*[472]).[473]

Evidently, customary law is challenged by three main factors: the relevance that requires a fast paced process of identification through interdisciplinary and empirical research as its solution, and technological neutrality to prevent strong influences by only a few business players; in addition, the challenge of uneven powers of influence geographically and culturally due to the uneven distribution of computers and penetration of electronic communication infrastructure globally

[469] CHIK, 2010, 10 et seq.

[470] To the customs as part of general law see KOSKENNIEMI, 2005, 389–397.

[471] See NADAKAVUKAREN, 2014, nos 1 and 2 referring to PHILIP ALLOTT.

[472] Over time the *opinio juris* can also be based on decisions of international courts and expert statements of renowned legal scholars.

[473] CHIK, 2010, 12; KULESZA/BALLESTE, 2013, 1340 referring to the State level; NADAKAVUKAREN, 2014, nos 7 and 8.

are to be taken into account.[474] Furthermore, mechanisms should be developed that allow a consensus reached within the fora of cyber-communities to be converted from soft law instruments to traditional international law regimes which would in turn lead to a harmonized legal environment.[475]

A custom comes into life if a well-established and identifiable practice or habit is observed, and if it has gained widespread acceptance and is expected as a right or obligation by the persons in the relevant communities that are affected by it.[476] As history shows (*"coutumes"* of the Middle Ages) custom is a rich resource and — combined with the respective *"opinio juris"* — an established source of legal rules (*"lex mercatoria"*) mainly with respect to economic and business practices.[477] As already seen in Roman times, customs exercised in private (peer-to-peer) relations can be codified as *jus*, as opposed to the statutory *lex*.[478] A similar development can be seen with Internet customs, evolving out of necessity, practical functionality, and transactional efficacy, through practices that became commonly accepted or expected at a period of time of widespread application. Customs organically developed by the Internet community as a whole have legitimacy as an autonomous legal system.[479] For obvious reasons, technology creators and system designers play an important role in cyberspace. However, the process of creating customs and then norms should not just be understood as the detection of behavior and attitudes of its participants, but as a special form of validating "norms" originating from other sources relevant in society.[480]

A norm-hierarchical perspective requires that customary rules (customary Inter-net-ional law) must be supplementary and complementary to other sources of law. Customs can help to interpret existing norms by elucidating ambiguities based on the reasonableness criterion or by filling in gaps if other sources do not contain an actual provision dealing with the relevant issue.[481] In case of a conflict between customary rules over time, the latter rule in time must prevail. Such kind of development is likely to occur since the changing infrastructure of the Internet and the

474 Chik, 2010, 14.
475 Kulesza/Balleste, 2013, 1341; see also Koskenniemi, 2005, 397–410.
476 See also Polanski, 2007, 99/100.
477 Chik, 2010, 15/16; for further details see Andreas Thier, Rechtsgewohnheiten, Ordnungskonfigurationen und Rechtsbegriff, Rechtsgeschichte 17 (2010), 40–45; particularly to the custom in the Canon Law being a legal body with a global scope (not restricted to specific territories) see Canons 23–28 and John M. Huels, Custom, in: Beal/Coriden/Green, 2000, 86–94.
478 Kulesza/Balleste, 2013, 1342.
479 See above II.B.2; Chik, 2010, 16; Braithwaite/Drahos, 2000, 50–54.
480 See also Chik, 2010, 18/19.
481 Chik, 2010, 19.

changing architecture of the World Wide Web lead to adapted practices that can again amount to new customary rules.[482]

4. Appendix: Importance of accountability

Accountability has become an important topic in the discussions about the legitimacy of international institutions. Due to the lack of a "global democracy" to which organizations must abide, global administrative bodies are confronted with requests to overcome accountability gaps.[483] This organizational accountability debate is of particular relevance in case of informal law-making since the respective rules might only be recognized if the rule-makers are accountable for their activities.

"Accountability" stems from the Latin word *accomptare* (to account), a prefixed form of *computare* (to calculate) developed in Ancient Greece and Rome. Accountability is the acknowledgment and assumption of responsibility for actions, products, decisions, and policies within the scope of the designated role.[484]

Various types of accountability can be distinguished, namely moral, administrative, political, managerial, market, legal/traditional, constituency related and professional accountability. Accountability is a pervasive concept, encompassing political, legal, philosophical and other aspects; each context casts a different shade on the meaning of accountability.[485] Nevertheless, a general definition that incorporates the basic elements remains recognizable in the sense that accountability consists in the obligation of a person (the accountable) to another (the accountee), according to which the former must give account of, explain and justify actions or decisions taken against criteria of the same kind, as well as assume responsibility for any fault or damage.[486]

Informal law-making must relate to democratic accountability including responsiveness to stakeholders, with both a substantive (output legitimacy) and a procedural component (input legitimacy). Since a clear tension exists between informal networks (focusing on the process-informality axis) and *ex post* institutionalized or formalized accountability mechanisms, some formal principles have to be implemented in order to achieve an adequate "control" framework.[487] Furthermore,

---

482 For a general overview of customs in the real world and in cyberspace see CHIK, 2010, 20/21.

483 WEBER, 2009, 133; for a detailed analysis of the accountability topics see WEBER, 2011b.

484 WEBER, 2009, 133.

485 WEBER, 2009, 133.

486 See also MALCOLM, 2008, 262.

487 PAUWELYN, 2011, 131/32.

preconditions that enable accountability (mandate/benchmark setting, transparency, disclosure of information) and other responsiveness-promoting measures need to be identified. In addition, two different directions of accountability are to be taken into account, namely internal accountability (or accountability to informal law-making participants and their constituencies) and external accountability (or accountability to actors that are not formally within the informal law-making network but that are affected by it).[488]

A chart looking at internal and external accountability under an international and a domestic perspective could have the following shape *(Table 14)*:[489]

	Accountability – International level		**Accountability – Domestic level**	
	Informal law-making network as such	**Individual participants**	**Individual participants**	**Informal law-making network as such**
Internal stakeholders	Internal decision-making and voting procedures Internal organizations; complaints procedures	New mechanisms? Complaints procedures, ombudsman	Control and oversight Comment procedures, judicial review	New constituencies' mechanisms? Court proceedings
External stakeholders	Transparency for observers Complaints procedures	New mechanisms? Complaints procedures, ombudsman	New mechanisms? Comment procedures, judicial review	New mechanisms? Court proceedings

The need for accountability mechanisms at the international level proportionally rises with the degree of autonomy and power exercised (*de jure* or *de facto*) by the informal law-making network; this assessment can be illustrated as follows *(Table 15)*:[490]

488 PAUWELYN, 2011, 132.
489 See also PAUWELYN, 2011, 133.
490 See PAUWELYN, 2011, 136.

	Internal accountability		
	Ex ante control (e.g. mandate, appointment)	**Ongoing control (e.g. participation, veto)**	**Ex post control (e.g. budget, regulation, sanction)**
No network autonomy or power (de jure or de facto)	No / less need	Complete ⬇	No / less need
Full network autonomy or power (de jure or de facto)	Crucial	Non-existing	Crucial

As a consequence, the conclusion may be drawn that effectiveness and accountability need not be (or be perceived as) polar opposites: Generally speaking for informal cooperation to be effective in the long term, accountability is needed; conversely, a core goal of accountability is the increase of effectiveness by learning from mistakes and feedback from stakeholders.[491]

D. Normativity-oriented regulatory concepts

In the last few years, not only theoretical concepts enshrining formal and procedural approaches were developed, but also substantive elements gained in importance. Scholars recognized that normative expectations have to be embedded into the design of regulatory frameworks for cyberspace. Therefore, the foundations of the main conceptual premises need to be outlined hereinafter.

1. Philosophical background

Contemporary legal theory started to question the understanding of law as command (the so-called command theory of law) by arguing that law rather provides people with reasons for actions. According to Joseph Raz, law mediates between different individual reasons in the process of what to choose and what to do; thereby, the authority of law stems from the service it provides in "mediating the people and the right reasons which apply to them".[492] The "service conception of authority" assesses law as a process that modifies the scope of other considera-

[491] PAUWELYN, 2011, 139.
[492] Raz, 1994, 214.

tions.[493] As a consequence, legal reasoning cannot be "dissociated from the overall process of practical reason"[494], since it changes the normative order and is reflected in the common institutions of everyday life.

John Finnis, in further developing this type of concept, expressed the opinion that the reasons provided by law would be inherently connected with the reasons of morality and those of politics; in a quite idealized "central case viewpoint" the manifold reasons are one and the same, consistent, attentive to all aspects of human opportunity and flourishing, aware of their limited commensurability, concerned to remedy deficiencies and breakdowns as well as conscious of their roots in the various aspects of human personality and in the economic and other material conditions of social interaction.[495] Even if the "central case viewpoint" seems to be rather theoretical, the processes of confluence, of identity between the reasons of law and other reasons of practical nature and of the relations between instances of law and social institutions cannot be overlooked.[496]

Law does translate the moral realms with its own legal lenses, irrespective of the fact whether an identity between legal and moral issues exists or not, and law does the same with politics, economics and other social systems, even if functionally differentiated.[497] Niklas Luhmann called this functional relationship a "structural coupling";[498] his approach is based on the assumption that the specific function performed by law lies in the stabilization of normative expectations translated by law from other social systems (and reflected in a coding of its own). In other words, the regulatory framework consists of a structural coupling between politics (or social sector mechanisms, based on spontaneous or organized spheres) and the reflexive measures of law.[499]

Following this approach, according to Gunther Teubner, law does not play a primary role in constituting societies; the main aspect is the self-constitution of a social system (for example politics, economy, media, communication).[500] Usually, law is indispensable in such environment but it only plays a supporting role. Consequently, the identification of law does not depend on the evaluation of its moral merits; in this theoretical model, moral criteria concern the law's legitimacy (the acceptance of its legal provisions) but they are foreign to and modified by the

493 Raz, 2004, 9; to the approach of Raz see also Reed, 2012, 19 and 86.
494 Thompson, 2011, 157.
495 Finnis, 1982, 15.
496 See also Thompson, 2011, 157.
497 Thompson, 2011, 158.
498 See also above III.C.3.b).
499 Luhmann, 1990; see also Teubner, 2012, 105.
500 Teubner, 2012, 103.

generally accepted legal propositions.[501] However, this assessment does not mean that any actor in society, from dutiful officials to anarchic programmers, are invited to abandon the pursuits of moral criteria altogether in practicing law or living life.[502] In addition, autonomy and value pluralism therefore need the political institutions of society to engage with conceptions, which enable individuals to pursue the good and to discourage evil.[503]

From a legal perspective, normative expectations can mainly be based in generally recognized substantive principles since they have two different core functions:[504] On the one hand, legal principles help to systemize and, by that, explain a set of legal rules, thereby they help to overcome the risk of an incoherent number of normative rules; on the other hand, principles can be considered elements of legal reasoning because they elucidate the object and the purpose of legal rules and influence the evolution of international customary law. In addition, the two functions facilitate the building of bridges between different actors in cyberspace with the aim of establishing interrelationships based on trust and confidence.

2. Hybrid economy and information society

The empowerment of the individuals, rather than the political system, also plays a role in the philosophical foundation of economic theories. Overcoming the old concepts of economic justification of regulation[505] the structural contours of a liberal model can be looked at from an informational economics perspective. In the meantime it is commonly accepted that the ideal of "free" information could erode economic interdependencies between individuals as well as between States.[506] The best-known approach of informational inclusion in cyberspace regulation is the concept of the so-called hybrid economy, which has attracted major attention through the extensive studies of Yochai Benkler[507] and the latest Internet-related book "Remix" of Lawrence Lessig.[508]

(i) As point of departure, Benkler expressed the opinion that the goal of a contemporary government must consist in assessing the needs and the values that are

501 Raz, 1994, 70.
502 Thompson, 2011, 159.
503 Raz, 1986, 133; see also Thompson, 2011, 181.
504 For more details to these elements see Weber, 2012b, 6; Uerpmann-Wittzack, 2010, 1246/47.
505 See above III.B.
506 See also Lanier, 2013, 193.
507 Benkler, 2004 and 2006.
508 Lessig, 2008.

crucial to its community.[509] Benkler then developed his approach by attempting to combine things, which do not seem to be combinable, namely the conciliation of the originally used notion of a "commercial economy" with the newly developed term "shared economy". The main target of the approach is the exchange of (valuable) information by individuals. In a broad sense this concept can lead to a sustainable information economy[510] and to an institutional ecology of the digital environment.[511]

Consequently, Benkler had to redefine the role of price in a world ruled by a hybrid economy.[512] In shared economies price does not play an exclusively relevant role anymore, but different other features take on this role.[513] The respective concept has been crystallized by Benkler in his book "Wealth of Networks" (2006) outlining a new phase in social evolution: According to Benkler the network economy is based on „peer production", which generates new resources, not those calculable with money.[514] Benkler is of the opinion that neither laws nor commercial barriers can halt the revolution initiated by peer production that will soon rule world markets.[515] In times of economic and cultural globalization it is imperative to look for global solutions that are sustainable and allow the handling of the most prevailing trends.[516]

Founded on this concept Benkler developed a theory of social production in the information environment that is marked by collaborative forms of development, which are common-based (relying on a common goal of informational resources) or peer-produced (driven by decentralized creative inputs).[517] Thereby, Benkler takes care of the effects that "law can have through the way it structures the relationship among people with regard to the information environment they occupy".[518] This approach optimistically designed as arising organically[519] attempts to develop a structural framework for coexistence in cyberspace. Benkler also stated that the structure of the information environment is constitutive of the autonomy,

509 See also Kulesza/Balleste, 2013, 1337.
510 See Lanier, 2013, 228.
511 See Franklin, 2013, 131 with reference to Benkler, 2006, 273.
512 Benkler, 2004, 275/76.
513 Benkler, 2004, 282.
514 Benkler, 2006, 115/16.
515 Benkler, 2006, 131; similarly Lessig, 2008, 266–268 addressing the limitations in copyright law.
516 In this connection Lanier, 2013, 238, 246, 248 refers to a unique commercial identity in a universal public market information system.
517 See Benkler, 2006, 169.
518 Benkler, 2006, 151; Lanier, 2013, 271–274, specifically refers to the economic network neutrality in this context.
519 For a critical assessment of this approach see Thompson, 2011, 178 et seq.

not only functionally significant to it,[520] and that communication is the basic unit of sociological existence[521], leading to the assumption of trust in the empowerment of the individuals, rather than in the political system constituting the structural contours of the environment.[522] Looking from that angle, i.e. a regulatory perspective, peer production is hydra-headed and largely out of any one jurisdiction.[523]

The problem of this approach lies in the fact that based on the liberal model of Raz which, however, is not fully reflected by Benkler[524] the proposal is made to defer substantive choices to the new collaborative forces characterizing the information society. As a consequence attempts by the State to intervene in the cultural discourse are considered neither justifiable nor feasible.[525] Benkler is advocating for an approach that takes up a "systematic commitment to avoid direct intervention on cultural exchange".[526] Several (practical) arguments question this conclusion:[527] (i) Cultural discourse tends towards polarization. (ii) It seems to be doubtful that frameworks which completely avoid cultural choice are available. (iii) The approach does not give an answer about what to do, politically, if the clay man happens to embody a wicked soul. (iv) The settlement of disputes arising out of substantive cultural matters of the information society is not addressed (challenge of adjudication). Therefore, the viability of acknowledging a difference of nature between rights and other cultural conceptions might have to be challenged.[528]

(ii) Lessig further analyzed Benkler's concept in his book "Remix" and came to the conclusion that the hybrid economy is the economic model best suited to reflect current trends in global online interaction.[529] According to Lessig, a hybrid economy combines elements of two well-established economic models, namely the commercial economy, conceiving the value of goods and services only in terms of money, and the sharing economy, exemplified by love and friendship which are invaluable in hard currency.[530]

520 Benkler, 2006, 146, 151, 169.
521 Benkler, 2006, 465; see also Kulesza, 2012, 150.
522 See also Thompson, 2011, 179.
523 See Brown/Marsden, 2013, 29
524 For a more detailed analysis see Thompson, 2013, 291–297.
525 Benkler, 2006, 151.
526 Benkler, 2006, 298.
527 For further details see Thompson, 2011, 182/83.
528 See also Thompson, 2011, 184.
529 Lessig, 2008, 248/49, 294.
530 Lessig, 2008, 118; see also Kulesza, 2012, 148/49.

According to Lessig, since cyberspace communities are organized in completely different ways than communities in the offline-reality,[531] the originally dichotomous classification distinguishing between commercial and sharing individual relationships can no longer be upheld in the online environment.[532] Netizens in cyberspace share time, ideas, knowledge, commercial activities, etc. free of charge or only subject to charge in case of a specific agreement. The best-known examples for this approach are Wikipedia and open source software such as Linux, which are based on the initiative of a few persons with free time and good ideas. Therefore, the sharing is likely to become commercial and insofar constitutes the hybrid economy.[533]

Assessing the merits of Lessig's approach it cannot be overlooked that his further developed concept is confronted with similar weaknesses as Benkler's approach since it does not take into account the States' interest in implementing a basic framework for social discourse. Furthermore, cultural differences in the perception of business and friendship are difficult to reflect even in online reality; this assessment appears to be in line with the fact that Wikipedia and Linux did not gain much higher importance in the last five years.[534]

3. Democracy, participation, constitutionalism

The involvement of civil society in decision-making processes of the online world makes it imperative to more closely analyze democratic and participatory models within a constitutional framework. Several theoretical approaches that deserve attention have been developed.

a) Concept of "civic virtue"

An early model for a democratic foundation of cyberspace rule-making can be seen in the concept of "civic virtue" as presented by David R. Johnson/David G. Post already in 1998. Since in cyberspace the system of rule-making based on borders between physical spaces is fundamentally subverted, the two scholars developed a detailed proposal for governing cyberspace, called a deeply democratic "Complex Systems Model for the Governance of Cyberspace": Instead of using statutory law and territorial State jurisdiction for governing transborder cyber-

531 Lessig, 2008, 225/26.

532 Lessig, 2008, 177–185; see also Kulesza/Balleste, 2013, 1335.

533 Lessig, 2008, 226–249; see also Mehra, 2011, 899–903, to the openness function of Wikipedia.

534 For a defense of the viability of the Wikipedia and Linux approaches see again Benkler, 2011b, 153–162, 212–233, 236–249.

space, the principle of civic virtue should prevail.[535] The problems caused by the new challenges of cyberspace would have to be countered by a tailor-made regulatory solution and not by an analogy-based application of traditional laws.[536]

Johnson/Post argue that the system would work solely embedded in the internalization and legitimization of the values enshrined within civic virtue.[537] Once the governed would accept the values as their own (internalize them) and recognize them as regulation that bind the community (legitimize them) the system would survive.[538] In order to be more concrete, Johnson/Post identified particular principles reflected in all online communities; such areas, occupied by cyber-communities, i.e. groups of Internet users sharing common ethical standards, could replace the traditional standards of the off-line societies. Rather than seeking a universal compromise for a statutory law consensus, Johnson/Post proposed "a form of civic virtue that can tolerate continuous conflict and can reside in the very architecture of a decentralized, diverse, complex adaptive system".[539] Such concrete values for all online communities would constitute a narrow catalogue of globally shared principles, created from the bottom-up.[540]

This concept, having some similarities with the model of the social contract,[541] has to rely on the assumption that the community members would feel bound by the values shared by the online community, which they decided to join. The rules shared by all of the communities would then facilitate the identification of the characteristics of the prevailing civic virtue, which could become the basis for the online (cyberspace) governance.[542]

The main critical argument expressed against the concept of Johnson/Post concerns the missing sense of reality.[543] More substantively it can be argued that the motivation of the members of the cyber-community to comply with the agreed ethical standards might be remote, if no power or authority would be charged with the surveillance of compliance, i.e. that a minimal level of an efficiently working legal system would have to be implemented.[544] Furthermore, it is argued that the civic virtue concept is against egoistic human nature since online communities might not act so morally stringent as not to give into the temptation authority

535 Johnson/Post, 1998, Congruence, Cyberspace, and Civic Virtue.
536 Johnson/Post, 1998, Introduction.
537 Johnson/Post, 1998, Congruence, Cyberspace, and Civic Virtue.
538 See also Kulesza/Balleste, 2013, 1334.
539 Johnson/Post, 1998, Introduction.
540 Johnson/Post, 1998, Introduction.
541 See above IV.C.1.
542 Johnson/Post, 1998, Congruence, Cyberspace, and Civic Virtue.
543 Shapiro, 1998, 709.
544 Goldsmith, 1998, 1200.

brings.[545] Nevertheless, with the development of a hybrid economy[546] the civic virtue approach could become less utopian because the common goal, strived for by all the governed, might go into the direction of peer production, whether monetary or not valued by price.[547]

b) Concept of "semiotic democracy"

In the last few years, attempts of applying democracy theory to the cyberspace "order" have been taken up again. Without any doubt, cyber-communities are diverse and reflect a variety of different cultures and social environments.[548] Therefore, the democratic ideals of cyber-communities must correspondingly be reflected in the legal order of cyberspace. A good example for a global knowledge community is Wikipedia.

In his highly debated book "The Regulation of the Internet and How to Stop It" (2008), Harvard scholar Jonathan Zittrain used the successful model of Wikipedia, understood as a very large online community, as basis for his concept of developing a "semiotic democracy" that should be able to meet the particulars of cyber-communities.[549] The term "semiotic democracy" was originally coined by media studies professor John Fiske in 1987 in the context of television; Fiske expressed the opinion that television treats its viewers as capable of assigning their own meaning to images they see on the screen.[550]

Zittrain's model of semiotic democracy is not founded on a regime of simple majority of votes, but it is construed as a more elaborate scheme valuating decisions based on the strongest, most convincing arguments.[551] In this context, Zittrain pointed to the fact that the involvement of people in the information they consume is an important goal itself. As a rule, according to Zittrain, arguments recognized and supported by the majority of the cyber-community should be acknowledged as the new community standards.[552]

Zittrain used Wikipedia for the concretization of his theoretical concept: Since the public views Wikipedia as a shared public resource, the expectations are comparatively high. But it should not be underestimated that besides Wikipedia many other online services have an impact on the Internet users' everyday life. Applying

545 KULESZA/BALLESTE, 2013, 1335; see also WEBER, 2009, 22 and BOWREY, 2005, 24–31.
546 See above IV.D.2.
547 See KULESZA/BALLESTE, 2013, 1339.
548 See above III.C.1.
549 ZITTRAIN, 2008, 147.
550 JOHN FISKE, Television Culture, London/New York 1987, 236, 239.
551 ZITTRAIN, 2008, 147.
552 ZITTRAIN, 2008, 147; see also KULESZA/BALLESTE, 2013, 1344.

the example of Google, Zittrain emphasized the impacts of the web search engine's ranking of search results on the users' assessment of which ideas have prominence and which do not.[553] However, contrary to Wikipedia the Internet users do not "govern" this institution. Therefore, the model of the semiotic democracy can hardly offer a broad theoretical foundation for participatory approaches in cyberspace.

c) Concept of societal constitutionalism

The question whether or to what extent the global civil society should be included into a specific kind of constitutionalization has already been debated for several years. Habermas developed a new constitutional order which is designed in a way that States are no longer solely members of international treaties, but rather "together with their citizens, they can now understand themselves as the constitutional pillars of a politically constituted world society".[554] According to Habermas, the UN Charter, together with other international treaties, has developed beyond its original character and has become a genuine constitution for the global community.

This approach, however, contains illusionary elements; national constitutions cannot so easily be transferred to a cross-border or even global level; the UN would be burdened with the production of norms that have a cosmopolitan character[555] and democratic participation of civil society might vanish completely. But notwithstanding this assessment it should not be overlooked that some constitutional norms have already emerged from the UN, particularly institutional norms creating a certain structure of international organizations.

As outlined[556], a constitutional fragmentation has occurred since some traditional principles of international public law (such as the sovereignty principle) were replaced by a number of regulatory spheres in which specific legal regimes are established. Constitutions in fact also have the task to react sensitively to social change.[557] For example, a "charter of human rights and principles for the internet" has been worked out by a so-called "Dynamic Coalition" in the context of the Internet Governance Forum (IGF)[558] and has subsequently not only been adopted by those members of civil society which participate in the IGF but also been signed

553 Zittrain, 2008, 147.

554 Habermas, 2006, 161.

555 See Teubner, 2012, 46; see also Diggelmann/Altwicker, 2008, 625/26 and 640–642.

556 See above II.B.; to the fragmentation aspect see Koskenniemi, 2006 (Report of International Law Commission).

557 See Diggelmann/Altwicker, 2008, 647/48.

558 See http://www.internetrightsandprinciples.org/site/charter.

by Dilma Rousseff, President of Brazil, as "Marco Civil da Internet" at the opening of the NetMundial in Sao Paulo on April 23, 2014.

There is a risk that tensions between different spheres of policy-making arise and the categories that separated universalism from relativism are blurred.[559] As a consequence, specialized regulatory regimes on human rights[560] tend to compete with the sovereign States as constitutional subjects[561], causing the problem of inter-constitutional collisions.[562] In this context, societal constitutionalism can explain developments in civil society and provide for general foundations of rule-making, however, this concept should be regarded more cautiously to avoid creating intensive competition for positions of power and social influence.

E. Assessment of regulatory theories and of possible future perspectives

The discussion of the manifold theoretical approaches trying to lay a convincing foundation for cyberspace regulation has shown that a single concept cannot explain the complex structure of cyberspace. Moreover, interrelated thinking seems unavoidable; therefore, a few general observations, combined with an assessment of the recently discussed regulatory models, are presented hereinafter.

1. Complexity of structured matrix

As outlined, socio-legal and socio-technical-legal elements play a major role in cyberspace; consequently, these elements are to be considered as key components of regulatory design and regulatory theory.[563] In addition, regulatory competition can lead to webs of regulation, thereby supporting the further development of network structures.[564] As a result, structural complexity occurs; the regulation of technology-based platforms and environmental layers contributes to the evolvement of (complicated) structures.[565]

The cyberspace "order" is caught in a web of conflicting constraints in which each element of the system influences other related elements; in addition, changing a

559 Teubner, 2012, 51/52.
560 For a detailed overview see Jørgensen, 2013, 33 et seq.
561 Teubner, 2012, 150.
562 To this aspect see in more detail Koskenniemi, 2006.
563 See above III.C.1.
564 Murray, 2007, 22 et seq.
565 See also Lessig. 1999a, 91–93.

single element has effects, which ripple out through the whole system.[566] Based on this perception, Murray developed the concept of a complexity matrix[567] allowing the rule-makers to intervene at each point of the matrix, but the complexity of the matrix means that it is impossible to predict the responses of any other point of the matrix.[568] Thereby, assuming that the matrix is a dynamic structure, rule-makers are offered the opportunity to produce effective complementary regulations.[569]

In light of this conceptual perception, Murray proposed a specific scientific methodology along the following lines: Regulators should produce a dynamic model of the regulatory matrix surrounding the "environment" that is subject to regulation (including a map of the communication networks already in place); based on this model the regulatory intervention is designed to offer a positive communication to the sub-systems, or nodes, within the matrix, thereby encouraging the support for the regulatory intervention. Subsequently, regulators should monitor the feedback that follows the intervention and modify it in case of an unsuccessful attempt or reinforce it in case of a positive feedback, making it more likely to succeed.[570]

This methodology, even if it might theoretically be justified, seems not only difficult to implement, but in practice almost impossible to adequately carry out.[571] Looking at the reality it cannot be underestimated that the complexities of the interactions between cyberspace users, the norms each of the many cyberspace communities espouses, the normative demands of all the rule-makers with claims over that activity, and the operation of markets and codes, seem to result in a model which is so complex that it is very hard to predict the effects of a regulatory intervention.[572] Even if a chaotic outcome could be avoided, this methodology would place enormous demands on rule-makers' resources that could hardly be met.

2. Polycentric and sectoral regulation

Notwithstanding the fact that the concept of the complexity matrix (Murray) does not appear to be a viable approach it cannot be contested that cyberspace regula-

566 Murray, 2007, 26.
567 For further details see above IV.B.3.
568 Murray, 2007, 234.
569 Murray, 2007, 237.
570 Murray, 2007, 250.
571 Reed, 2012, 220 uses even the word "completely" instead of "almost".
572 Reed, 2012, 220/21.

tion is moving from a static rule-making model to a dynamic regulatory matrix.[573] This dynamic development leads to a "hypercomplex structural match".[574] From a general perspective, complexity is part of the concept of decentralization as it is based on networks of interdependencies.[575] However, a decentered (complex) regulatory concept also causes fragmentation since the model has to encompass a whole range of interactions among the State and civil society as well as among individuals and private organizations.[576] In view of such complex structures the term "polycentric regulation" was coined which is often described as the "undertaking" of subjecting human conduct to the governance of external controls, whether State or non-state, intended or unintended.[577]

In an order of polycentric regulation the different communities involved in the rule-making processes become important actors. If their participants have a shared set of normative beliefs, shared causal beliefs, shared notions of validity, and a common policy, scholars use the term of "epistemic communities".[578] According to Senn, the process of digitization is governed by transnational epistemic communities (being genuine representatives of the globalization development) and networks, resulting in a polycentric structure or a decentralized network of networks[579], for example as epistemic communities in competition enforcement.[580] In order to overcome fragmentation, digitization can help to improve connections and (closely linked) also leads to increased interdependencies of economies and societies.[581]

The weakness of the formal concept of polycentric regulation consists in the fact that the problems of rule-making pluralism[582] and fragmentation are not (critically) assessed. A global phenomenon such as cyberspace needs a (at least partially) coordinated set of rules; discretionary pluralism would destroy the value of its global reach. Furthermore, the activities developed by epistemic communities and transnational networks raise issues of legitimacy and democratic deficit which merit particular attention.[583]

573 Murray, 2007, 241.
574 See Jørgensen, 2013, 22/23.
575 See Senn, 2011, 30; for a general overview see Musiani, 2013, 43–72.
576 Senn, 2011, 31.
577 Murray, 2007, 47 and 234/35.
578 Braithwaite/Drahos, 2000, 24 and 622/23; Senn, 2011, 73 and 101 qualifying these communities as part of civil society.
579 Senn, 2011, 169.
580 Braithwaite/Drahos, 2000, 620 and 622/23.
581 Senn, 2011, 170.
582 The term „pluralism" is used by Senn, 2011, 252, but its drawbacks are not assessed.
583 This aspect is mentioned by Senn, 2011, 170.

However, the concept of polycentric regulation may lead to the conclusion that rule-making activities in cyberspace should not necessarily cover the whole range of possible legal issues that arise in cyberspace. Moreover, a functional differentiation according to given needs and requirements appears to be appropriate. This assessment creates the impression that a shift from territorial to sectoral regime affiliation must take place in cyberspace rule-making.[584] The functional differentiation might best be linked to the substantive regulatory topics in cyberspace.[585] Depending on whether privacy in social networks, file sharing or deep pocket inspection should be regulated, the "organization" of the involved online participants can differ.

As a consequence, each of the functionally differentiated regulatory regimes has its own operative rationality and develops its own dynamics.[586] In addition, such regimes might cover different environments and reflect the designs and patterns of the concerned communities' interests. The fact, however, that these rules are sector-oriented, modeled according to the prevailing perceptions, and applicable in any area of society usually leads to a lack of coherence in the global cyberspace.[587]

3. Hybrid and mesh regulation

In parallel to the concept of polycentric regulation with functional differentiation (or sector-specific regulation) the concept of hybrid regulation has been developed which tries to overcome the weaknesses of a complex structured matrix. Elaborate network structures are composed of a variety of "hybrid" elements making the notion of "hybridity" useful to elucidate the networks' complexities.[588] The term "hybrid" is described as a combination of a contradictory difference, marked not by either/or, but by both-and, guiding the search for new tendencies in law and society[589], i.e. hybrids are the combination of both sides of a difference.[590] Hybridity can also be seen as a tool to help analyzing and understanding the limits of traditional legal categories and descriptions with the objective of trying to develop ways to reconcile any contradictions resulting from categorization.[591]

The problem with the concept of hybrid regulation consist in the fact that it does not allow any assessment as to whether individual stakeholders in the network

584 See also SENN, 2011, 78.
585 The substantive topics are outlined below V.C.2.
586 SENN, 2011, 254.
587 See also SENN, 2011, 254.
588 WEITZENBOECK, 2014, 62.
589 SAND, 2009, 874.
590 WEITZENBOECK, 2014, 62.
591 See WEITZENBOECK, 2014, 65.

pursue their personal interests or (also) pursue a common interest shared by the other stakeholders in order to reach an overarching network purpose. Since the respective interests do not have to be identical it is important to not only have a procedural framework available but also a system that evaluates the expressed opinions and executed activities. In view of this substantive aspect a system of checks and balances must be put in place, which provides for mechanisms to balance potentially differing interests.[592]

Another approach questions the traditional system of law that structures the rule-making authority in the form of a pyramid with the national legislator on top representing the sovereign State. According to Ost/van de Kerchove a paradigm shift has occurred due to the profound transformation of the State and of modern law in the sense that the pyramidal model with the government at the top is replaced by the network (*réseau)* model even if some remnants of the old model still exist.[593] This shift is justified with the generally acknowledged fact that State sovereignty is not an intangible status anymore, that the will of the State legislator ceases to be received as dogma, and that different powers (State, private enterprises, civil society) need to interact.[594]

Ost/van de Kerchove base their approach, called mesh theory, on the insight that in the era of globalization and internationalization a State's internal legal order cannot survive as stand-alone solution anymore. Furthermore, the move towards mesh regulation[595] is considered the result of two major transformations in the legal and political landscape, namely (i) the move from the use of the statute as the primary instrument of control to different other forms of regulation and (ii) the increased use of the notion of governance instead of government.[596] The first transformation leads from a centralized sovereign authority to a flexible, decentralized, adaptive and often negotiated regulation.[597] The second transformation causes a process that co-ordinates the efforts of actors and social groups not attached to the State or State-owned entities to attain their objectives in fragmented and uncertain environments.[598] Thereby, the concept of mesh regulation comes close to Reed's approach of consensus-building by way of communities' under-

[592] See also WEITZENBOECK, 2014, 67.

[593] OST/VAN DE KERCHOVE, 2002, 14.

[594] OST/VAN DE KERCHOVE, 2002, 14.

[595] The term "mesh" is also used in the network theory describing the creation of a local networking that perches small routers throughout the area to produce a mesh.

[596] For more details see OST/VAN DE KERCHOVE, 2002, 26–32.

[597] See WEITZENBOECK, 2014, 69.

[598] OST/VAN DE KERCHOVE, 2002, 29.

standing[599] or Murray's approach of "network communitarism" being a process of discourse and dialogue between the individual and society.[600]

Without any doubt, numerous stakeholders are present in cyberspace and the traditional system of centralized sovereign State regulation cannot survive the technological developments in the communication networks. The concept of hybrid regulation and mainly of mesh regulation applied to such networks leads to the insight that the relative importance of each source of rule depends on the nature of the activity and the other stakeholders (participants) being regulated.[601] But the identity and regulatory strength of this concept is endangered by the fact that it leaves substantial discretion for the assessment of the quality of the rule-making and does not give any guidance as to the values of the norms agreed by the communities.

A similar approach conceptualizing a world of hybrid legal spaces has been developed by Berman under the heading of "global legal pluralism" that encompasses more than one legal, or quasi-legal, regime in the same social field.[602] Since neither the primacy of territorially-based authority nor the universal harmonization seems to be appropriate in a hybrid reality with overlapping legal spheres, the creation or preservation of multiple parallel legal systems might be an alternative if the concerned actors at least acquiesce to procedural mechanisms, institutions or practices.[603] Legal pluralism envisages providing a "jurisgenerative" model that "focuses in the creative interventions made by various normative communities drawing on a variety of normative sources in ongoing political, theoretical, and legal iterations".[604] According to Berman a pluralist approach to managing hybridity should not attempt to erase the reality of that hybridity, but should recognize the normative conflict and try to overcome it by bringing the actors into a shared social space.[605] The main problem of the legal pluralism concept, however, remains the uncertainty of being able to identify the applicable rules since clear guidance on how to substantiate the pluralism is missing.

599 Reed, 2012, 11.

600 Andrew Murray, Information Technology Law: The Law and Society, Oxford 2012, 68.

601 Weitzenboeck, 2014, 72.

602 Berman, 2007, 1158/59.

603 Berman, 2007, 1162–1165.

604 Berman, 2007, 1166.

605 Berman, 2007, 1192/93; to the possible subsidiarity schemes see Berman, 2007, 1207–1209.

4. Interim conclusion

Summarizing the considerations on the normative foundations of cyberspace regulation it can be stated that the manifold theoretical approaches offer different insights on which a global cyberspace framework could be built. Philosophers and legal sociologists of more than two thousand years contribute to the picture without being able to present the all-convincing solution. But many voices have expressed the importance of some kind of social contract, which is nicely shown in the following picture *(Table 16)*:[606]

Assessing the most recent theoretical approaches which have at least partly dealt with the cyberspace challenges the conclusion appears to be justified that the concepts of polycentric and sectoral regulation as well as of hybrid and mesh regulation that are based on the informal law-making or the Internet-ional customary law model have the inherent value that the variety of legal instruments, the need of including all concerned stakeholders and the increased importance of govern-

606 Picture from Diplo Foundation, Geneva, available at: http://diplo.smugmug.com/ILLUSTRATIONS/Internet-Governance/More-illustrations-1/i-mqJbvkT/A

ance are shown. But these concepts do not substantially help in designing the legal framework for cyberspace in a substantively satisfactory manner since guidelines on how the processes of decision-making should be structured are not part of these theories.

In view of the difficulties related to the given theoretical concepts academia has tried to "escape" the specific discussions by introducing the phenomenon of the so-called meta-regulation (or the regulation of regulation). Meta-regulation puts its focus on procedures rather than on the determination and prescription of behavior through rules, i.e. meta-regulation attempts to offer a method that should serve to analyze the existing regulatory framework.[607] Methodologically, the meta-regulation concept raises questions in relation to determining possible ways to compare different forms of State or private regulation and, thereby, to configure regulation.[608] This fact links meta-regulation to public policy issues[609] and makes it also dependent on these.[610] Thereby, meta-regulation as theoretical concept is confronted with the same challenges as other similar concepts of not being in a position to give clear guidelines for the substantive contents of the regulatory environment.

Another escape approach has very recently been presented by de Búrca/Keohane/Sabel who plead for a "global experimentalist governance" (called "GXG process"). An ideal-type of GXG regime comprises five key steps[611], namely (i) the initial reflection and discussion among stakeholders, (ii) the articulation of a framework understanding with open-ended goals, (iii) the implementation of these broadly framed goals, (iv) the continuous feedback provided from local contexts, and (v) the periodic and routine re-evaluation of the goals and practices (including their possible adaption or revision). Certain similarities of the GXG approach with the multi-layer or network governance model are given, however, GXG puts more emphasis on new forms of learning.[612] A condition for GXG is that States are unable to formulate a comprehensive set of rules and effectively monitor compliance. Furthermore, States must not be stymied by disagreement over basic principles and the cooperation of civil society actors either as agenda setters or as problem solvers is normally indispensable.[613] A problem with the

607 Senn, 2011, 34/35; for further details see Bronwen Morgan, The Economization of Politics: Meta-Regulation as a Form of Nonjudicial Legality, Oxford 2003, 489 et seq.; Lipton, 2012, 147, refers to cyberlaw as "meta-field".

608 Senn, 2011, 35 and 36.

609 For a general overview to the policy issues see the contributions in Brousseau/Marzouki/Méadel, 2012.

610 See also Senn, 2011, 36/37.

611 See de Búrca/Keohane/Sabel, 2014, 2.

612 See de Búrca/Keohane/Sabel, 2014, 4.

613 For more details to those conditions see de Búrca/Keohane/Sabel, 2014, 13/14.

GXG approach consists in the vulnerability to manipulation and unintended consequences, even if GXG has the potential to increase participation in, and thus the democratic legitimacy of, institutions.[614] Additionally, the foreseeability and the predictability of legal norms are low.

Evaluating the described theories it often seems the case that the link to the international legal setting is missing. Even if cyberspace is considered a new world and if global experimentalist governance could be a challenging approach, manifold linkages to the (further) existing real or physical world continue to exist. It is also not imaginable that a completely new system can be implemented as of January 1, 20XX.[615]

Moreover, the design discussion should more intensively address the relations between (theoretical) regulatory concepts and the decision on how to have them embedded into the ongoing (and further developed) international normative order. In addition, a theoretical model always has to reflect the regulatory needs vested with the substantive issues as mainly developed by the *lex informatica* approach.[616] Looking from that perspective, convincing future-oriented approaches should include the social contract and the customary law perception and in particular the establishment of common principles that the different cyber-communities have to comply with.[617]

As a consequence, in a nutshell, only the development of a heuristic and simultaneously holistic approach to rule-making in cyberspace can be managed, i.e. an approach which enshrines the cyberspace universality concept and also addresses the probability of compliance with norms by the concerned communities.[618] Therefore, the following considerations in the last main Chapter V attempt to design a "Global Cyberspace Framework" that is based on the elaboration and implementation of some central guiding principles.

---

614 See DE BÚRCA/KEOHANE/SABEL, 2014, 14/15.

615 WEBER, 2012b, 6.

616 See above IV.A.2.

617 WEBER, 2012b, 6.

618 See also REED, 2012, 221.

V. Development of a "Global Cyberspace Framework" (GCF)

A. Introductory Remarks

The first four chapters have evidenced that the classical forms of rule-making can hardly cope with the challenges of cyberspace and that many new approaches of norm-setting have been developed without, however, establishing a systematic framework which could govern cyberspace. Obviously, such new regime is difficult to design and implement in view of the manifold requirements to be met in order to come to stable and reliable normative terms. Therefore, this concluding chapter does not promote specific rules to be adopted by legislators on a global or a national level but envisages drafting general principles suitable for application in a changing technological and social environment.

Without any doubt it is difficult to forecast the future as experience has shown for centuries. Prognostications and definitive statements are always risky in times of uncertainty. This assessment is true for social and natural sciences notwithstanding the fact that technical developments have been subject to anticipations that were quite correct as the following examples show:[619]

- Already in the fifteenth century Leonardo da Vinci who was not only a famous painter and thinker, but also a visionary, was sketching parachutes, helicopters, hang gliders, and even airplanes.[620] When engineers started to build the respective machines based on Leonardo's sketches some twenty to thirty years ago it became apparent that in fact the constructed machines did function as expected.
- The famous French novelist Jules Verne published a prophetic book in the year 1863, called "Paris in the Twentieth Century";[621] in this ambitious project Verne described new inventions that seemed to be unthinkable at the time of publication. In fact, the manuscript was lost for almost 130 years and was only published in 1994. At the time of its re-discovery, the surprised public was astonished to see that Verne predicted that Paris would have glass skyscrapers, air conditioning, television equipment, elevators, etc. within the following hundred years. Shortly after the mentioned book, Verne published two other

619 For an overview see also WEBER, 2012b, 1/2.

620 For further details see FRITJOF CAPRA, The Science of Leonardo: Inside the Mind of the Genius of the Renaissance, New York 2007.

621 JULES G. VERNE, Paris au XXe siècle, Paris 1863, only published in 1994.

Co-Publication with Schulthess Juristische Medien AG

Published by Springer-Verlag GmbH Berlin Heidelberg 2015
R.H. Weber, *Realizing a New Global Cyberspace Framework*,
DOI 10.1007/978-3-662-44677-5_5

novels, namely "From the Earth to the Moon" (1865)[622] and "Around the Moon" (1870)[623], outlining numerous details of the missions of the US astronauts to the moon some hundred years later (1969). Verne predicted the size of the space capsule, the duration of the voyage and the weightlessness of the astronauts.[624] Notwithstanding the fact that Verne was not a scientist, he amassed a vast archive encompassing the great scientific discoveries of his time.

- In the year 1949 George Orwell gave a quite accurate forecast on the expected technological environment in the year 1984.[625] Particularly after Snowden's numerous revelations since June 2013 that made transparent the vast collection of data by secret services' entities and supervisory authorities, most individuals now do have the impression that "big brother is watching you".

Obviously, technologies are quickly changing the environment, thereby confronting mankind with partly unexpected challenges. To ensure that the legal framework for cyberspace is based on reliable technological foundations the following developments have to appropriately be taken into account:[626]

- Information technologies including cloud computing and big data analytics will increasingly become utilities ("mass technologies"). As for electricity or telecommunications, utilities are required in case of need; in principle, users do not care about the provider. Nevertheless, it should not be underestimated (mainly by natural science experts) that technological equipment', in particular robots, will not be able to perform certain human activities, at the forefront pattern recognition and exercise of common sense.[627] These human abilities enable and require the creation of multiple models that are more easily apt to meet the diverse forthcoming developments and to approximate future events.
- Fast technological developments are responsible for the acknowledgment of the so-called Moore's law saying that the number of components in integrated circuits doubles every year (later corrected to two years). However, queries have been raised regarding the viability of Moore's law in the long run. Gordon Moore himself, when asked about a possible collapse of the celebrated law named after him, predicted in the year 2005 that it would end in ten to

622 Jules G. Verne, De la Terre à la Lune, Paris 1865.
623 Jules G. Verne, Autour de la Lune, Paris 1870.
624 Kaku, 2011, 5.
625 George Orwell, Nineteen Eighty-Four, London 1949.
626 See also Weber, 2012b, 2/3
627 Kaku, 2011, 83; to the risk for humans of being (partly) replaced by machines see Lanier, 2013, 5/6.

twenty years.[628] Some futurists (Ray Kurzweil, Bruce Sterling, Vernor Vinge) who are of the opinion that this law will ultimately lead to a technological singularity expressed more fundamental concerns; in other words, the period in which progress in technology occurs becomes almost instant.[629] In addition, technology on its own is neither the cause of, nor a solution to a particular constellation of problems.[630]

- Looking from a general perspective of human development it can be argued that individuals seem to be in a transition phase from being passive observers of law to becoming the choreographers of nature and finally conservators of nature. As a consequence, human beings will have to be able to control objects of the environment and the technical equipment would need to have the ability to decipher an individual's wishes in order to subsequently carry them out.[631]

Another important aspect concerns the likelihood of a fundamental political influence exercised by new technologies. Science in general, if developed in a future-oriented way, can question political structures by causing an unsettling effect:[632] (i) A good historical example is the controversy between Galileo Galilei presenting the idea of a round world (thereby questioning religious assumptions) and the Catholic Church represented by the pope; in the year 1633 an inquisition ban on reprinting Galileo's work was released by the pope which was only lifted in 1718.[633] (ii) Recently, representatives of several social sciences' disciplines have expressed the opinion that the "Arab spring movements/revolutions" could not have happened without the available information technology instruments such as mobile phones and social networks.[634]

Drawing a preliminary conclusion from these observations it must be acknowledged that technology is also a social endeavor. Internet technologies in particular (as well as their legal implementation) are to be understood through the lens of social interpretation since they have an identifiable socio-legal effect beyond their direct contribution to the fabric of society.[635] As a consequence, this (last) chapter exploits the legal settlements that design the cyberspace environment.

---

628 See Manek Dubash, Interview, Techworld 2005, retrieved from http://news.techworld.com/operating-systems/3477/moores-law-is-dead-says-gordon-moore/.

629 See Ray Kurzweil, The Singularity is Near: When Humans Transcend Biology, New York 2005.

630 Franklin, 2013, 94.

631 See Kaku, 2011, 58.

632 Weber, 2012b, 3.

633 See John L. Heilbron, Censorship of Astronomy in Italy after Galileo, in: Ernan McMullin (ed.), The Church and Galileo, Notre Dame 2005, 279–304.

634 See the special issue of the International Journal of Communication, Vol. 5, 2011, 1435 et seq. with the title "The Arab Spring and the Role of ICTs".

635 Weber, 2012b, 3; Murray, 2007, 37–42.

B. Policy parameters for cyberspace rule-making

Discussions so far have shown that legal instruments are exposed to challenges in cyberspace and that the implementation of legal means must be executed with great care and prudence in order to avoid undesired effects. Before the basic parameters and the guiding principles of an international cyberspace framework will be analyzed it seems justified to assess the political visions of rule-making as well as their inherent scope and limits.

1. Political visions of rule-making

Looking at the experience of the last few years it seems obvious that the success of an appropriate legal framework governing the future of cyberspace depends on the ability of the policymakers to embrace new approaches using different tools from the still dominant and traditional model of command-and-control regulation.[636] Furthermore, the identification of underlying structures and the basic shortcomings as well as the assessment of the international legal order's rational potential merit greater attention.[637]

Usually, two visions of political power exist, namely (i) the dominance of State power and (ii) the power distribution.[638] State power is founded on the sovereignty concept; power distribution relies on a variety of stakeholders. Questions in assessing possible political systems refer to the structure of the international rule-making agenda, the extent and form of supra-state institutions and the role of sovereign States.[639]

Political forces have always intended to get involved in the organization and administration of cyberspace, irrespective of the fact that scientific communities and private actors were responsible for the main developments. The attempt of States to regain power became particularly obvious prior to and mainly during the World Conference on International Telecommunications (WCIT) in Dubai (December 2012); the advocates of a "cyber-sovereignty" approach raised their voices louder, expressing the opinion that for public interest and security reasons control

636 Weber, 2012b, 3; Weiser, 2009, 538/39 refers to a "multiparty contracting problem".

637 This theoretical discussion cannot be deepened hereinafter; for a recent overview see Altwicker/Diggelmann, 2014, 69 et seq.; to the constellations of regulatory instruments in global governance see Michèle Rioux/Nicolas Adam/Biel Company Pérez, Competing Institutional Trajectories for Global Regulation — Internet in a Fragmented World, in: Roxana Radu/Jean-Marie Chenou/Rolf. H. Weber (eds.), The Evolution of Global Internet Governance. Principles and Policies in the Making, Zürich 2013, 37, 49–54.

638 Klimburg, 2013, 1.

639 Weber, 2013, 95.

over the Internet should remain in the competence of national governments including the right to regulate the activities occurring in the Internet as far as accessible by the domestic population.[640] The negotiations in Dubai showed that some countries such as Russia, China or Saudi Arabia are attempting to subordinate the management of the Internet to governmental control, mainly by referring to security and public order interests, even if such a development would lead to a (national) fragmentation of the Internet. Quantitatively, the promoters of cyber-sovereignty had a slight majority amongst the ITU members in Dubai, thus also making it difficult to develop a moderate approach by introducing more flexibility in the decision-making processes.

At first, the differentiation between (i) the proponents of a liberal structuring of cyberspace, having confidence in a private-economic fulfillment of tasks with as little State interventions as possible and (ii) the representatives of a concept featuring national control interests, may appear rather insignificant.[641] However, this distinction points into the direction of different regulatory approaches, namely one in which the political power is increasingly distributed and includes non-state actors, and one in which State power is dominant.[642] After the WCIT, a binary global scene seems to have emerged, most of the developing world (with the exception of India) sided with the cyber-sovereignty advocates. The WCIT morphed into a "battle", partly (and problematically) even called a "digital cold war" of the liberal West against the rest of the world.[643]

The process of international regime formation was already confronted with diverging opinions in the past; insofar, the discussions at the WCIT did not come as novelty. Usually the globalists pleading for international legal harmonization are confronted with the objections of the skeptics; the respective general arguments are summarized in the following diagram *(Table 17)*:[644]

640 For further details see WEBER, 2013, 98.

641 WEBER, 2013, 101.

642 KLIMBURG, 2013, 1; see also KATHERINE MAHER, The New Westphalian Web, Foreign Policy, February 25, 2013.

643 WEBER, 2013, 101; for a detailed discussion of the political initiatives prior to and during the WCIT see HILL, 2013, 79 et seq.

644 See ANTONOVA, 2008, 67/68, and WEBER, 2009, 93.

	Globalists	*Skeptics*
Concepts	— One world, shaped by extensive, intensive and rapid flow of goods/ services/ data	— Internationalization, not globalization — Regionalization
Power	— Rise of multilateralism — Decline of Nation State — Erosion of State sovereignty, autonomy and legitimacy	— Nation State rules — Intergovernmentalism
Culture	— Emergence of global popular culture	— Resurgence of nationalism and national identity
Economy	— Transnational economy — Global informational capitalism	— Development of regional blocs — New imperialism
Inequality	— Growing inequality within and across societies — Erosion of old hierarchies	— Growing North-South divide — Irreconcilable conflicts of interests
Order	— Global civil society — Multilayered global governance — Cosmopolitanism	— International society of States — Political conflicts among States — Communitarianism

Obviously, the above diagram cannot be directly mirrored in cyberspace but it contains valuable elements. In addition, there is clearly no easy way forward to overcome the emerging tensions between the cyber-sovereignty and the civil society-inclusive approaches. Moreover, different routes exist and the choice of the way forward depends on the specific environment.[645] Generally, it can be said that the traditional understanding of political structures as command must be reflected by a new understanding which allocates to the rule-makers the incentive of inducing civil society to execute certain actions in the sense that people think about what to choose and what to do in a decentralized system.[646] Guiding principles for humanity do have a global nature, even if influenced by smaller entities; in other words, the absence of hierarchical structures and the fact that new issues are com-

[645] WEBER, 2013, 105.
[646] REED, 2012, 248 et seq.

plex must be acknowledged; flat structures on different appropriate levels facilitate decision-making by including the relevant persons and organizations at the actual point of their concern.[647]

The current challenges in the context of cyberspace regulation by nature require a broader and more collective decision-making than in a traditional State. As already Fukuyama mentioned, the normative order was established to limit discretion of exclusive State power.[648] Therefore, the movement towards global governance is unavoidable and the structure of international law will need some adaptions.[649] Global governance refers to a new order encompassing States, non-state actors, and new geographic and/or functional entities in a power-sharing framework.[650] The crucial point concerns the appropriate balance of power between sovereign States' governance and non-territorial and privatized mechanisms.[651]

Therefore, global governance must encompass collective efforts enabling the concerned persons to identify, understand, and address worldwide problems that go beyond the capacity of individual States to solve.[652] The respective efforts must acknowledge that changes with regard to the separation of the traditional power model (Montesquieu) seem unavoidable.[653] As a further insight it must be recognized that the failures attributed to the multilaterism approach cannot easily be remedied by a minilaterism concept, at least not in the – globally oriented – cyberspace field.[654] Consequently, different levels at which political theory may operate are to be taken into account: (i) A global framework needs to be combined with domestic political theory, i.e. it must be assessed to what extent notions of domestic importance are to be adapted at the global level, and if so, how it should be done. (ii) A global political theory must be able to provide guidance as to what principles should be adopted and which institutions should be put into practice. (iii) Finally, the question is to be tackled how general principles should be applied to specific issues.[655]

647 Weber, 2013. 106.
648 Fukuyama, 2004, 98/99.
649 To the discussion about the structure of international law see Altwicker/Diggelmann, 2014, 78–81.
650 Winchester, 2009, 22.
651 See also DeNardis, 2014, 23.
652 Weber, 2010a, 15.
653 For more details see Burkert, 2012, 100–109.
654 Brummer, 2014, 165 et seq. proposes a minilaterism approach in the fields of international finance and international trade.
655 Caney, 2006, 2/3.

In order to cope with the globalization of (inter-)governmental relations and governance, the political theorists are referring to the notion of "cosmopolitanism" which embraces three elements, namely individualism, universality, and generality.[656] A broad understanding of "cosmopolitanism" in decision-making procedures reflects and even extends the Kantian framework highlighting global distributive justice besides launching civil and political rights.[657] Future democratic iterations will make interconnectedness and interdependence deeper and wider; this development does not undermine democracy but shows the emergence of new political configurations.[658] In order to overcome the existing gap in the regulatory perceptions for cyberspace, it is necessary to strengthen the efforts (i) to establish appropriate structures and organizational elements for the implementation of decentralized decision-making procedures involving a variety of stakeholders and (ii) to implement adequate fora for debates and discussions.[659]

2. Scope and limits of rule-making approaches

The analysis of the different regulatory models, which can lead to a new legal order,[660] has shown that fresh approaches are needed in order to build an appropriate legal framework for cyberspace. If a regulatory need is recognized in cyberspace, the concerned members of civil society as well as businesses may not be satisfied with national legal provisions and may not be willing to wait for multilateral treaties. Consequently, as experience evidenced over the last two decades, soft law has spread out with the objective to fill the gaps emerging in traditional legal regimes; later, the vagueness of the soft law notion has led to the concept of informal law-making. However, even if these (new) models will play an important role in practice, such assessment does not suffice to build an appropriate legal framework as long as the models are not embedded into the international legal regime.[661]

Therefore, the identification of scope and limits of rule-making approaches and particularly the establishment of reliable pillars in a future cyberspace environment gain importance. In view of the reliability issue, light should be shed on different debated ideas:

656 Pogge, 1994, 89/90.
657 Lane, 2013, 22; see also Koskenniemi, 2005, 611.
658 See Benhabib, 2006, 74.
659 Weber, 2013, 113.
660 See above Chapter IV.A.-E.
661 Weber, 2012b, 7.

(i) As mentioned, any legal order has social impacts.[662] Therefore, the setting of a legal framework for cyberspace should consider realizing optimal conditions for a perfect society. Such an approach does have a long standing tradition: Almost five hundred years ago, in 1516, Sir Thomas Morus published the novel "Utopia", envisioning a paradise on a fictional island in the Atlantic Ocean.[663] Again in the nineteenth century, many social movements in Europe searched for various forms of utopia or utopian environments.[664]

During the last fifty years scholars have tried to better incorporate a utopian environment into the structure of legislative (national and international) frameworks. Forty years ago, autonomous cultural arrangements were qualified as "framework of utopia", thereby giving a structure to the utopian environment itself.[665] More recently, the eminent scholar Martti Koskenniemi assessed the structure of international legal reasoning through the lens "From Apology to Utopia", outlining the descriptive and normative concerns of the international legal order. Koskenniemi argues that in respect of the relevant issues grammar has not changed extensively, but new topics such as human rights and environment emerged.[666] Nevertheless, even with a higher degree of concretization, "utopia" is not an ideal concept for the design of an appropriate cyberspace framework since it is difficult to identify sufficiently clear contours in this concept and since it seems quite impossible to draw structural elements, possibly aiming at future developments, from this concept.[667]

(ii) Nearly half a century ago, Louis Henkin phrased the often cited sentence that "almost all nations observe almost all principles of international law and almost all of their obligations all of the time".[668] This assertion does not seem very convincing anymore.[669] Compliance is not only doubtful in the military and political arena (for example in view of interventions into the sovereignty of other countries) but also in the cyberspace field; more and more States undermine the globality of the Internet by interfering into the free cross-border information flow, thereby jeopardizing the freedom of expression through a national fragmentation of the Internet, or by applying wide-spread communication surveillance mechanisms, thereby violating the right of privacy, both fundamental human rights

[662] See above III.C.1.

[663] THOMAS MORUS, The Utopia, 2002, retrieved from http://www.idph.com.br/conteudos/ebooks/Utopia.pdf.

[664] For further details see HERBERT GEORGE WELLS, A Modern Utopia, Leipzig 1905.

[665] ROBERT NOZICK, Anarchy, State and Utopia, Oxford 1974.

[666] KOSKENNIEMI, 2009, 562–573.

[667] WEBER, 2012b, 7; see also MACKINNON, 2012, 232–236.

[668] HENKIN, 1979, 47.

[669] WEBER, 2012b, 8.

being guaranteed by international and regional legal instruments (for example the UN Convention on Human Rights).[670]

Moreover, it cannot be overlooked that the increasingly dense framework of rules with different legal qualities rather leads to uncertainties than clear acknowledgments in respect of compliance with (international) rules by States.[671] At best it can be said that the international legal framework provides instruments for reconciling conflicting interests and settling disputes.[672] In addition, it should not be overlooked that narrowly designed and oriented rules usually are not apt to comply with the challenges of rapidly changing technologies;[673] as a consequence, a polycentric regulatory approach should be chosen.[674]

Other models are based on specific compliance aspects: For example, Chayes/Handler express the opinion that States obey international rules not because they are threatened, but because they are persuaded by the dynamic created in form of treaty regimes to which they belong.[675] Instead of persuasion (or reputation) the substantive fairness of international rules can also be considered as decisive element; particularly Franck relies more on fairness concepts than on managerial processes in the international domain.[676]

Both approaches, however, underestimate procedural elements, i.e. the complex processes of institutional interactions in a transnational legal setting as well as the processes of internalization of global norms.[677] Apart from procedural objections, structural reasons also do not support the ideas of persuasion and fairness.[678] Furthermore, from a historical perspective, Hobbes' famous concept, outlined in his Leviathan,[679] based on the assumption that law is to be defined in political terms, which means in terms of power, does not fit the structures of cyberspace anymore since the regulatory environment is linked to the multistakeholder participation (and the civil society's involvement in the decision-making processes).[680]

670 Jørgensen, 2013, 37–41.
671 Weber, 2012b, 8.
672 Kaufmann, 2011, 1199; Howse/Teitel, 2010, 127 et seq.
673 See above III.C.1.
674 See above IV.E.2 and Senn, 2011, 186 et seq.
675 Chayes/Handler Chayes, 1998.
676 Franck, 1995, 1 et seq.
677 See Weber, 2012b, 8; Shaffer, 2010, 10 et seq.; Koh, 1997, 2599, 2602, 2645/46, 2655/56.
678 See Howse/Treitel, 2010, 128–130.
679 Hobbes, 1651.
680 Weber, 2012b, 8; Frydman, 2004, 231; to the multistakeholder approach in particular see below V.C.3.

3. Structured rule-making processes (multi-layer governance)

The design of a legal framework must be based on the acknowledgement that its principles are to be embedded into the global governance debate. This concept is described as new "order, characterized in part by porous borders and power sharing amongst States, non-state actors, and new geographic and functional entities".[681]

a) Principles of a multi-layer approach

Notwithstanding the manifold facets of global governance the widely accepted statement might be made that "there is no such thing as" a sole global governance.[682] Moreover, global governance has to be looked at from a multi-layer (multi-level) perspective,[683] i.e. different layers (levels) are to be taken into account depending on the actors involved, the topics at stake and the problems to be solved.

Multi-layer governance requires the development of common foundations applicable to all relevant layers, while at the same time it must respect diversity and pluralism in order to be commensurate with the respective level of integration.[684] An important aspect of this movement is the acknowledgment of the need for increased cooperation when trying to achieve a multi-layer consistency.[685] Therefore, multi-layer governance addresses normative guidance as to how relations between different layers of governance should be framed in a coherent and not fragmented manner, encompassing both analytical and prospective issues in building upon observations of legal phenomena.[686] The definition of the proper interaction of the different levels has a direct impact on an ideally coherent regulatory architecture of multi-layer governance, i.e. multi-layer governance "proposes a process and direction".[687] If common legal rights and obligations can be identified, the ensuing legal framework enjoys special legitimacy, which is essential for the operation and effectiveness of law.[688]

681 See WINCHESTER, 2009, 22.
682 WEBER, 2012b, 7.
683 For a general overview see WEBER, 2010c, 689/90.
684 COTTIER, 2009, 656/57.
685 See BREINING-KAUFMANN, 2005, 118.
686 WEBER, 2010c, 689.
687 COTTIER, 2009, 656.
688 WEBER, 2010c, 690; COTTIER, 2009, 659/60.

Since regulatory frameworks evolve within a given societal and political context,[689] private regimes are part of the overall legal design, particularly if their weaknesses can be eliminated or at least diminished;[690] these regimes have a certain place in a multi-layer structure, if developed with the objective of establishing an appropriate institutionalization, based on broad initiation and wide building support.[691] Other elements are the significance of the institutional environments, the dynamics of relationships, and how non-sovereign bodies respond to multiple legitimacy claims in complex and dynamic regulatory situations.[692] In relation to non-state or private networks and organizations, the governance emphasis should not be based on normative validity; moreover, the trend towards efficiency and public value maximization also needs to be supported.[693]

b) Development of normative multi-layer governance principles

Multi-layer governance is a topic, which is discussed in many fields outside cyberspace regulation, particularly in the field of financial markets.[694] The inclusion of several layers into the regulatory considerations is a consequence of the acknowledgment that State law is not solely capable of designing an appropriate legal framework anymore and that private and semi-autonomous rule-making can make valuable contributions to the implementation of a reasonable normative order. However, the multi-layer structure should not be understood as a hierarchical order but as a polycentric network of participating entities.

Notwithstanding the fact that some elements, which define multi-layer governance in a global context, seem diffuse, important core themes can be distilled:[695]

- Future regulatory problems by their nature will require broader and more collective decision-making than applied in traditional regimes; global interactions necessitate the establishment of a multistakeholder regime.[696]
- Responses to new problems are complex on the global level and flat structures on different sub-levels facilitate decision-making by including the relevant persons and organizations in the process at the actual point of their respective concern.

689 Following Weber, 2012b, 7.
690 To the weaknesses of private regimes see above II.C.4 and the examples given by Tambini/Leonardi/Marsden, 2013, 296/7.
691 Bernstein/Cashore, 2007, 347–371.
692 Black, 2008, 137–164.
693 Senn, 2011, 228 and 259.
694 See Weber, 2010c, 689/90.
695 Waters, 2009, 33; Weber, 2010c, 692.
696 See below V.C.3.

- The ongoing processes of globalization and integration necessarily lead to an altered perception and notion of State sovereignty and ask for new elements of legitimacy in this respect.

Furthermore, globalization is not a clearly defined term. Commercial globalization reflects the fact of having increased transnational businesses and economic activities. Cultural globalization addresses the issues related to the manifold social policies. Legal globalization looks at the harmonization of the States' normative orders or the implementation of cross-border legal rules.

In this context, the new dimensions of global administrative law merit further attention since this concept looks at institutional differentiations and elaborated procedural techniques.[697] Assessing the dichotomy of regulatory sources and the emergence of new regimes introduced by civil society, adapted transnational concepts need to be developed in the administrative law field.[698] Institutions can lead States to a more cooperative behavior than they otherwise might have, building mutual connections from peripheral points, in federative or associate forms.[699]

Hand in hand with the development of global administrative law the regulatory system and design has increasingly accepted the importance of public notice and consent procedures.[700] Recently the fruition of these ideas was mainly seen in connection with the execution of functions by the G-20 in respect of financial regulation.[701] However, lessons from the respective experiences can also be drawn for other segments of society.[702]

c) Macro-legal and micro-legal level approach as alternative

Another theoretical approach does not differentiate between a multiple of layers, but between the macro-legal and the micro-legal level. The foundation of this approach is based on the assessment that the legal character of different objects might not be identical. Some scholars have coined the term of "yet unidentified legal objects" in the context of the attempt to develop a global law, encompassing the objects, which have a "doubtful" or "controversial" legal character.[703] Such objects require the acceptance of a certain degree of normativity since they are pragmatically implemented (in practice).[704] Departing from the well-known dis-

697 Kingsbury/Casini, 2009, 319 et seq.
698 See also Senn, 2011, 71.
699 See also Cassese, 2005, 674; Senn, 2011, 215/16.
700 Barr/Miller, 2006, 41.
701 Wouters/Ramopoulos, 2012, 12 et seq.
702 Weber, 2012b, 7.
703 Frydman, 2012, 17, 20.
704 Duss, 2012, 21.

tinction between «objective law» and "subjective rights" the approach differentiates between the macro-legal and the micro-legal level;[705] thereby, the model provides for the possibility to assume a micro-legal concept of normativity without the need to implement a macro-legal framework.[706]

This approach has been hardly tested in cyberspace reality but it appears possible that the respective ideas can be made fruitful in connection with the implementation of appropriate organizational rules in social communities. On the one hand, for example, moral norms falling under the notion of "netiquette"[707] are relevant for online macro-communities.[708] On the other hand, communities built around email and discussion lists or bulletin board systems could be seen as micro-communities, however, such narrow understanding hardly corresponds to the perceptions of the users themselves.[709] Even if the classification of online micro-communities causes major difficulties, a certain taxonomy can be done, for example by distinguishing commercial communities, online/offline communities, gaming communities, cafe communities, knowledge communities, and creative communities[710], allocating to each class a primary purpose. However, from a regulatory perspective this taxonomy does not provide for major substantive insights.

4. Legitimacy of cyberspace rule-making

The multi-layer concept and the hereinafter discussed multistakeholder participation approach challenge the traditional legal and political understanding of legitimacy as a notion primarily relevant to sovereign States as subjects of the international legal order according to the prevailing doctrine. As a consequence, several questions arise:[711] Who can be a legitimate stakeholder in a multi-layer framework (for which layer)? Do the same criteria for legitimacy apply in a multi-layer regime as in the traditional regime? What importance does legitimacy have in a multi-layer environment? Is not the inclusion of many stakeholders legitimizing enough?

Legitimacy can be perceived as a justification of authority giving the governed the feeling that their own values are represented in a decision-making context;[712] an

705 See also WEBER, 2012b, 7.

706 FRYDMAN, 2012, 21.

707 For examples see above II.C.5.

708 See MURRAY, 2007, 141–144.

709 For a detailed description of the various studies done in this field see MURRAY, 2007, 145–148.

710 This is the approach of MURRAY, 2007, 148.

711 See also WEBER, 2009, 105/06.

712 WEBER, 2002, 46/47.

authority's "right to rule" is to be traced back to a translation of the Latin word "legitimus" as meaning "lawful, according to law".

In the sociological perspective of Max Weber three models *("Idealtypen")* of governance exist, the rational or legal, the traditional and the charismatic authority; legitimacy in a wider sense also encompasses an ethical-philosophical dimension, which heaves legitimacy above positive law.[713] Some scholars differentiate between "normative theories" on legitimacy, which set out general criteria for evaluating the right to rule, and "empirical theories", which focus on belief systems of those subject to government.[714] As a result, legitimacy can either be justified by formal ideas as the rule of law rationale (legality) or by substantive value rationality based on morality and justice.[715]

According to a source-oriented perception of legitimacy, an authority may be qualified as legitimate when referring to democratic States, which base their authority on the "demos", the public.[716] In reality, procedural aspects within the different governing entities may enhance the legitimacy of policy-making decisions in cyberspace.[717] This comprehension of legitimacy can be traced back to Luhmann who argued that legitimization could be effected through adequate procedures.[718] Franck described legitimacy as "the aspect of governance that validates institutional decisions as emanating from a right process. What constitutes right process is described in a society's adjectival constitution or rules of order, or is pedigreed by tradition and historic custom".[719]

The procedural approach[720] may be complemented by a result-oriented type of legitimacy, i.e. a substantive conception which looks at the outcome of the legitimizing procedures; this result-oriented approach depends on the values deemed as "right" by the stakeholders concerned, thus in part justifying them as legitimizing sources.[721] But such an approach reveals a particular difficulty, because it relies on subjective perceptions of legitimate values, which are related to cultural and societal differences and evolve over time.[722] For such reasons, Habermas tried to link the procedural aspects with specific notions of contents ("discourse princi-

713 For a detailed discussion of Max Weber's concept see Weber, 2009, 110.
714 Clark, 2005, 18.
715 Clark, 2005, 19.
716 Habermas, 1992, 117.
717 Weber, 2009, 110.
718 Luhmann, 1975, 9–53.
719 Franck, 1995, 1.
720 To the elements of the procedural legitimacy (transparent and accountable operations) see also Brownsword, 2012, 257/58.
721 Weber, 2009, 110/11.
722 Clark, 2005, 13.

ple"), assuming that just those norms can claim validity that receive the approval of all potentially effected people, insofar as they participate in a free and rational discourse.[723] The problem with the discourse principle, however, consists in the fact that it is challenged by particular aspects of fair processes of consensus-building.

Legitimacy must also be measured in light of constitutional values and principles. Such a constitutional approach to cyberspace regulation, based on particular architectural principles, could provide important inputs. Clark specifies "three cognate concepts — legality, morality, and constitutionality", which are set to "mark out the terrain within which the practice of legitimacy tends to take place".[724] Legitimacy is thereby perceived as a reconciling norm, enabling consensus on how these three elements can be accommodated amongst each other.[725] In addition, legitimacy should be assessed from the perspective of regulatory purposes and standards, regulatory instruments, regulatory effectiveness, and regulatory connection.[726]

Such perceptions of legitimacy emphasize the origins of the concept in political sciences, which – in contrast to cyberspace governance – does not specifically focus on States. As a "virtual province", cyberspace is mainly "managed" through a bottom-up approach with a large number of stakeholders; apart from this fact, with international law gaining importance, legitimacy questions are becoming weightier not only for the international society in general, but also for the stability of the international order.[727]

---

723 Habermas, 1992, 161.
724 Clark, 2005, 19.
725 Clark, 2005, 20.
726 For more details see Brownsword, 2012, 258–264.
727 Weber, 2009, 111; Clark, 2005, 12–17.

C. Guiding principles of a Global Cyberspace Framework

1. Formal/procedural principles of a Global Cyberspace Framework

a) Need for a dynamic and flexible approach

The fast technological developments make it necessary to apply a dynamic and flexible approach in the regulatory design of a global cyberspace framework. The traditional way of norm-setting does not meet the requirements of a fast moving environment anymore. State legislators often do not have sufficient "technical" knowledge of the matter to be regulated and are therefore exposed to industry lobbyists. Furthermore, the legislative democratic process is usually long and the risk exists that legal norms will be enacted and implemented only at a time when technology has already changed (so-called regulatory lag).[728]

User dynamism can also be seen in a competitive market environment: As experience in the online world has shown, network platforms with interactive users resemble (dynamic) communities rather than two-sided versions of perfectly competitive markets.[729] User dynamism within a community is beneficial in terms of generating content, creativity, and quality accounts for a larger share of value on these platforms.[730]

A dynamic and flexible approach should lead to a taxonomy, which allocates functional areas and tasks to specific institutional actors being most apt to deal with the respective issues. DeNardis/Raymond recently developed such taxonomy for the specific area of Internet governance; this taxonomy may serve as example how relevant issues of cyberspace and the corresponding institutional actors can be structured *(Table 18)*:[731]

728 WEBER, 2002, 59.
729 MEHRA, 2011, 905.
730 MEHRA, 2011, 905/06 and 952.
731 DENARDIS/RAYMOND, 2013, 4/5.

Functional Area	*Tasks*	*Primary Institutional Actor*
I. Control of "Critical Internet Resources"	Central Oversight of Names and Numbers	ICANN, IANA, US DoC
	Technical Design of IP Addresses	IETF
	New Top-Level Domain Approval	ICANN
	Domain Name Assignment	Internet Registrars
	Oversight of Root Zone File	US DoC/NTIA
	IP Address Distribution (allocation/assignment)	IANA, RIR, LIR, NIR, ISP
	Management of Root Zone File	IANA
	Autonomous System Number Distribution	IANA, Regional Internet Registries
	Operating Internet Root Servers	VeriSign, Cogent, others
	Resolving DNS Queries (Billions per Day)	Registry Operators (VeriSign, others)
II. Setting Internet Standards	Protocol Number Assignment	IANA
	Designing Core Internet Standards	IETF
	Designing Core Web Standards	W3C
	Establishing Other Communication Standards	ITU, IEEE, MPEG, JPEG, ISO, others
III. Access and Interconnection Coordination	Facilitating Multilateral Network Interconnection	Internet Exchange Point Operators
	Peering and Transit Agreements to Interconnect	Private Network Operators, Content Networks, CDN
	Setting Standards for Interconnection	IETF
	Network Management (Quality of Service)	Private Network Operators
	Setting End User Access and Usage Policies	Private Network Operators
	Regulating Access (e.g. Net Neutrality)	National Governments/ Agencies

Functional Area	*Tasks*	*Primary Institutional Actor*
IV. Cybersecurity Governance	Securing Network Infrastructure	ISP, Network Operators, Private End User Networks
	Designing Encryption Standards	Standards-Setting Organizations
	Cybersecurity Regulation/ Enforcement	National Statutes/Multilateral Agreements
	Correcting Software Security Vulnerabilities	Software Companies
	Software Patch Management	Private End Users
	Securing Routing, Addressing, DNS	Network Operators, IETF, Registries
	Responding to Security Problems	CERT/CSIRT
	Trust Intermediaries Authenticating Web Sites	Certificate Authorities (CA)
V. Information Intermediation	Commercial Transaction Facilitation	E-Commerce Sites, Financial Intermediaries
	Mediating (of) Government Content Removal Requests (Discretionary Censorship)	Search Engines, Social Media Companies, Content Aggregation Sites
	App Mediation (Guidelines, Enforcement)	Smartphone Providers (e.g. Apple)
	Establishing Privacy Policies (via End User Agreements and Contracts)	Social Media, Advertising Intermediaries, Email Providers, Network Operators
	Responding to Cyberbullying and Defamation	Content Intermediaries
	Regulating Privacy, Reputation, Speech	Statutory and Constitutional Law
	Mediating Govt. Requests for Personal Data	Content Intermediaries, Network Operators

Functional Area	*Tasks*	*Primary Institutional Actor*
VI. Architecture-Based Intellectual Property Rights Enforcement	Domain Name Trademark Dispute Resolution	ICANN UDRP, Registrars, Accredited Dispute Resolution Providers
	Removal of Copyright Infringing Content	Content Intermediaries
	Algorithmic Enforcement (e.g. Search Rankings)	Search Engine Companies
	Blocking Access to Infringing Users	Network Operators/ISP
	Domain Name System IPR Enforcement	Registries/Registrars
	Regulating Online IPR Enforcement	National Statutes, International Treaties
	Standards-Based Patent Policies	Standards-Setting Organizations
	Enacting Trade Secrecy in Content Intermediation	Search Engines, Reputation Engines

b) Need for a user-centered and community-related approach

Due to the lack of equivalence,[732] a replication of the physical world model is not possible in cyberspace.[733] Obviously the most serious consequence of embedding the wrong (business) model in cyberspace rule-making is its effect on the behavior of those who are subject to the law: Cyberspace participants may adopt behaviors which they believe will enable them to comply with the respective cyberspace rules, but these rules are often different from what the rule-makers originally intended.[734] Instead of purely replicating physical world models the online rules are to be designed in a way which addresses the needs and requirements of cyberspace communities, i.e. the approach must be user-centered and community-related in order to be suitable for cyberspace.

The user-centered approach may be described in short as follows: "Digital information is really just people in disguise".[735] In more moderate words it could be said that persons and information about them are very closely linked in cyber-

732 For a detailed analysis see Reed, 2010, 248 et seq.

733 See the detailed analysis (incl. the aspects of guessing wrong and rigging the market), underlined by many examples from the (mainly European Union) legislation, outlined by Reed, 2012, 158 et seq.

734 Reed, 2012, 170.

735 Lanier, 2013, 15.

space. On the basis of the information available online a clear picture of an individual is usually identifiable; therefore, the individual must have a direct influence with regard to the design and contents of such information. The user-centered approach includes the task of rule-makers to design a normative order for the benefit of the "citizens" of cyberspace.[736]

Openness also encompasses the need to implement neutral rules not favoring any specific (societal) model, i.e. rules based on a clear identification of the regulatory objectives; this process helps to release rules seeking to persuade cyberspace stakeholders to comply with them, not impose laws with command and control functions.[737] A particular measure in the neutral rule-making context is the realization of the network neutrality principle[738] that also needs regulatory action in transparency, switching and contract exit.[739]

Furthermore, the fundamental rights of individuals are only guaranteed if several specific issues are properly addressed:[740] (i) What measures should be taken to create greater transparency and dialog between consumer groups, other civil society stakeholders, and standards experts? (ii) How can it be ensured that the benefits of rapid standards-making are maintained even with the additional scrutiny suggested in increasing multistakeholder arrangements?

A stronger emphasis on user-orientation has been expressed for example in the context of privacy protection. Cyberspace users should be provided with understandable and (in the light of the good faith principle) acceptable terms of service including options to influence the collection of personal information as follows *(Table 19):*

Example: Privacy
The following general principles are to be considered as milestones of an online privacy system:[741] (i) Individuals should have the choice of sharing or not sharing their information. (ii) The technical system must be designed in a way that choice can be easily executed by the individuals. (iii) Individuals whose information is used by third persons are to be notified about such use. (iv) The legal framework should provide means to verify whether the information is correct and in compliance with existing privacy policies. (v) The legal framework must provide mechanisms that ensure compliance with applicable privacy policies and give recourse for legal action.

736 See also KULESZA/BALLESTE, 2013, 1326.

737 See REED, 2012, 173–178 giving many examples from legislations not taking into account the mentioned fact.

738 See below V.C.4.c)(i).

739 See BROWN/MARSDEN, 2013, 185/86.

740 See BROWN/MARSDEN, 2013, 200.

741 WEBER, 2012c, 281.

The user-orientation of rule-making can also be seen in the recent Recommendation 2014/6 of the Council of Europe releasing a Guide to human rights for Internet users (April 2014).[742] Amongst others, users should receive support to understand and effectively exercise their human rights online in case their freedoms have been restricted and interfered with; furthermore, users should be empowered to use the Internet as participatory form of democratic life (No. 4).

An interesting user-centered approach has been developed by Brown/Marsden who argue that the term "user" as such would correspond to a poor description of the potential creativity of the individual user in cyberspace; rather the (in fact ugly) term *prosumer* (the online creator, after Toffler[743]) should show "the potential for the individual to move far beyond a caterpillar-like role as a producer of raw silk and encompass their ability to regenerate into a butterfly or a moth".[744] Reality evidences that the verb "to surf" is indicating the user-generated agenda of the prosumer, as does the weaving of the web by billions of prosumer-created sites.[745]

A partly similar approach has been outlined by Braithwaite/Drahos, pleading for the transformation of the consumer movement into a pro-competitive constituency.[746] Since the consumer movement has credentials in competition law and policy it could offer trained vigilance for regulatory transformation that diminishes monopolization and enhances economic efficiency, thereby simultaneously increasing the sovereignty of civil society.[747] In this understanding, consumer advocates, organized in epistemic communities, would constitute a distributed network of information workers who are competition watchdogs.[748]

2. Identification of the relevant substantive principles of cyberspace

A global legal framework for cyberspace regulation with a broader scope than Internet governance, which mainly looks at protocols, technical standards, and address allocation system issues, should identify the most relevant substantive principles and seek to find the appropriate regulatory mechanisms that are suita-

742 Recommendation CM/Rec(2014)6 of the Committee of Ministers to member States on a Guide to human rights for Internet users of April 16, 2014 (adopted at the 1197th meeting of the Ministers' Deputies).

743 Alvin Toffler, The third wave, New York 1980.

744 Brown/Marsden, 2013, 184.

745 Brown/Marsden, 2013, 184.

746 Braithwaite/Drahos, 2000, 620 and 623–628.

747 Braithwaite/Drahos, 2000, 623.

748 Braithwaite/Drahos, 2000, 625; for further details of the concept see *ibid.*, 625–628.

ble for the implementation of a normative order. Such framework cannot be developed purely in an abstract way; moreover, the rule-makers must have an understanding of how cyberspace is actually used (or how an expected use can occur) in order to identify the behaviors, which the norms should attempt to influence.[749]

In theory, two groups of principles (with some grey zones) can be distinguished, namely (i) those principles of the real world which can be applied in cyberspace without major adjustments or amendments (for example many fundamental rights) and (ii) those principles which need significant adjustments or amendments in order to cover the particularities of cyberspace.[750] The inherent advantage of principles compared to legal norms consists in the fact that principles functioning as guidelines do not require strict compliance or observance.[751]

The list of possible substantive principles[752] is (or can be) quite long; as mentioned, sometimes the topics are relatively similar to the offline world, at other times completely new issues arise.[753] Notwithstanding the existing or lacking neighborhood of cyberspace norms to traditional provisions, however, there is no way that an easy analogy may be drawn. Even if some (vague) routes to meaningful equivalence between offline and online problems can be established, the importance of equivalence should not be exaggerated, but it might have a symbolic value since cyberspace users might be more inclined to follow an equally applicable general offline/online rule than two different rule-sets whose combination and outcome merely aspire to be equivalent.[754]

The objective of this book consists in the attempt to assess possible normative foundations of cyberspace regulation, not to discuss specific legal issues being of concern to cyberspace lawyers, not at least due to the fact that vast literature is available on most of these issues. Therefore, only a short overview to the substantive principles is given hereinafter.

The structuring of the substantive topics can be done in different ways, for example by distinguishing market entry, infrastructure stability, ownership and distribution systems (intellectual property rights, privacy), and content as broad category.[755] In order to exemplify the substantive topics by way of easily understandable charts without going into the details of a legal interpretation, the

749 Reed, 2012, 156.

750 See also Kulesza, 2012, xiv.

751 See Uerpmann-Wittzack, 2011, 1248.

752 Mathiason, 2009, 59, uses the notion "regulatory imperatives" instead of substantive principles.

753 A thorough discussion of the substantive topics is not the objective of this book; for a detailed description of current national practice see Kulesza, 2012, 85–124.

754 See also Reed, 2012, 119–121 and Reed, 2010, 248 et seq.

755 This approach has been chosen by Weber, 2002, 101–203.

categories chosen by Brown/Marsden will be shown in form of an overview. The five substantive topics discussed are (i) privacy and data protection[756], (ii) copyright[757], (iii) censorship/filtering[758], (iv) social networking services[759], and (v) smart pipes.[760]

The main merits of the classification of Brown/Marsden can be seen in the fact that special attention is allocated to social networking services and smart pipes which opens the possibility to specifically address new issues such as user-generated contents and their regulation[761], the specific data protection requirements for social networking services[762] and the regulatory problems related deep pocket inspection[763]. However, some important substantive issues are not covered by this classification, for example the general application of human (fundamental) rights in cyberspace[764], the provisions on electronic commerce[765], the rules related to the liability of Internet service providers,[766] or the legal environment for cybersecurity.[767]

The mentioned five substantive topics[768] can be put into relation with the relevant impact and policy driver issues. The respective diagram allows drawing lessons for public policy and market failure as follows *(Table 20)*:[769]

756 Brown/Marsden, 2013, 47–68; see also Reed, 2012, 158–163; Kulesza, 2012, 54–62; for a recent detailed analysis of the international perspective see Bygrave, 2014.

757 Brown/Marsden, 2013, 69–91; see also Murray, 2007, 169–202; Reed, 2012, 152–155; Kulesza, 2012, 33–41.

758 Brown/Marsden, 2013, 93–116; see also – under the heading digital content – Murray, 2007, 205–229.

759 Brown/Marsden, 2013, 117–138.

760 Brown/Marsden, 2013, 139–162; to the systems convergence in particular see Kulesza, 2012, 49–54.

761 Brown/Marsden, 2013, 126–128.

762 Brown/Marsden, 2013, 134/35.

763 Brown/Marsden, 2013, 146–148.

764 To this topic see Kulesza, 2012, 44–49; Jørgensen, 2013.

765 To this topic see Kulesza, 2012, 69–75.

766 To this topic see Tambini/Leonardi/Marsden, 2008, 6–9 and 14–19; Kulesza, 2012, 62–65; Lipton, 2012, 144 and 147/48, re-conceptualizes cyberlaw mainly from an Internet service provider angle which appears to be too narrow as a perspective.

767 To this topic Kulesza/Balleste, 2013, 1313/14 with further references.

768 To the basic considerations for doing the five case studies see Brown/Marsden, 2013, 18/19 and 163 et seq.

769 This diagram is based on Brown/Marsden, 2013, 168/69.

	Data protection	Copyright	Censorship/ filtering	Social networking	Smart pipes
Social impact of technology	Bandwidth, processing capacity, storage scope, surveillance	Digital reproduction at marginal cost, peer-to-peer nets, cyberlocker sites	Ubiquitous use of broadband, widespread use of blogs, private censorship, governmental surveillance	Mass diffusion of information, need for protection (children, etc.)	Monitoring of traffic, mobile broadband, streaming video
Policy drivers: entry barriers, networks, scale effects, competition	Single market in data flows, data hoarding by enterprises and governments	Incentivation of creativity, granting of exclusive rights, highly concentrated markets (music, film, software)	Entry costs through technology for blocking, traffic monitoring enables surveillance	Costs of providing safer environment, tipping effect of dominant network	Quality-of-service technology imposes network costs (but reduced by scale economies)
Fundamental rights in policy design	International legal instruments available (ICCPR, ECHR)	Right to remuneration and moral right accepted	Lack of due process and appeal, little democratic scrutiny	Little effective government policy, mainly private actor business model	Limited regulatory oversight and rights-based discussion
Lessons	Privacy as key human right, to be protected by government	Higher protection of creators' rights at the expense of freedom of speech/privacy	Improved transparency needed; focus on content producers desirable in the long term	Only self-regulation	Risk of implementation of invasive systems, telecom regulations with too limited perspective

The five substantive issues can also be related to the institutional political economy of cyberspace regulation showing an interesting dialogue between property rights holders and governments as illustrated in the following diagram *(Table 21)*:[770]

[770] This diagram is based on BROWN/MARSDEN, 2013, 170/71.

	Data protection	Copyright	Censorship/ filtering	Social networking	Smart pipes
Key actors: national, global, regional	Data protection regulators, consumer protection agencies, coordination in EU, APEC, etc.	Rightsholder associations, State legislators (US, EU, Japan) and international instruments (WIPO, ACTA)	ISPs, multinational content companies, user groups, multinational coders (WWW Consortium)	ISPs, intermediaries, local user groups, child protection groups, coders in Silicon Valley	Telecoms regulators, ISP, intermediaries, content companies, surveillance-industrial complex
How legitimate and accountable?	If legislative, democratically accountable, less so with self-regulatory solutions	Much policy laundering, forum shifting, exclusion of civil society and developing world	Limited transparency and accountability, remote engineering ethics	Some control by user-generated regulation, opaque terms and application means	Parliamentary supervision of telecom regulators, less so with self-regulatory solutions
Multistake-holderism	Internet governance through IGF, RFID process	Civil society involvement in WIPO, actions against ACTA	Little representation for free speech organizations (except in hotline governance)	Little formal multistake-holder consultations by corporates	Limited activities of stakeholders in telecoms regulatory environment
Key technical actor buy-in	Apple Safari, Firefox (DNT), privacy framework of RFID industry	Trusted Computing Group (TCG) and operating system vendors with limited effect involved, partial role of ISP	ISP-level filtering, need for standards and best practices	More open environments needed, prevention of high-walked gardens	Corporate vendors and mobile industry support quality-of-service, technical opposition given
Lessons	Strong intervention from legislators/ regulators is needed	Code instead of business innovation, limitation of freedom of expression, low multistake-holder involvement	Private censorship, limited governmental initiatives, control of "critical" material	Ineffective user-generated regulation, civil society ineffective	Little traction for policy initiatives, some initiatives of technical community

A further perspective concerns the various layers of protocol stack, not merely the application layer, which can be mirrored against the five case studies according to the following diagram *(Table 22)*:[771]

	Data protection	**Copyright**	**Censorship/ filtering**	**Social networking**	**Smart pipes**
Layer	RFID focus, browser code (do not track, cookies), privacy by design, privacy impact assessment	Failure of technological protection measures, ISP blocks, three-strikes	Application or network or both, supported by filtering software	Application and platform	Network or transport-layer
Location (manufacturer, ISPs, servers, clients)	Software and system architects	Previously hardware and software vendors, now ISP	Transport-level filters and clients filters	Server side with some mobile-based features	DPI solutions (hardware/ software vendors), traffic management solutions
Enforcement of code	Threat of data protection rules' enforcement	Ban of devices and circumvention measures	"Plug pulling", Green Dam local filter, Golden Shield national solution	Terms of use (amended by contractual terms with third parties)	Termination monopoly of ISP, nontransparent terms, competition regulation

A specifically important perspective concerns the outcomes and divergences of the five substantive issues in respect of key parameters of cyberspace regulation as of the following diagram *(Table 23)*:[772]

[771] This diagram is based on Brown/Marsden, 2013, 176.

[772] This diagram is based on Brown/Marsden, 2013, 179/80.

	Data protection	Copyright	Censorship/ filtering	Social networking	Smart pipes
Transparency	Limited impact of opaque privacy policies and user education	Unclear causation: Does more transparency lead to more just solutions?	Private block lists, no generic reporting duty on ISP	Often obscure in software updates and privacy policy changes, little evidence of good practice	Creating greater transparency through regulation
Enforcement	Data breach requirements and code solutions, limited effect of State enforcement	Problem of second user, business models and licenses effective in enforcement, three-strikes dispropor-tionate	Private censorship limits user rights, put-back "enforcement"	Nudges and defaults (not individual reuses of data) useful ("distributed enforcement")	Network neutrality as solution to prevent protocol and application blocking
Inter-operability	Cross-border-adequacy assessments drive interoperability	DRM closes off interoperability	Cleanfeed instead of DNS blocking	Portability not sufficient	Limited transparency related to adaption of vender off-the-shelf solutions to ISP
Efficiency	Efficiency by internalized data controller self-enforcement?	New business models required	Source treatment: Tackling producers not blocking views	Improvement of corporate governance conformity needed	Co-regulation between legislators and industry desirable

3. Realization of multistakeholder participation

Without any doubts, civil society is the most active user of the Internet and therefore the most affected player; in the meantime, practically all aspects of the Internet have an impact on the daily life of civil society. Therefore, whether the organization of the Internet, its governance, access, operability or other topics are concerned, the understanding of members of civil society and non-state actors has to be taken into account.[773] This concept of including all possibly concerned actors in a participatory framework is now usually called multistakeholder model.

773 Weber, 2011a, 6–8; Weber/Weber, 2009, 94.

For the time being, the multistakeholder discussion is mainly of a descriptive nature. Further research should rather concentrate on normative aspects.[774]

a) General foundations

Internet governance is not the first field attempting to implement multistakeholder models. Participatory democracy having directed the way for multistakeholder participation can already be found in the debates of economic governance models.[775] Furthermore, the realization of the interests of global public goods requires the involvement of all stakeholders concerned.[776]

Multistakeholder participation must be designed in view of the applicable social and environmental conditions. Commonly used evaluation criteria encompass the following aspects:[777]

- *Level of the standards:* The level issue can concern different objectives to be realized, for example high technical security standards or limits to living standards.
- *Completeness of the standards:* The completeness aspect depends on the question whether the standards refer to multiple issues or are limited to a single issue only.
- *Market coverage:* The broader the market coverage, the more likely is a widespread functionality of the multistakeholder involvement.
- *Accountability:* It is important to ensure that the standards contain regulations regarding the monitoring, reporting or verification of actions taken by an entity as well as potential sanctions.
- *Economic model:* A decentralization of economic decisions and an easy market access lead to a higher chance of having several stakeholders involved.
- *Extent of the involvement of stakeholders:* Entry barriers for stakeholders should be lowered and participation possibilities facilitated.
- *Impact of the existing standards on the decision-making of an entity:* Corporate governance frameworks as well as corporate social responsibility concepts are supporting the involvement of multistakeholders in participating in the entity's decision-making processes.

774 Normative aspects are discussed hereinafter, however, this book's objective does not allow extending the considerations into all potential details and must remain the topic of another publication.

775 See Elinor Ostrom, Governing the commons: the evolution of institutions for collective action, Cambridge 1990.

776 See Weber/Menoud, 2008, 24–27; Doria, 2013, 119.

777 Van Huijstee, 2012, 45.

Already Aristotle explained the best regime to be a combination of various features for the sake of the commons, however, he did not perceive democracy as the mandatory best regime, but rather aristocracy.[778] In aristocratic regimes, only a few are able to act as representatives for the benefit of the community; these ruling persons should act "with a view to what is best for the city and for those who participate in it".[779] This (historic) perception shows that the bottom-up process may be implemented in practice by establishing a hierarchical framework encompassing representatives from various parts of civil society and/or from different regions who themselves can elect legitimate individuals for the participation in the final decision-making processes.[780]

From a theoretical perspective, it should be differentiated between the groups of involved actors and the authority relations between these actors. A possible approach may be structured as follows:

Often four different groups of actors are distinguished playing a role in the multi-stakeholder debates related to cyberspace regulation, namely (i) States, (ii) formal intergovernmental organizations (IGO), (iii) business entities, and (iv) non-governmental organizations (NGO), technical and academic community, civil society and the individuals acting on their own behalf. The last group obviously combines a wide variety of actors but a further refinement would lead to an unmanageably complicated typology.[781]

Apart from the distinction of different actors governance arrangements can also vary according to the authority relations between these actors. Four ideal-typical possibilities are available for consideration, namely (i) hierarchy, (ii) homogeneous polyarchy, (iii) heterogeneous polyarchy, and (iv) anarchy.[782] Hierarchy entails relations of super- and subordination (command and obey structure), usually given in the context of States, polyarchy encompasses situation where the authority is distributed among several actors, having either (homogeneously) similar formal powers or (heterogeneously) different formal powers. In case of anarchy no authority relations exist.

778 Aristotle, The Politics of Aristotle, translated by Benjamin Jowett, Oxford 1885, Vol. 1, Book III, Chapter 7, 1279b.

779 *Ibid.*, 1279a.

780 See also Weber/Weber, 2009, 94/95.

781 See also DeNardis/Raymond, 2013, 9.

782 DeNardis/Raymond, 2013, 10.

b) Important elements of multistakeholder participation

The analysis of the general foundations of multistakeholder participation has shown that the inclusion of civil society calls for a bottom-up process. Even if the various actors of civil society are independently organized, common strategies and goals can be developed; the bottom-up approach also enables the creation of new networks and facilitates the enlargement of the fundament for the active participation of Internet users.[783] The multistakeholder models must rely on ever increasing participation by those with interests, capacities, and needs.[784]

In elaborating the substantive issues of multistakeholder participation in more detail, the specific legitimacy strategies are to be developed; thereby, the following factors should be taken into account:[785]

- *Openness:* Access to discussions, negotiations and decisions must be open for interested and concerned persons.
- *Transparency:* Procedures have to be transparent in formal and substantive respects thus ensuring an appropriate representation of the situation.
- *Accessibility:* Information sources need to be accessible for interested and concerned persons.
- *Accountability:* Decision-makers must be accountable to those being exposed to the respective decisions, i.e. responsibility is an important element in corporate structures.
- *Credibility:* Decision-makers should seek to achieve an acknowledgment of their credibility by the persons concerned.
- *Adequately resourced:* Multistakeholder involvement and participation requires sufficient human and financial resources in order to enable the respective processes.
- *Consensus-based:* Acceptability for decisions taken will increase if they are reached by consensus of all concerned persons and not by (sharp) majority votes;
- *Opportunity for appeal/challenge:* An entity of any nature should provide for the possibility to file a complaint against a given decision to an independent panel of „judges“.
- *Ability to resist capture:* Decision-making bodies must avoid to be captured by lobbying groups.

---

783 Weber/Weber, 2009, 94.

784 Doria, 2013, 135.

785 Waz/Weiser 2012, 242/43; to the strategies see Tamm Hallström/Boström, 2010, 141 et seq.

A proper treatment of these aspects requires an enlargement of the scope of traditional research. A multidisciplinary examination of the relevant questions incorporating social-legal, economic, policy-oriented and game theory studies as well as interdisciplinary information studies drawing on socio-economic and political analysis is indispensable.[786] For the time being, an integrated approach has not yet been developed: The disciplines still remain "somewhat stove-piped in different silos"[787] without bringing together the many approaches into a holistic and coherent scientific framework as well as associated evaluation and design methodologies. Developing a multidisciplinary catalog of methodologies as well as the corresponding multidisciplinary tools can improve comprehension of challenges of better participative decision-making, including consideration of governance concepts.[788]

Major substantive issues of the multistakeholder concept are the access to and the participation in cyberspace rule-making. By enhancing the respective possibilities for the multistakeholder communities, better use can be made of the public service value of the Internet. In fact, no other medium is able to spread information within such a short period of time, making it possible for members of civil society to communicate on current topics. Furthermore, organizing events as has been shown during the Arab spring[789] and helping persons in need is facilitated due to the easy information flow and the activation of people.[790]

The realization of the multistakeholder participation is particularly appropriate if a co-regulation system exists which balances the often mutually exclusive interests of the State, the businesses, and civil society.[791] If society becomes more integrated, a more "communitarian" framework will evolve over time.[792]

A specific problem related to responsiveness and participation concerns the scope of impact actually reached. Obviously, a multistakeholder regime is not accomplished by merely providing the preconditions for the participation of civil society; moreover, a real opportunity to shape policy output needs to be provided.[793] Therefore, an evaluation of the influence that the voices of the various stakeholders have on the decision-making process should be conducted; listening to

786 Brown/Marsden, 2013, 200.
787 Brown/Marsden, 2013, 200.
788 Brown/Marsden, 2013, 201.
789 See for example Rolf H. Weber, Politics Through Social Networks and Politics by Government Blocking: Do We Need New Rules?, International Journal of Communication 5 (2011), 1186–1194.
790 See Weber/Weber, 2009, 101.
791 See Tambini/Leonardi/Marsden, 2013, 30o; Dutton/Peltu, 2007, 73.
792 See also Koskenniemi, 2005, 599.
793 Dany, 2008, 61.

the voices of the members of civil society may not become an alibi since in this case the outcome of the deliberations will not result in everyone's welfare.[794] In addition, attempts by certain groups to advance their own interests must be critically analyzed.

In addition, the multistakeholder concept should not be viewed as a value in itself to be applied homogenously to a multiple of governance functions, i.e. the concept is not a one-fits-all solution for cyberspace governance.[795] For example in respect of cyberspace regulation, an appropriate and effective approach must attempt to determine what types of governance are optimal for promoting a suitable regime in any particular functional and political context. As the NetMundial in late April 2014 showed, the multistakeholder concept has to be seen as a compromise with caveats, and a couple of "blocks" stand in the way of a reloaded multistakeholder development.[796] The multistakeholder concept should be based on a granular taxonomy which most likely leads to different results in respect of the manifold substantive topics such as freedom of expression, cybersecurity, standard setting (protocols, routers), interoperability, operational stability, treatment of Internet service providers, etc.[797]

c) Multistakeholder participation in Internet governance debates

Notwithstanding the fact that other markets and areas have known the inclusion of a variety of stakeholders for quite some time[798], the multistakeholder debate has particularly evolved in connection with Internet governance. The discussions are based on the definition contained in the Tunis Agenda for the Information Society: "A working definition of Internet governance is the development and application by governments, the private sector and civil society, in their respective roles, of shared principles, norms, rules, decision-making procedures and programs that shape the evolution and use of the Internet."[799]

After the agreement on the Tunis Agenda and the implementation of the Internet Governance Forum the topic of multistakeholder participation (or – in shorter form – multistakeholderism[800]) became a major discussion issue in the context of

794 WEBER/WEBER, 2009, 101.

795 DENARDIS/RAYMOND, 2013, 2.

796 See FRANCESCA MUSIANI/JULIA POHLE, NETmundial: only a landmark event if „Digital Cold War" rhetoric abandoned, available at http://policyreview.info/articles /analysis/netmundial-only-landmark-event-if-digital-cold-war-rhetoric-abandoned.

797 See also DENARDIS/RAYMOND, 2013, 2.

798 See the examples listed by MENA/PALAZZO, 2012, 534/35.

799 World Summit on the Information Society (WSIS), Tunis Agenda for the Information Society, WSIS-05/TUNIS/DOC/6(Rev.1)-E, 18. November 2005, Para 34.

800 To the -ism discussion in more details see DORIA, 2013, 117/118.

Internet governance.[801] The multistakeholder concept is more than a bottom-up process or an equal footing principle and cannot be replaced by a sole democracy understanding[802] even if Drake (in his own words "misquoting" Winston Churchill on democracy) argues that "multistakeholderism is the worst form of governance, except all others that have been tried".[803]

Governance policies involve a variety of actors operating at different layers of a structured system, from the physical infrastructure to content and behavior; these activities encompass the development of standards and protocols as well as the offering of applications and services with the consequence that a cross-mapping governance should be realized.[804] This fact clearly shows that non-state actors such as engineers, entrepreneurs, and citizens need to find appropriate cooperation forms.[805] Civil society can even be considered to be the glue making cyberspace regulation happening in reality.

The key to the multistakeholder concept must be seen in the concretization of the "respective roles" of the stakeholders.[806] The Report of the Working Group on Internet Governance (WGIG) of June 2005 and the Tunis Agenda are silent on the interpretation of the term "respective roles".[807] The problems for the interpretation of this term due to its ambiguity have caused substantive impediments to the success of the multistakeholder model.[808] The reference to the technical and academic community does also not help to describe the involvement of civil society. The complexity of defining the "respective roles" has led to the assessment that the cyberspace is left with an unfinished task.[809]

The already described four groups of actors and the four ideal-typical possibilities of authority relations between these actors need a concretization in respect of Internet governance; a first attempt has been undertaken by DeNardis/Raymond.[810]

801 To the historical development of the multistakeholder concept in the WSIS I and WSIS II context see Mathiason, 2009, 97–125.

802 Doria, 2013, 120–123; see also Weber, 2011a, 7/8.

803 Drake, 2011, 69.

804 See also Brown/Marsden, 2013, 202.

805 See Mathiason, 2009, 32–48.

806 Doria, 2013, 123–127; Uerpmann-Wittzack, 2011, 1261/62; Kulesza/Balleste, 2013, 1329/30 and 1342.

807 See de la Chapelle, 2011, 15, calling the wording "in their respect roles" a perfect example of what diplomats usually describe as constructive ambiguity, namely an agreement on terms that conceal a disagreement of substance.

808 Doria, 2013, 123.

809 Doria, 2013, 126/27.

810 See DeNardis/Raymond, 2013, 11/12.

Their approach, which convincingly excludes the anarchy relation, can be summarized as follows *(Table 24)*:[811]

Stakeholder Types	Authority Relations		
	Hierarchy	Polyarchy	
		Homogeneous	Heterogeneous
States, IGO, Firms, NGO	ITU		ICANN
States, IGO, Firms		IOSCO	
IGO, Firms, NGO			Global Compact
States, Firms, NGO		IETF, W3C	

Apart from the more theoretical aspects practical considerations must also gain importance, for example in respect of the following questions: (i) How can greater transparency and dialog between different civil society groups and standards experts be introduced? (ii) How can it be ensured that the benefits of rapid standard-making are maintained even with the additional scrutiny due to increasing multistakeholder arrangements?[812]

Recently, the European Commission has also taken up the multistakeholder concept and in its Communication of February 2014 proposes the principle "to defend and promote fundamental rights and democratic values, and multistakeholder governance structures that are based on clear rules that respect those rights and values",[813] " (…) governed by a genuine multistakeholder model (…) where the necessary inter-governmental discussions are anchored in a multistakeholder context in the full understanding that the Internet is built and maintained by a variety of stakeholders, as well as governments; (…) where decisions are taken on the basis of principles of good governance, including transparency, accountability, and inclusiveness of all relevant stakeholders" as a basis for a common European vision for Internet governance.[814] In No. 5 of the mentioned Communication, the European Commission describes the multistakeholder process under the headings of transparency, inclusiveness and balance, and accountability[815] leading to the following conclusion *(Table 25)*:[816]

811 The chart is a shortened version taken from DeNardis/Raymond, 2013, 12.
812 See also Brown/Marsden, 2013, 200.
813 European Commission, 2014, 2.
814 European Commission, 2014, 3.
815 European Commission, 2014, 6.
816 European Commission, 2014, 7

• The European Commission is firmly committed to the multistakeholder model of Internet governance. The Commission calls upon stakeholders to further strengthen the sustainability of the model by making actors and processes more inclusive, transparent and accountable.
• The Commission will work with stakeholders on the exchange of best practice.

On the national level, many countries do now have an event comparable to the Internet Governance Forum conference that gathers interested stakeholders for a yearly exchange of ideas and comments. In particular Brazil has made remarkable experiences of multistakeholder cooperation for the discussion of Internet-related issues, embodied in the Brazilian Internet Steering Committee (CGI.br).[817] The regional IGF for Europe, namely the European Dialogue on Internet Governance (EuroDig), nicely combines the theoretically contradicting terms of "dialogue" and "governance".

In the context of Internet governance, Wolfgang Kleinwächter developed a sophisticated model composed of the "United Nations" as organization of sovereign States and the "United Constituencies" representing networks, non-governmental groups, businesses, technical/academic community and civil society. Even if the two governance cultures are rather different, they do not need to be antagonistic, but can co-exist in a meaningful way.[818] A formal and rough comparison between "national hierarchies" of the "United Nations" and "global networks" of the "United Constituencies" could lead to the following diagram *(Table 26)*:[819]

817 See OII-Paper, 2013, 13–16.
818 Kleinwächter, 2011, 571.
819 Kleinwächter, 2011, 571/72.

Issue	United Nations	United Constituencies
Actors	Governments	Private Industry/Civil Society
Structure	Hierarchies	Networks
Codification	National Laws	Universal Codes
International Agreements	Legally Binding Treaties	Memorandum of Understanding
Mission	Broad	Narrow
Policy Development	Top Down	Bottom Up
Decision-Making	Formally specified Majority Voting	Informally specified Rough Consensus
Representation	Elections by All	Delegation by competent Constituencies or via NomComs
Policy-Making	Formally Restricted Access and limited Participation	Formally Open Access and broad Participation
Negotiations	Mainly closed to outsiders	Mainly transparent and open for outsiders
Result	Stability and Predictability	Flexibility

The table shows that both the "real places" and the "virtual places" are linked to each other; since reality does not allow a separation, an objective need for collaboration in a multistakeholder framework is given.

Furthermore, it is important that all stakeholders need to recognize the dynamic nature of the respective roles of the stakeholders in the cyberspace environment.[820] Not only do new actors appear and have to be integrated, but also iterative consultation processes and governance workflows change over time.[821] Therefore, pitfalls in the design of participatory processes need to be avoided, for example by ensuring really inclusive participation, by fighting information overload, by synthesizing discussions, by preventing capture(s), and by ensuring the neutrality of the framework.[822]

820 Doria, 2013, 135.
821 De la Chapelle, 2011, 16/17 and 20.
822 De la Chapelle, 2011, 22/23.

4. Compliance with basic socio-legal values

a) Acknowledgement of cultural diversity

In view of the global extension of the Internet it appears to be obvious that different cultural attitudes and expectations about the best possible way of implementing a legal framework exist and may cause conflicts. Culture can be defined as the integrated system of socially acquired values, beliefs, and rules of conduct delimiting the range of accepted behaviors in any given society.[823]

Due to the vast new opportunities offered by cyberspace, many Internet cultures exist, made up by different members of civil society, all trying to maintain their own voice and identity.[824] Virtual communities and online identities are spreading out, showing how people interact within a given social space; "meet" and "face" are becoming different notions as compared to the real world; inclusion and exclusion from communities follow different patterns.[825] Therefore, Lovink calls for a new kind of cultural criticism, capable of analyzing different positions that are the hallmarks of potential conflicts.[826] The form of governance in view of different perceptions also depends upon the fact that technologies do not only tie up with changes in society, but that the organizational power of communication is adequately realized.[827]

Sociologists argue that globalization creates entirely new kinds of social relations, i.e. new ways of identifying, managing, disciplining and profiting from human relations through the use of the technologies that connect people.[828] As a consequence, studies of cyberspace culture have started to focus on new virtues such as the commons-based-peer-production (Benkler)[829], on youth practices[830] and on social network sites.[831] Furthermore, culture also influences the way online practices affect the formation of identity.

Upholding the values of openness and sharing in the Internet leads to the promotion of a free culture movement. According to Lessig, the social practices associated with cyberspace represent a creative revolution fostering new means for participation in cultural production.[832] The new forms of collaboration create the

823 Jørgensen, 2013, 122; to the aspect of solidarity in particular see Benkler, 2011b, 89–95.
824 Bowry, 2005, 14/15.
825 Jørgensen. 2013, 123.
826 Lovink, 2003, 10.
827 Bowry, 2005, 25–29.
828 Bowry, 2005, 177.
829 For further details see above IV.D.2.
830 Palfrey/Gasser, 2008.
831 Jørgensen, 2013, 125.
832 Lessig, 2004.

situation that "many minds produce knowledge"[833]; thereby, the contributors develop a distinct attitude towards authorship no longer based on the notion of "owner" but of partnership.[834]

In this context, it should not be underestimated that law itself can be seen as a cultural product; treating law as a cultural reality means looking at the material structure of the law to see it in play and at play as signs and symbols, fantasies and phantasms.[835] The analytical problem for rule-makers consists in the attempt to escape the artificial construction of autonomous categories and principles of law.[836] Cultural analysis should strive to combat common sense understandings of law as formal and rule-bound, and instead seek to justify an alternative approach showing the law as discipline moving beyond legal realism.[837]

Consequently, rule-makers should look at broader ways of thinking about what law is and about how law was constituted. A cultural analysis of law not only helps in challenging traditional ideas of culture, it also may help advance new concepts of law.[838] For example, as experience over the last two decades showed, international law and some human rights (for example right to development and right to cultural/linguistic diversity) must accommodate broader aspirations for all members of civil society. From a scholar point of view, empirical research on civil society advocacy should be improved.[839]

The acknowledgment of cultural values, however, should not be misinterpreted in a way that "maintaining social habits", the protection of "morality", and safeguarding "social standards" may be used to interfere with central fundamental rights. Practice has shown that governments of many countries refer to such terms as justification for interventions into open communication networks by declaring these values part of "national security".[840] Thereby, cultural values are perverted into political interests of the individuals that hold the power in a State.

During the last decade, cultural diversity has become a legally established principle for the international community. Foremost, the UNESCO Universal Declaration on Cultural Diversity, adopted by the UN Assembly in 2005, merits more at-

833 Sunstein, 2006, 151.
834 See also Jørgensen, 2013, 132.
835 Austin Sarat/Jonathan Simon, Cultural Analyses, Cultural Studies and the Situation of Legal Scholar-ship, in: Austin Sarat/Jonathan Simon (eds.), Cultural Analyses, Cultural Studies, and the Law: Moving Beyond Legal Realism, Durham 2003, 13.
836 Bowry, 2005, 19.
837 See the respective title of the book of Sarat/Simon (note 835).
838 Bowry, 2005, 17.
839 Bowry, 2005, 190.
840 Kulesza, 2012, 120/21.

tention.[841] In fact, nowhere is the diversity of the world's communities more vivid than in cyberspace, enabling cultures to simultaneously interact at all possible levels.[842] The need to respect and promote cultural diversity is specifically enshrined in many WSIS documents.[843] The practical application of the principle of cultural diversity in the context of the Domain Name System also led to the introduction of internationalized domain names in early 2010.[844]

b) Recognition of cyberspace openness

Freedom of information/communication and freedom of access to networks are of utmost importance in the cyberspace environment.

(i) In line with the well-known slogan "information wants to be free"[845] Lessig proclaimed in his book "The Future of Ideas"[846] that free resources are essential for creativity and innovation. The importance of "free information" became most obvious with the beginning of the age of convergence, which allowed a cheap and simple cross-media delivery, some thirty years ago. Communications theorist Ithiel de Sola Pool popularized the term "convergence" in his seminal book "Technologies of Freedom" stating that "electronic technology is bringing all modes of communication into one grand system".[847] As follow-up to Pool's pronounced vision and the emergence of the World Wide Web in the early nineties of the last century Nicholas Negroponte predicted in his famous book on digitization ("Being Digital") that by 2005 (i.e. 10 years later) Americans would spend more hours on the Internet than on watching network television[848]; this prediction turned out to be quite wrong at the time, partly due to the lack of sufficient digital distribution chains for information deliveries.[849]

---

841 UNESCO, Convention on the Protection and Promotion of the Diversity of Cultural Expressions, 20 October 2005, available at http://portal.unesco.org/en/ev.php-URL_ID=31038&URL_DO=DO_TOPIC&URL_SECTION=201.html.

842 Kulesza, 2012, 140; see also Kurbalija, 2012, 163/64.

843 WSIS, Plan of Action, WSIS-03/GENEVA/DOC/5-E, 12 December 2003, para. 23; WSIS, Declaration of Principles, Building the Information Society: a global challenge in the new Millennium, WSIS-03/GENEVA/DOC/4-E, 12 December 2003, paras. 52–54; WSIS, Tunis Agenda (note 799), 20.

844 Kim Davies, ICANN Blog, First IDN ccTLDs now available, 5 May 2010, available at http://blog.icann.org/2010/05/idn-cctlds/.

845 This slogan was coined by Stuart Brand at the first Hackers' Conference in fall 1984; see Murray, 2007, 76/77 note 7.

846 Lessig, 2001.

847 Pool, 1984, 28.

848 Negroponte, 1995, 58.

849 See Murray, 2007, 78.

Notwithstanding the fact that Lessig also assumed a faster realization of convergence his theoretical analysis about the available options for society is correct. According to Lessig, on the one hand, there is the model of the perfectly controlling cable providers (owning and controlling the physical, logical and content layer of its network); on the other hand, there is the Internet model in principle not exerting any control over a physical layer beyond the decision to include specific equipment and enabling the free exchange of content over a code layer that remains open.[850] Vertical integration and anticompetitive behavior, however, could jeopardize the second model driving at openness.

(ii) As Benkler stated, networks can be characterized as systems partly overlapping and, therefore, requiring "bridges"; freedom and power are affected by the degree of openness, i.e. by the extent "to which individuals can bob and weave between networks to achieve their designed behavior, perceptions, or outcomes".[851] The relation between freedom and the mentioned three objectives can be described as follows *(Table 27)*:[852]

- **Relation freedom/behaviors:**
  "A facility that allows a user to get a desired content without being exposed to advertising provides a degree of freedom and affordance to be free of this particular modality of power."
- **Relation freedom/actions or perceptions:**
  "A system of unencrypted music gives users technical freedom to use music files as they please. Note: They may still not be "free" of all restraints, due to, say, the legal system's constraints, but they do have freedom in the technical distribution system from the particular kind of technical power."
- **Relation freedom/outcomes:**
  "Critiques of systems designed to bundle payment for cultural materials with the basic ISP service have so far succeeded in preventing this pathway of exerting power over outcomes from being established. Users may still be susceptible to power over behavior in the form of digital rights management (DRM), but not to power over outcomes in this form."

850 Lessig, 2001, 167.
851 Benkler, 2011a, 721.
852 Benkler, 2011a, 732–734.

The relations can be deepened and combined to complex configurations depending on the democratizing environment. In preparing norms it is important to understand the level of freedom and its sources, thereby enabling the rule-makers to design a structure that leads to an equilibrium of the diverging interests.[853]

(iii) The openness of cyberspace is also threatened by governmental and private control regimes: The security-industrial complex applying extensive surveillance measures even by co-opting private actors has a significant potential in the hand of dictatorial regimes; its technologies of control and lobbying power, mostly obscured from public gaze, might increase over the coming decade and thereby cause serious threats to individual human freedoms in the cyberspace.[854]

In addition to the above mentioned encrypted music and the digital rights management by rightsholders, the openness of cyberspace can only be ensured on the private side if dominant stakeholders are restricted in blocking rival content threatening their own commercial interests, for example by transforming open platforms into "walled gardens".[855] A vigorous enforcement of the openness rules to maintain access to innovation is needed in times of increasing establishment of horizontal and vertical bottlenecks over distribution.[856]

(iv) Recently, the inventor of the World Wide Web, Tim Berners-Lee, proposed to implement a "Magna Carta" in order to protect and enshrine the independence of cyberspace since the web he had created 15 years ago has come under increasing attack from governments and corporate influence making it necessary to ensure an "open, neutral" system.[857] Berners-Lee's Magna Carta plan is supposed to be taken up as part of an initiative called "the web we want" which calls on people to generate a digital bill of rights and an open Internet.[858]

Openness of cyberspace corresponds to the principle that the Internet must be seen as a public sphere in a universality concept encompassing multiple publics with manifold interests.[859] Looking from this perspective, openness is also a prerequisite for combatting the fragmentation of network structures. As outlined by the European Commission, the vision for cyberspace governance must consist in a single, un-fragmented network.[860] The aspect of one un-fragmented resource is

853 See also Benkler, 2011a, 751.
854 See also Brown/Marsden, 2013, 162.
855 See Mehra, 2011, 894 et seq.
856 See also Brown/Marsden, 2013, 199.
857 See http://www.theguardian.com/technology/2014/mar/12/online-magna-carta-berners-lee-web.
858 See also the statements of Vint Cerf as cited by Kulesza/Balleste, 2013, 1312.
859 Jørgensen, 2013, 83–89; Uerpmann-Wittzack, 2011, 248.
860 European Commission, 2014, 2.

endangered if each State develops its own national network with the objective to intervene into the cross-border flow of information.

The right to free Internet access being an emanation of the right to free speech and free communication was mentioned in all WSIS documents.[861] In 2011, universal Internet access has been declared a human right in the Report of Frank La Rue, presented to the United Nations General Assembly.[862] Regional and national human rights instruments also know this principle; Switzerland was the first of several countries[863] introducing a universal right of access to the broadband Internet as part of the widely acknowledged universal service obligation. Notwithstanding these principles many countries still apply extensive Internet filtering and censorship. Recently, the Council of Europe clearly included the right of access to the Internet into the Recommendation 2014/6 on a Guide to human rights for Internet users.[864] Therefore, the implementation of an "openness" principle is to be seen as a central pillar for an international cyberspace framework.[865]

The openness of cyberspace also is a key element of the "Internet Universality" concept of UNESCO as presented in a working paper in September 2013. The "Internet Universality" is constituted by the R-O-A-M approach designing Rights, Openness, Accessibility, and Multistakholder.[866] Based on this approach the relevant issues can be summarized in a diagram as follows *(Table 28):*

861 See Kulesza, 2012, 141 with further references.

862 La Rue, 2011.

863 Not Finland as stated in many publications (for example Brown/Marsden, 2013, 38) only looking at EU countries.

864 Recommendation CM/Rec(2014)6 of the Committee of Ministers to member States on a Guide to human rights for Internet users of April 16, 2014 (adopted at the 1197th meeting of the Ministers' Deputies).

865 See also Kulesza, 2012, 143.

866 See http://www.unesco.org/new/fileadmin/MULTIMEDIA/HQ/CI/CI/pdf/news/internet_universality_en.pdf.

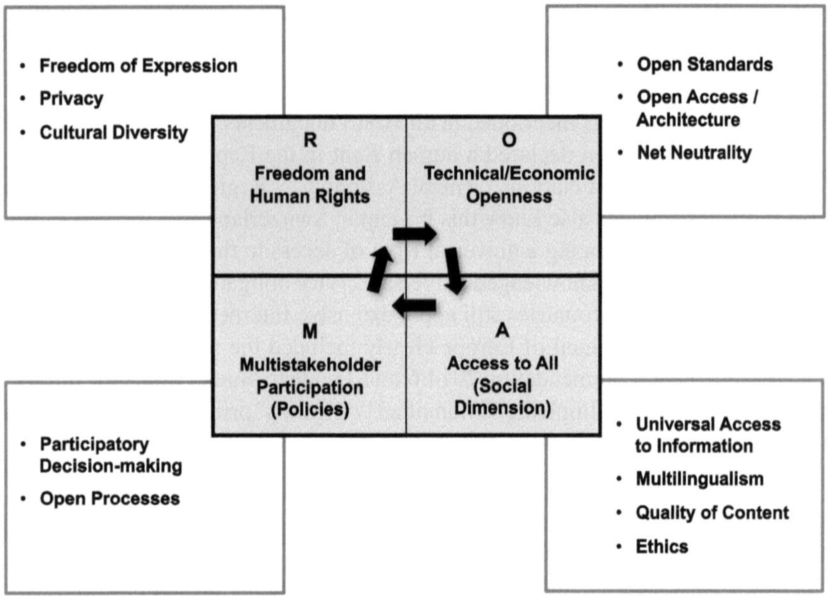

c) Implementation of corresponding technological values: neutrality and interoperability

The technological environment also contributes to the realization of social values. Two principles are insofar of major importance, namely the principle of technology neutrality and the principle of interoperability.

(i) The term *technology neutrality* means that normative rules should abstain from favoring or discriminating against any particular technology. The basic nature of this principle is clear, however, the implementation can cause problems. Often, at least if the rule-maker is careful, a legal norm does not opt for a specific technology, but the norm could lead to the result that technology 1 is norm-compliant without further modification, whereas technology 2 needs a (possibly expensive) modification. In such a situation, the norm would have an indirectly discriminating effect.[867]

Other objectives to be achieved by applying the technology neutrality principle can encompass (i) the achievement of particular effects (for example related to the behavior of people or the outcome of activities), (ii) the functional equivalence between different modes of activities (for example offline and online), (iii) the

[867] See REED, 2012, 192.

non-discrimination between technologies with equivalent effects, and (iv) the drafting techniques in respect of the developed rules (for example flexible norms in order not to hinder the future design of technologies and sustainable norms which do not require over-frequent revisions to cope with technological change).[868]

Rule-making techniques to be adopted for the realization of technology neutrality encompass the technology indifference model, the implementation neutrality principle, and the concept of potential neutrality.[869] Indifferent laws are applicable irrespective of the technology used. If a specific technology is preferred for policy reasons the law should at least not favor one or more implementations of that technology. Finally, a rule-maker can achieve a basic level of neutrality between different technological implementations by providing the possibility to modify a non-compliant implementation in a way that it becomes compliant.

Certain doubts that technology neutrality can achieve its aims, however, have been expressed and need to be overcome.[870] Apart from the fact that neutrality is not always desirable (for policy reasons or competition concerns) the business models often change with the consequence of jeopardizing technology neutrality irrespective of the technological developments. Furthermore, language is not always technology-neutral and literal interpretation can keep the law connected to the technology.

(ii) The term *interoperability* is open to be defined in a broad way, namely as a tool to interconnect networks (including the aspect of standardization), but also as measure to interconnect individuals. Palfrey/Gasser distinguish interoperability functions on four broad layers of complex systems:[871] (i) The first layer concerns technology (ability to transfer and render data and other information across systems, applications, or components). (ii) The second layer is the data layer (ability to read the data). (iii) The third layer is the human layer (ability to communicate, for example through a common language). (iv) The fourth layer looks at institutional aspects (ability to work together).

Open participatory standards (for example an open source operating system such as Linux) are partly claimed to be better for the development of fundamental rights and to grant better access to information than a proprietary operating system (such as Windows).[872] Interoperable systems usually make life easier and in-

868 See Koops, 2006, 83–90.
869 For more details see Reed, 2012, 193–199.
870 See Reed, 2012, 199–204.
871 Palfrey/Gasser, 2012, 5/6.
872 Further to this discussion Brown/Marsden, 2013, 22.

crease efficiency.[873] An open environment can also stimulate innovation since State censorship and corporate control of the value chain might be more difficult; the wider the choice that is available to users, the higher their ability to take advantage of their freedoms will be, however, a guarantee of fundamental rights is not given.[874] Usually, a combination of instruments is needed to get optimal levels of interoperability.[875]

Interoperability, mostly addressed from the perspective of technology, is a widely discussed topic among cyberspace scholars. In a broad sense, conditions for open interoperability can encompass (i) access to the decision-making process, (ii) transparent and undistorted procedures, (iii) pro-competitive goals, (iv) objective and relevant criteria for technology selection, and (v) no over-standardization.[876] In a more narrow sense, interoperability between networks refers to the possibility to easily link two different structures; this issue has been dealt with in the literature to a very detailed extent.[877]

From a theoretical perspective interoperability issues can be mapped by differentiating between private-sector-led approaches and government-driven measures on the one hand, as well as between unilateral and collaborative approaches on the other.[878] Private initiatives are reverse engineering, licensing, technical collaboration, and open standards initiatives; governmental actions are disclosure of information, transparency for consumer, public procurement, and framework for cooperation.[879]

In respect of the mentioned private interoperability the possibility of encryption as user-led regulation must be considered:[880] Encryption software gives the individual the possibility to protect the exchange of information against interference by third persons, however, this technical measure can also make communication more difficult and thereby jeopardize human interoperability. Additionally, the use of encryption software is confronted with governmental prohibition provisions in many countries and the software's application is partly complicated.

873 Palfrey/Gasser, 2012, 11; to the competitive advantages of interoperability see Palfrey/Gasser, 2012, 168/69, 173/74 and 232.

874 See also Brown/Marsden, 2013, 23.

875 Palfrey/Gasser, 2012, 160.

876 Brown/Marsden, 2013, 28/29; to the legal operability in particular see below V.D.2.

877 Instead of repeating the contents of previous valuable studies reference is made to the detailed publications of Palfrey/ Gasser, 2012, and DeNardis, 2011; see also Beydogan, 2010, 304–317; Brown/Marsden, 2013, 36–43, 157/58 and 187–192; to the common carriage regulation in particular see Weiser, 2009, 537 et seq.

878 See Palfrey/Gasser, 2012, 14 who, however, label (contrary to this study) a private-sector-led-approach as "non-regulatory" approach.

879 Palfrey/Gasser, 2012, 15.

880 See Brown/Marsden, 2013, 22–28.

5. Implementation of structural governance principles

a) Organizational management requirements

A cyberspace regulatory framework also needs to address organizational elements: a stable order will only be realizable if the degree of "organization" is high enough, enabling and facilitating the implementation (and enforcement) of the agreed harmonized substantive standards. As past experience has shown, the implementation of autonomous soft law and non-state standards based on the principle that they are considered by the concerned persons as benchmark for the behavior can lead to a gradual process of institutionalization.[881]

Such insight has led the school of institutional analysis to develop the concept of the new institutional economics, acknowledging the contribution of sociological institutionalism on historical institutional path dependency and thus providing a broader explanation of the incremental development of policy.[882] Similar considerations are discussed in connection with the constitutionalism of global developments.[883] Relevant questions are the institutional response to dynamic economic change, the functionality of the utility and geometry of regulation and the democratic deficit in case of institutional underdevelopment.[884] Responses to these aspects with regard to available tools can encompass the following aspects: (i) Responses of regulatory institutions to dynamic change in economic conditions; (ii) influence of political, social, cultural, ideological, and economic factors on governance reforms; (iii) divergence of national and regional regulators in their response to global technological factors.

Organizational and decision-making procedures are not any longer solely defined by States and established international organizations; moreover, representatives of other "public" groups (such as business and civil society) have taken a seat at the negotiation table, i.e. these "social actors" have also become accredited participants in the relevant fora.[885] In the last few years, not only private persons and businesses, but also representatives of national governments and international organizations have recognized that the establishment of adequate decision-making structures is important, irrespective of the legal quality of the normative order (hard law or soft law).[886] Without any doubt, appropriate coverage of concerned

881 WEBER, 2010b, 517/518.

882 For further details see NORTH, 1990.

883 See DIGGELMANN/ALTWICKER, 2008, 643–645.

884 To these issues and the following questions see BROWN/MARSDEN, 2013, 16.

885 FRANKLIN, 2013, 50.

886 KOSKENNIEMI, 2007, 1; see also SENN, 2011, 200 and 270 et seq. to the institutional transformation.

stakeholders with adequate reputational and retaliatory rules can generate a sufficient degree of compliance.[887] Reputational constraints are usually derived from the fact that illegitimacy itself can create "costs", i.e. members in standard-setting bodies must keep reputational discipline by refraining from overtly biased or self-serving decision-making.[888]

New organizational structures also require the development of new governance principles enshrining a range of meanings such as regulating influence, directing, controlling, commanding etc.[889] Typical assays of globalized governance, encompassing the notion of government (in the perception of Foucault) and of governed behavior or regulatory techniques[890] can be seen in the following aspects that need to be addressed:[891]

- Governance must refer to an "order, characterized in part by porous borders and power sharing amongst states, non-state actors and geographic/or functional entities".[892]
- Governance must encompass collective efforts enabling the concerned persons to identify, understand and address worldwide problems going beyond the capacity of individual States to solve.[893]

As the observations to the substantive cyberspace legal framework have evidenced, the future problems by their nature require a broader and more collective decision-making process than in the past; the different interests and needs call for the mentioned establishment of multi-layer mechanisms ensuring that the voices of all concerned participants are heard and appreciated.[894] In terms of a well-known approach of economic theory, law should not mainly use sticks, but through global governments mechanisms rather prefer to use carrots.[895]

The absence of hierarchical structures and the fact that responses to new issues are complex must be acknowledged. Flat structures on different appropriate levels facilitate the decision-making by including the relevant persons and organizations at the actual point of their respective concern. Thereby, the interests of the parties involved should not be defined by any specific group, but through procedural par-

887 WEBER, 2012b, 9.
888 BRUMMER, 2011, 309.
889 See also SENN, 2011, 256/57; MATHIASON, 2009, 16–18.
890 See also SENN, 2011, 257/58; for the sake of completeness it may be added that the Canon Law already dealt with the power of governance (see Canons 129–144 and MYRIAM WIJLENS, in: BEAL/CORIDEN/GREEN, 2000, 183–194).
891 WATERS, 2009, 33; WEBER, 2010a, 15.
892 WINCHESTER, 2009, 22.
893 See WEISS/THAKUR, 2006.
894 WEBER, 2010a, 15.
895 FRYDMAN, 2004, 231.

ticipatory mechanisms that reflect the views of the whole society.[896] The mentioned multistakeholder approach calls for different forms of "co-governance" in a multi-layer multi-player mechanism of coordination and collaboration.[897] In practice, these mechanisms are now tested in different forms of "enhanced cooperation";[898] for Internet governance the task of making policy recommendations regarding future forms of multistakeholder inclusion into the regulatory cyberspace processes is mainly performed by the Working Group on Enhanced Cooperation (WGEC).[899]

Based on such an understanding, future governance can be seen as a broad "array of changes in the distribution of authority, legitimacy, decision-making and participation by individuals and organizations in ordering human society, in response to similarly broad changes to material, social, technological, and economic conditions".[900] Consequently, an increased interconnectedness and complexity of life must be taken into account, leading to the formation or legitimization of aggregated networks of sub- or cross-state communities as rule-producing and rule-enforcing actors.[901]

If this kind of governance regime is implemented in social life, civil society will act according to (aligned) incentives with the public interest;[902] this is even more the case with market participants in business matters. Consequently, the degree to which rules are binding should not be conflated with whether they imply a formal legislative obligation; insofar, hard law and soft law are not dichotomous or qualitatively different forms of regulatory control.[903] Lack in confidence in the organizational law and skepticism about the legal framework of governance is detrimental and cannot be helpful in relation to the institution that provides a regime with which civil society and the commercial world should operate.[904]

The problem of soft law or "informal" law-making consists in the fact that such kind of law can hardly provide a protection against extraneous influences. This issue concerns the relationship between the system's own design and the environment in which it operates.[905] This fact calls for the development of new elements covering accountability, institutional differentiation and elaborated procedural

896 Weber, 2012b, 8.
897 Kleinwächter, 2011, 573.
898 See also Franklin, 2013, 191.
899 See http://unctad.org/en/Pages/CSTD/WGEC.aspx.
900 Waters, 2009, 35.
901 Cottier/Hertig, 2003, 261 et seq.; Petersmann, 2011, 23 et seq.
902 Weber, 2012b, 9.
903 Brummer, 2011, 306.
904 Susskind, 1996, 40.
905 Weber, 2012b, 9.

techniques. In the last few years the international regulatory system has undergone a significant evolution and accepted increasing prominence of public notice and consent procedures.

b) Enforcement and dispute resolution requirements

The establishment of an effective and efficient dispute settlement mechanism with the objective to complement and "enforce" soft law or informal international/Internet-ional rule-making is of major importance in order to attribute higher acceptance to a newly established substantive normative order.[906] As many examples show,[907] the possibility of invoking a dispute settlement mechanism tends to lead to better voluntary compliance with the rules.[908]

The need to improve the system of judicial review is especially apparent in connection with decisions taken by the ICANN board. The possibility of appealing against an ICANN decision to the competent court in California is not a suitable solution; moreover, new appeals procedures need to be implemented, for example the establishment of an independent body of experts being vested with the power to review the respective decisions and to release new guidelines, if necessary.[909]

The term dispute settlement mechanism should be understood in a broad sense, including not only theoretical "proceedings" in a traditional form (such as arbitration), but also all conceivable forms of mediation. Governmental legislators and private rule-makers have developed different forms of alternative dispute resolution (ADR) mechanisms; these models apply many types of binding effects of norms and range from negotiated solutions to clear recommendations and finally to enforceable judgments. The suitability of the discussed approaches depends on the given circumstances.[910]

Dispute settlement mechanisms can equally be necessary to clarify which legal obligations are potentially incomplete or inadequate. In this respect, the dispute settlement regime should be able to establish the predicate for, and limit the scope of, retaliation. There is no suitable forum for complaints in the cyberspace world available yet; however, consideration should be given on how to implement new structures dealing with the settlement of disputes.[911]

906 See Thompson, 2011, 183.
907 For example consumer disputes, financial services disputes etc.
908 Weber, 2012a, 17.
909 For more details see Weber/Gunnarson, 2012, 68 et seq.
910 For an overview see the still basic contribution of Harry T. Dewards, Alternative Dispute Resolution: Panacea or Anathema?, Harvard Law Review 99 (1985/86), 668 et seq.
911 Weber, 2012b, 9/10.

The availability of dispute settlement mechanisms is also a pre-condition for the introduction of (reputational or/and monetary) sanctions. Examples could be the imposition of some sort of disciplinary and enforcement powers, that would attach costs to the failure of complying with applicable rules. The universally applicable Canon Law of the Catholic Church also contains reputational sanctions. However, such a "sanctioning" requires the implementation of adequate mechanisms making the "environment" of the normative order clearly transparent and including accountability principles that bind the responsible persons.[912]

D. Incorporation of a Global Cyberspace Framework

Based on the assessed policy parameters for cyberspace rule-making and the guiding principles of a normative online order the structural design of a corresponding framework can be outlined. Cyberspace should not be a regulatory vacuum; global challenges require global solutions. The core of the concept must consist in a "Global Cyberspace Framework" (GCF), which should be embedded into internationalized policy structures, and a procedural regime, which relies on the multi-layer/polycentric governance model and on multistakeholder participation and which takes proper account of the functional dimensions of a normative order. Shown in a table the house to be built may have the following shape *(Table 29)*:

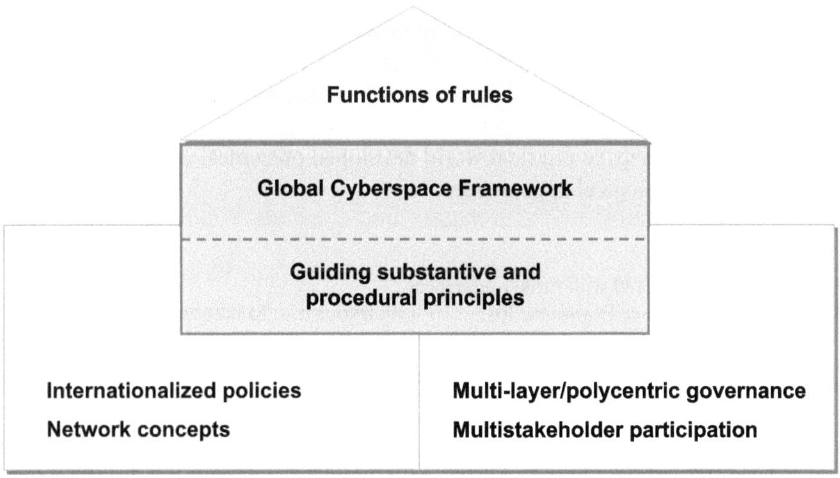

[912] See above IV.C.4.

1. Need for internationalization of policy structures

The question of who should run the Internet is intrinsically political because it is a sociocultural concern[913], i.e. cyberspace regulation cannot evade political considerations.[914] However, the question remains whether the power of digital networks is so great that traditional politics can no longer retain their former status.[915] A preliminary answer has already been given by Marshall McLuhan more than fifty years ago: The communication networks allow a "collective interplay" and constitute a "global village".[916]

Without any doubt, cyberspace requires (and deserves) universal protection and regulation.[917] Since cyberspace functions independently of State borders, online human activities need a minimal legal framework giving guidelines as to the compliance with important substantive principles of the concerned community. In addition, sensitive topics might even need surveillance and intervention mechanisms, which led Vint Cerf to propose the creation of a "cyber fire-department".[918] Nevertheless, the "crossing the Rubicon" metaphor recalling Julius Caesar's river crossing on the way to Rome from Gaul appears to overestimate the changes needed to adapt international policies.[919]

Since traditional rule-making is connected to the physical territory according to the sovereignty principle, civil society might be prepared to comply with norms stemming from an authority which acts in the territory of domicile. In contrast, a legal framework that has been developed at another place and is "transported" through cyberspace can hardly expect to become acceptable. This assessment is particularly true for the enforcement of rights against cyberspace actors that do not have assets in the concerned jurisdiction.[920] Looking from a general perspective, rule-makers need to avoid becoming unwitting prisoners of history by looking at the pre-cyberspace physical world developed piecemeal instead of addressing the new technological appearances.[921]

913 Franklin, 2013, 139 with further references.

914 For more details see Franklin, 2013, 176–180; Brousseau/Marzouki/Méadel, 2012.

915 Lanier, 2013, 328.

916 McLuhan, 1962, 5.

917 See also Kulesza, 2012, 136.

918 Vint Cerf mentioned the "cyber fire-department" being an international organization that would stand guard over international cybersecurity and coordinate international efforts in fighting cyber-crime at the IGF Meeting 2010 (Session 123) in Vilnius, Lithuania; a transcript is available at http://www.afilias.info/webfm_send/138.

919 Demchak/Dombrowski, 2011, 32, evoke this metaphor in connection with the Stuxnet worm attack.

920 Reed, 2012, 223; Goldsmith, 1998, 1216/17.

921 See also Reed, 2012, 151.

Therefore, Post has (recently again) proposed[922] that national legislators should abandon all their claims in the cyberspace context and not act as authority over cyberspace anymore, but – moreover – recognize a right to self-determination for cyberspace actors, namely "their right – perhaps even their inalienable right – to govern themselves as they see fit".[923] According to Post this approach is a consequence of the fact that national law can no longer guide the behavior of those subject to it in any meaningful way.[924] Surprisingly enough, these statements do not stem from the early days of cyberspace, but only date a few years back (2009). Nevertheless, as Reed points out, this "proposition is more than a little idealistic".[925] It can hardly be imagined that States would be willing to give up their law-making authority and their jurisdiction, to the contrary, as the recent experiences during and in the aftermath of the WCIT 2012 (Dubai) have shown, national interventions are in the process of being strengthened.[926]

However, even in view of the expressed reservation it cannot to be excluded that an incentive exists for States to substantially reduce their claims to authority over cyberspace.[927] The reason for this assumption lies in the growing awareness of States that reality does not allow them to make a claim with a global extension and does not offer the corresponding power. Competences could potentially be moved from the State level at least to a regional level.[928] The effectiveness element calls for a limitation of the claim for compliance with national laws to those cyberspace actors who are likely to recognize the implemented norms since they consider themselves part of the concerned community (civil society). Such a limitation would also contribute to a certain reduction of confusion with respect to the normative force of available laws and overcome the dilemma of existing power paradoxes.[929]

922 Already at a time when the Internet became more widely used by civil society the promoters of the libertarian movement proclaimed the independence of cyberspace (see above II.B.2).

923 Post, 2009, 185.

924 Post, 2009, 168.

925 Reed, 2012, 223.

926 See above V.B.1.

927 Reed, 2012, 224.

928 From a technological perspective the most recent attempts of network engineers, mainly of a team of the Swiss Federal Institute of Technology in Zurich, developing a decentralized structure (instead of a global structure) of the Internet with some regional outlets (as far as network order and control authority is concerned) should not be overlooked (see NZZ am Sonntag of June 1, 2014, 53–57).

929 See also Franklin, 2013, 18–20.

Nevertheless, this assessment is subject to two reservations which merit attention:

- Members of civil society in cyberspace cannot be divided into two categories, namely those who deliberately break the law ("bad people") and those who intend to act lawfully ("good people"). Such a distinction[930] does not reflect reality in cyberspace and the assumption that "good" norm-compliant persons would benefit from better laws can hardly be defended.[931]
- The States' acknowledgement of the fact that a practically unlimited extension of their laws' applicability does not correspond to the nature of cyberspace should not be interpreted as a complete denial of the need for a legal framework. Moreover, apart from the existence of voluntarily observed social norms based on soft law arrangements or customary habits, some basic principles need universal protection (and regulation).[932] As a result, a basic set of commonly accepted rules will allow for efficient and flawless international cooperation in all cyberspace-related matters.[933]

Summarizing this aspect in a nutshell it can be stated that the political dimensions of rule-making in cyberspace must take into account the manifold interests of cyberspace users and rule-makers acting in different cultural environments.

2. Need for multi-layer/polycentric approach with multistakeholder participation

For the time being, the attempt of introducing cyberspace regulations takes place in multiple international, regional and national fora according to the described multi-layer approach based on polycentric rule-making processes.[934] Most fora, however, that have not been established according to binding multilateral agreements (and not many fora in the cyberspace field fulfill this requirement of a multilateral incorporation) so far lack decision-making power; this assessment is particularly relevant for the most important forum, namely the Internet Governance Forum (IGF). Its establishment at the second WSIS in Tunis (2005) was conditional of a design only allowing discussions and deliberations (often in form of so-called dynamic coalitions) without extending the right to release binding motions.[935]

930 This distinction is partly made by Reed, 2012, 55–57.
931 Critical to this approach also Julia Hörnle, Book Review, International Journal of Law and Information Technology 20 (2012), 370, 380/81.
932 Kulesza, 2012, 136; to these generally acknowledged principles hereinafter V.D.3.
933 See also Kulesza, 2012, 138.
934 See above V.B.3.
935 See Weber, 2009, 70/71; Franklin, 2013, 154 et seq.; Brown/Marsden, 2013, 13/14.

This fact, however, does not mean that fora such as the IGF should be vested with sovereign power. Moreover, the principle of a multi-layer regime requires accepting different forms of rule-making developed by different institutions and stakeholders. This assessment is particularly relevant in view of the fact that many types of cyberspace users are actors in the online world and conflicts of interest between them need to be balanced and solved.[936] The realization of a multistakeholder regime is not an easy task; all participants need to build and constantly regain trust and confidence.

Notwithstanding the different perceptions of the various stakeholders in cyberspace the principles agreed upon in the manifold fora need to be linked into a comprehensible structure. This objective can be achieved if — apart from the technical interoperability[937] — the legal interoperability is also improved. Legal interoperability is the process of making legal rules work together across jurisdictions.[938] Whether new laws are implemented or existing laws are adjusted/reinterpreted depends on the given circumstances. Due to the increasing fragmentation of cyberlaw, efforts should be undertaken to achieve higher levels of legal and policy interoperability in order to reduce costs in cross-border business and to drive innovation and economic growth.[939]

In view of the complex cyberspace structures that make it advisable to implement a multi-layer regime composed of polycentric rule-making processes[940] and in consideration of the impossibility to define an optimal level of legal interoperability the model of total harmonization should not be the approach to follow even if the judgment based on a specific national law does not comply with general principles of another national law as the case "LICRA c. Yahoo!" demonstrated.[941] Moreover, it is important to find the appropriate degree of legal interoperability (instead of an all-or-nothing solution), which considers the substantive principles (such as freedom of expression, privacy, etc.) in different circumstances.[942] In-

936 Reed, 2012, does not really differentiate between the manifold cyberspace users and follows a relatively "monolithic" approach; see also the critical remark made by Julia Hörnle, Book Review, International Journal of Law and Information Technology 20 (2012), 370, 381.

937 See above V.C.4.c) (2).

938 Palfrey/Gasser, 2012, 178.

939 Palfrey/Gasser, 2012, 178/79.

940 See above V.B.3.

941 The "Tribunal de grande instance" in Paris confirmed the illegal nature of the sale of memorabilia of the Nazi period under French law in 2000 (thereby approving the competence of the French courts in a complaint against the US firm Yahoo!; decision RG:00/0538 of May 22 and November 22, 2000). Later Yahoo! started legal action in the US arguing that the sale's prohibition would contradict the First Amendment of the US Constitution.

942 For more details see Palfrey/Gasser, 2012, 180–183.

stead of debating a multilateral treaty system against a multistakeholder approach a new collaborative approach should be realized.

Furthermore, some variability is also caused by the enforcement mechanisms ("law in action") that might drive the decision on implementing a top-down approach (governed by large international bureaucracies) or a bottom-up process (developed step-by-step within multistakeholder institutions).[943] The multi-layer model attempting to achieve the suitable legal interoperability can insofar be seen as variable geometry model or as example of the described polycentric regulation.[944]

3. Need for consensus on guiding principles

In order to avoid a fragmentation of the applicable legal regime and to improve legal interoperability, the academic perspective calls for the implementation of a Global Cyberspace Framework (GCF); such a Framework should (i) adhere to the specific nature of cyberspace, (ii) envisage implementing the multistakeholder concept in the decision-making processes by realizing an appropriate multi-layer regime and (iii) incorporate the mentioned substantive principles into the framework.[945]

a) General declaration and additional protocols

The form of a Global Cyberspace Framework should not be identical to the traditional multilateral treaties designed as agreements between sovereign States, but should rather have the character of a declaration, a protocol or a commitment, based on the creation of a wide contractual consensus[946] acceptable to sovereign States, international organizations, businesses, and civil society.[947] The inclusion of private actors in internationally binding regimes has already been executed in other fields (for example Montreux Protocol[948]) and is also achievable in future cyberspace regulations.

943 Palfrey/Gasser, 2012, 184/85.

944 See above IV.E.2.

945 See also Kulesza, 2012, 152–154 with a proposal for an "Internet Framework Convention" which, however, is not fully identical with the proposal in this book; the idea of the "Convention" has been taken up in Kulesza/Balleste, 2013, 1345.

946 Such kind of consensus corresponds to the notion of "social contract" (see above IV.C.1).

947 Kulesza, 2012, 153.

948 The Montreux Document on pertinent international legal obligations and good practices for States related to operations of private military and security companies during armed conflict, 17 September 2008, available at: http://www.icrc.org/eng/assets/files/other/icrc_002_0996.pdf; see also Weber, 2011a, 11–13.

The "agreement" on a global normative order is not a completely new thing that never happened in the past: the (ecclesial) *jus canonicum* of the Catholic Church is a legal body with a global reach being independent from national legislation. The Canon Law is usually defined as a set of norms created by reason enlightened through faith that intends to bring order into the life of ecclesial community,[949] i.e. the Canon Law attempts to assist people in the reception of God's saving mysteries. Law is a specific instrument in this process, prompting and binding the community to strive for its perfection and giving directions for its progress.[950] This comparison does not mean that Canon Law should be taken up (by analogy) in cyberspace, however, it shows that normative orders can exist for centuries in parallel to the traditional national legislation.

A Global Cyberspace Framework could be complemented by additional protocols addressing specific social policy issues.[951] The respective topics might often be of a substantive matter (guiding principles)[952] but also encompass specific Internet issues (e.g. protocol standards and their interoperability, domain name allocation system). Such an approach leads to a desirable sequential rule-making process according to the prevailing needs. In addition, heuristic categories could be developed building a system and further evolving into a normative order.

Potential material topics are civil law (e.g. protection of privacy), trade law (e.g. provisions on e-commerce and international consumer protection as well as copyright and trademark principles), administrative law (e.g. trans-border online offer of medical services), financial law (e.g. e-banking), or criminal law (in particular cybersecurity).[953] Further input could be drawn from the 2005 WGIG Report[954], even if it cannot be overlooked that this document mainly addresses social policy issues essential to Internet governance and its already existing supervisory mechanisms.[955]

949 See Ladislav M. Örsy, in: Beal/Coriden/Green, 2000, 6.
950 *Ibid.*, 2.
951 See also Kulesza, 2012, 154.
952 See above V.C.2.
953 See Kulesza, 2012, 137/38.
954 Report of the Working Group on Internet Governance, June 2005, available at: http://www.wgig.org/docs/WGIGREPORT.pdf.
955 For this reason the approach of Kulesza, 2012, 154, for the design of the additional protocol appears to be too narrow.

b) Agreement on guiding principles

The most central issue of a Global Cyberspace Framework consists in the need for reaching a consensus on the applicability of some guiding principles.[956] Since law cannot operate as a mechanism for controlling the behavior of all cyberspace actors in a satisfactory way[957], the model with normative principles helps to systemize and explain a set of appropriate normative rules; furthermore, principles are an element of legal reasoning.[958] General principles are a recognized source of international law according to Article 38 (1) (c) of the Statue of the International Court of Justice; furthermore, general principles should be observed by the States and other cyberspace stakeholders since compliance with them leads to foreseeability in respect of the other actors' behavior; insofar, compliance pays off.[959] Even if different cultural identities do not necessarily acknowledge the same substantive principles some key values appear to be globally accepted.[960] At the forefront, human (fundamental) rights, ethics, and democratic participation merit strong protection. Such an approach could systematically benefit from the concept of "regulatory gravity".[961]

Human rights can be seen as values common to a major part of (or even the whole) global community. Not only are there several international legal instruments in place protecting human rights for more than fifty years, but also human rights are not exclusively a matter, which concerns States. Private enterprises are equally bound to conduct their business in a way that individuals are able to exercise their guaranteed freedoms. The efforts of the Global Network Initiative encompassing the major IT and Internet firms show that the cyber-community no longer relies on States as the only capable entities to protect fundamental rights.[962] In a comparative view, the mentioned Canon Law is also perceived as normative

956 At the NetMundial in Sao Paulo the participants agreed in the Multistakeholder Statement of April 23/24, 2014, on a set of governance principles, available at http://www.netmundial.br/.

957 See Reed, 2012, 242.

958 Uerpmann-Wittzack, 2010, 1246.

959 Kulesza/Balleste, 2013, 1344.

960 To the freedom of expression in the global governance debate see in particular MacKinnon, 2012, 2013–219; Anne-Claire Jamart, Internet Freedom and the Constitutionalization of Internet Governance, in: Roxana Radu/Jean-Marie Chenou/Rolf H. Weber (eds.), The Evolution of Global Internet Governance. Principles and Policies in the Making, Zürich 2013, 57 et seq.

961 See Reed, 2012, 100; Murray, 2010, 195 et seq.

962 See Global Network Initiative, available at: http://www.globalnetworkinitiative.org; see also Kulesza/Balleste, 2013, 1348.

order for a truly human community; some norms are borne from a human need for order, entrusted to individuals and linking the order to values.[963]

Ethics is another central principle. By identifying ethical standards, common to civil society (and thereby also to cyber-communities), a consensus as far as behavior in cyberspace is concerned might be achievable.[964] For quite some time ethics has not been deeply addressed in cyberspace rule-making circles, however, recently the perspective seems to convincingly change. For example, the European Commission expressed the intention to include ethics in the efforts for implementing suitable governance structures in cyberspace.[965] Ethical behavior enshrines many related principles, such as acting in good faith or building trust.

Experience in cyberspace has shown that the online civil society is more likely prepared to acknowledge general principles that have become customary ("Inter-net-ional rulemaking") instead of strict laws. General principles need to be derived from the acknowledged perceptions of the civil society's members. Therefore, an important element of the Global Cyberspace Framework conception should consist in designing customary legal rules for online communities that are based on recognized general principles; by identifying, for example, ethical standards, common to all online communities (along the concept of the "civic virtue" as developed by Johnson/Post), a consensus satisfying all concerned individuals and entities in cyberspace might be achievable.[966]

A further issue of a Global Cyberspace Framework concerns the delineation of the addressed actors in cyberspace. Apart from the usually mentioned multistakeholders (States, international organizations, businesses, civil society), Internet intermediaries also merit special attention. Particularly with respect to their role in cyberspace activities, that may cause harm and require remedies, a more intermediary-focused approach of a Global Cyberspace Framework seems justified.[967] As mentioned[968], appropriate dispute settlement mechanisms can equally be helpful in clarifying which legal obligations are potentially incomplete or inadequate. There is no suitable forum for complaints in cyberspace matters available yet; therefore, it appears to be reasonable to consider implementing new structures dealing with the settlement of disputes.

963 See Ladislav M. Ösry, in: Beal/Coriden/Green, 2000, 2 and 4.
964 See also Kulesza, 2012, 151.
965 European Commission, 2014, 9.
966 See Kulesza, 2012, 151.
967 Lipton, 2012, 148.
968 See above V.D.5.b).

c) Quality of rule-making

As outlined, a Global Cyberspace Framework should be composed of basic principles, not of narrowly worded legal norms. Therefore, the body of these principles can hardly be called a "law". Consequently, no specific term such as *"lex digitalis"* or *"Jus Internet"*[969] is proposed as terminological classification for the Global Cyberspace Framework.

Irrespective of the chosen form of a Global Framework Convention it is necessary to ensure that the norm-setting reaches an adequate level of quality. A consensus of all concerned cyberspace actors on the rule-making body does not suffice if the norms are so defective that they do not achieve the envisaged normative objectives. Three problems are particularly noteworthy in this context:[970]

- In developing new norms rule-makers have to avoid creating conflicts with other rules that are already part of the cyberspace users' law system. Therefore, rule-makers should research the norms currently applied and considered to constitute a part of the concerned community and only then define the new rules in a way that they fit into the existing framework; this kind of procedure can contribute to the required regulatory quality of a Global Cyberspace Framework.[971] Depending on the given circumstances, new rules may be able to modify existing norms by gradually extending their scope into the rule-makers' desired direction, if this direction is not irreconcilable with the existing framework.[972]
- Another problem consists in the concrete drafting of new rules; if cyberspace actors do not understand the wording, compliance with the rules can hardly be expected and/or achieved. In other words, the linguistic quality of norms is of importance; insufficient quality is a widely known issue in rule-making processes.[973] In addition, if new rules do not take up the requirements of the socio-technological environment obedience by cyberspace actors is not facilitated.[974]
- A third pitfall occurs if the law is framed in terms, which have no apparent connection to what the cyberspace actors actually do.[975] If the relation between the demands of the rule-maker and the behavior of cyberspace actors is not recognizable, a rejection (non-compliance with new rules) by cyberspace

[969] This is the terminology recently used by Kulesza/Balleste, 2013, 1343–1345.
[970] For further details see Reed, 2012, 226–228.
[971] For more details to the regulatory quality requirements see above III.C.2.
[972] Reed, 2012, 227.
[973] See Reed, 2012, 129 et seq.
[974] To the aspect of respect for the implemented normative order see Reed, 2012, 20–25.
[975] Reed, 2012, 228.

actors is likely since the new rule does not appear to be established on the basis of a meaningful concept.[976] Only meaningful and respectful laws will not encounter resistance from the addressees of the norms (i.e. civil society).[977]

As known from general law-making theories, an appropriate trade-off between simplicity and certainty in respect of the application of new rules is difficult to achieve; as a consequence, rule-makers have to carefully assess the cyberspace actors' required intentions, behaviors, and outcomes in some detail.[978] Furthermore, as designed by the form of a Global Cyberspace Framework, it appears to be imperative to have a flexible rule-making regime in an open systems' design.

Another general observation consists in the acknowledgement that law should be embedded in a social concept[979] and that law can hardly operate as a mechanism for controlling the behavior of cyberspace actors.[980] Therefore, the purpose of a rule-making process should be to regulate functions and effects, not means.[981]

The preparation, design, and implementation of an appropriate Global Cyberspace Framework cannot be the exclusive task of legally educated scholars. Moreover, a multidisciplinary approach should be applied and must include impact assessments in respect of different market structures and their dynamics, the development of pioneering international policies for cyberspace regulation and the monitoring of efficiency exercised by the implemented legal cyberspace framework.[982] The IGF has become a forum for multidisciplinary exchanges; the respective deliberations could even be made be more fruitful if comprehensive discussions between representatives of different disciplines, professional backgrounds, and cultural/geographical expertise would take place.

4. Need for improved emphasis on the functions of rules

When designing the future cyberspace legal framework[983] the fact should be considered that building designers, i.e. architects, are the experts in sketching "constructions". More than a hundred years ago the famous architect Louis H. Sullivan said: "It is the pervading law of all things, organic and inorganic, of all things, physical and metaphysical, of all things human and all things superhuman, of all

976 To the elements constituting meaning laws see also above III.A.1.

977 For more details to these aspects see Reed, 2013, 20–23.

978 See Reed, 2012, 241.

979 See Koskenniemi, 2005, 573.

980 See Reed, 2012, 242.

981 See Thompson, 2013, 45.

982 See also Brown/Marsden, 2013, 203.

983 The following comments are based on Weber, 2012b, 10.

true manifestations of the head, of the heart, of the soul that the life is recognizable in its expression, that form ever follows function. This is the law."[984]

The architect Sullivan uses twice the word "law" consisting in the key notion of making form dependent from function. Therefore, when designing an international legal framework for cyberspace, the function of law has to be considered in more depth; following Bentham's principle of utility and Luhmann's approach of stabilization of normative expectations, a functional approach that bodes for the political project should determine the normative order.[985] As a result, the main question could be phrased as follows: What social impacts should be caused by law? The answer is to be founded on the expectations of civil society. These expectations change over time, but some elements remain the same, such as legal certainty, stability, and reliability. In times of fast developing information technologies civil society is able to better rely on these principles in an informal law-making process and context than in the traditional legal regime.

Coexistence in an increasingly informal law-making environment makes it necessary to implement governance elements which encompass collective efforts enabling a proper identification and understanding of worldwide problems needed for global solutions, to have organizational structures in place which allow widespread participation by way of a multistakeholder model and to establish a dispute settlement mechanism which strengthens the accountability of all involved members of States' powers, international organizations, businesses, and civil society.

[984] Louis H. Sullivan, The tall office building artistically considered. Lippincott's Magazine 57, March 1896, 403–409, reproduced in: Leland M. Roth (ed.), America builds: Source Documents in American Architecture and Planning, New York 1983, 340, 345.

[985] See Thompson, 2013, 48/49; to the functional approach see also Reed, 2012, 179.

Index

Co-Publication with Schulthess Juristische Medien AG

Published by Springer-Verlag GmbH Berlin Heidelberg 2015
R.H. Weber, *Realizing a New Global Cyberspace Framework*,
DOI 10.1007/978-3-662-44677-5

H

I

J

K

L

T

U

V

W

Publikationen aus dem Zentrum für Informations- und Kommunikationsrecht der Universität Zürich

erschienen bei Schulthess Juristische Medien AG, Zürich

Band 1 **Neues Fernmelderecht – Erste Orientierung**
WEBER ROLF H. (Hrsg.),
mit Beiträgen von Fischer Peter R., Geiser Jean-Maurice, Gunter Pierre-Yves, Haag Marcel, Hoffet Franz, Maurer François, Ramsauer Matthias, Rieder Pierre, Stampfli Katharina und Weber Rolf H., Zürich 1998

Band 2 **Symposium Schluep – Querbezüge zwischen Kommunikations- und Wettbewerbsrecht**
WEBER ROLF H. (Hrsg.),
in Zusammenarbeit mit von der Crone Hans Caspar, Forstmoser Peter, Zäch Roger und Zobl Dieter,
mit Beiträgen von von der Crone Hans Caspar/Groner Roger, Mestmäcker Ernst-Joachim, Nobel Peter, Schwarz Mathias/Klingner Norbert und Weber Rolf H., Zürich 1998

Band 3 **Informatik und Jahr 2000 – Risiken und Vorsorgemöglichkeiten aus rechtlicher Sicht**
WEBER ROLF H.
Zürich 1998

Band 4 **Daten und Datenbanken – Rechtsfragen zu Schutz und Nutzung**
WEBER ROLF H./HILTY RETO M. (Hrsg.),
mit Beiträgen von Druey Jean Nicolas, Gaster Jens-L., Hilty Reto M., Kemper Kurt, Sieber Ulrich und Weber Rolf H., Zürich 1998

Band 5 **Neustrukturierung der Rundfunkordnung**
WEBER ROLF H.
Zürich 1999

Band 6 **Rechtsschutz von Datenbanken (EU – USA – Schweiz)**
KÜBLER PHILIP
Zürich 1999

Band 7 **Informationsqualität – Ein Beitrag zur journalistischen Qualitätsdebatte aus der Sicht des Informationsrechts**
ZULAUF RENA
Zürich 2000

Band 8 **Werbung im Internet – Rechtsvergleichende, lauterkeitsrechtliche Beurteilung von Werbeformen**
JÖHRI YVONNE
Zürich 2000

Band 9 **Rechtlicher Regelungsrahmen von raumbezogenen Daten**
WEBER ROLF H.
Zürich 2000

Band 10 **Geschäftsplattform Internet – Rechtliche und praktische Aspekte**
Weber Rolf H./Hilty Reto M./Auf der Maur Rolf (Hrsg.)
Zürich 2000

Band 11 **Finanzierung der Rundfunkordnung**
Weber Rolf H.
Zürich 2000

Band 12 **Der Softwarepflegevertrag**
Widmer Michael
Zürich 2000

Band 13 **Datenschutzrecht vor neuen Herausforderungen**
Marketing – E-Commerce – Virtuelle Bank – Sachdaten
Weber Rolf H.
Zürich 2000

Band 14 **Geschäftsplattform Internet II – Rechtliche und praktische Aspekte**
Weber Rolf H./Hilty Reto M./Auf der Maur Rolf (Hrsg.)
Zürich 2001

Band 15 **Digitale Verbreitung von Rundfunkprogrammen**
und Meinungsvielfalt – Entwicklungen, Probleme, Lösungen
Weber Rolf H./Dörr Bianka S.
Zürich 2001

Band 16 **Die Übernahme von Allgemeinen Geschäftsbedingungen in**
elektronisch abgeschlossene Verträge
Schwab Karin
Zürich 2001

Band 17 **Geschäftsplattform Internet III – Kapitalmarkt – Marktauftritt – Besteuerung**
Weber Rolf H./Hilty Reto M./Auf der Maur Rolf (Hrsg.)
Zürich 2002

Band 18 **Rechtliche Rahmenbedingungen für verwaltungsunabhängige**
Behördenkommissionen – Untersuchung am Beispiel der geplanten
Fernmelde- und Medienkommission
Weber Rolf H./Biaggini Giovanni
Mitarbeit: Dörr Bianka S./Peduzzi Roberto
Zürich 2002

Band 19 **Elektronische Signaturen**
Schlauri Simon
Zürich 2002

Band 20 **Zugang zu Kabelnetzen – Spannungsfeld zwischen**
Netzbetreiberfreiheit und offenem Zugang
Weber Rolf H.
Zürich 2003

Band 21 **Elektronische Signaturen und Haftung der Anbieter von Zertifizierungsdiensten – Eine Darstellung am Beispiel der Regelungen in der EU, Deutschland, Grossbritannien und der Schweiz**
DÖRR BIANKA S.
Zürich 2003

Band 22 **Geschäftsplattform Internet IV**
WEBER ROLF H./BERGER MATHIS/AUF DER MAUR ROLF (Hrsg.)
Zürich 2003

Band 23 **IT-Outsourcing**
ICT: Rechtspraxis I
WEBER ROLF H./BERGER MATHIS/AUF DER MAUR ROLF (Hrsg.)
Zürich 2003

Band 24 **Rechtsfragen rund um Suchmaschinen**
WEBER ROLF H.
Mitarbeit: Spacek Dirk
Zürich 2003

Band 25 **Schweizerisches Filmrecht**
WEBER ROLF H./UNTERNÄHRER ROLAND/ZULAUF RENA
Zürich 2003

Band 26 **Kinofilmverwertung in der Schweiz**
UNTERNÄHRER ROLAND
Zürich 2003

Band 27 **E-Health und Datenschutz**
BERGER KURZEN BRIGITTE
Zürich 2004

Band 28 **Unternehmensinformation und Recht – Eine Übersicht**
STÜCKELBERGER BALZ
Zürich 2004

Band 29 **Schutz von TV-Formaten – Eine rechtliche und ökonomische Betrachtung**
SPACEK DIRK
Zürich 2005

Band 30 **Kulturquoten im Rundfunk**
WEBER ROLF H./ROSSNAGEL ALEXANDER/OSTERWALDER SIMON/SCHEUER ALEXANDER/WÜST SONIA
Zürich 2006

Band 31 **Zugang zu Premium Content**
WEBER ROLF H./OSTERWALDER SIMON
Zürich 2006

Band 32 **Sorgfaltspflichten bei der Datenübertragung**
FAVRE KATIA
Zürich 2006

Band 33 **IT-Sicherheit und Recht – Grundlagen eines integrativen Gestaltungskonzepts**
WEBER ROLF H./WILLI ANNETTE
Zürich 2006

Band 34 **Privatvervielfältigung im digitalen Umfeld**
BAUMGARTNER TOBIAS
Zürich 2006

Band 35 **Das Recht der personenbezogenen Information**
WEBER ROLF H./SOMMERHALDER MARKUS
Zürich 2007

Band 36 **Staatliche Massnahmen gegen Medienkonzentration**
KELLERMÜLLER HANSPETER
Zürich 2007

Band 37 **Der Mehrwertdienst im Fernmelderecht**
HUBER KARIN
Zürich 2007

Band 38 **Telecommunications Competition and Its Driving Force**
WU JUN
Zürich 2008

Band 39 **Media Governance und Service Public**
WEBER ROLF H.
Zürich 2007

Band 40 **The Information Society and the Digital Divide Legal Strategies to Finance Global Access**
WEBER ROLF H./MENOUD VALÉRIE A.
Zürich 2008

Band 41 **Netzzugang in der Telekommunikation**
AMGWERD MATTHIAS
Zürich 2008

Band 42 **IT-Governance als Aufgabe des Verwaltungsrates – Kriterien einer sorgfältigen Pflichterfüllung unter Berücksichtigung der strategischen Rolle der IT im Unternehmen**
WILLI ANNETTE
Zürich 2008

Band 43 **Der ASP-Vertrag**
CHRISTIAN M. IMHOF
Zürich 2008

Band 44 **Zivilrechtliche Haftung von Internet-Providern bei Rechtsverletzungen durch ihre Kunden**
FRECH PHILIPP
Zürich 2009

Band 45 **Public Key Infrastructure**
MARKWALDER DANIEL
Zürich 2009

Band 46 **Shaping Internet Governance: Regulatory Challenges**
WEBER ROLF H.
Zürich 2009

Band 47 **Rundfunkübertragungsrechte an den Olympischen Spielen im europäischen Kartellrecht**
Medienmärkte, gemeinsamer Erwerb durch die European Broadcasting Union und Exklusivvergabe
HELLWIG IRENE
Zürich 2009

Band 48 **Spyware**
Rechtliche Würdigung ausgewählter Fragen sowie Empfehlungen an die Praxis unter besonderer Berücksichtigung des Eidgenössischen Datenschutzgesetzes
BUCHER MANUEL
Zürich 2010

Band 49 **Internet of Things**
Legal Perspectives
WEBER ROLF H./WEBER ROMANA
Zürich 2010

Band 50 **Datenschutz v. Öffentlichkeitsprinzip**
Erläuterungen zu den Spannungsfeldern am Beispiel des Zürcher Informations- und Datenschutzgesetzes
WEBER ROLF H.
Zürich 2010

Band 51 **Online Marketing und Wettbewerbsrecht**
WEBER ROLF H./VOLZ STEPHANIE
Zürich 2011

Band 52 **Internet-Access-Providing-Verträge mit geschäftlichen und privaten Endkunden**
Eine vertragsrechtliche Analyse nach schweizerischem Recht unter besonderer Berücksichtigung des Rechts der Europäischen Union
ORSOLYA FERCSIK SCHNYDER
Zürich 2012

Band 53 **Classification of Services in the Digital Economy**
WEBER ROLF H.
Zürich 2012

Band 54 **Neuer Regulierungsschub im Datenschutzrecht?**
WEBER ROLF H. / THOUVENIN FLORENT
Zürich 2012

Band 55 **Die Erzwingung unangemessener Preise im Kartell- und Fernmelderecht – Eine rechtsvergleichende Untersuchung**
VLCEK MICHAEL
Zürich 2013

Band 56 **The Evolution of Global Internet Governance**
Principles and Policies in the Making
RADU ROXANA / CHENOU JEAN-MARIE / WEBER ROLF. H.
Zürich 2013

Band 57 **The New International Telecommunication Regulations and the Internet**
A Commentray and Legislative History
HILL RICHARD
Zürich 2013

Band 58 **Trennungsgebot und Internet**
Ein medienrechtliches Prinzip in Zeiten der Medienkonvergenz
VOLZ STEPHANIE
Zürich 2014

Band 59 **Big Data und Datenschutz – Gegenseitige Herausforderungen**
ROLF H. WEBER / FLORENT THOUVENIN (Hrsg.)
Zürich 2014

Ausserdem erschienen:

Regulatory Models for the Online World
WEBER ROLF H.
Zürich 2002

Towards a Legal Framework for the Information Society
WEBER ROLF H.
in collaboration with Roduner Xenia
Zürich 2003

MIX
Papier aus verantwortungsvollen Quellen
Paper from responsible sources
FSC® C105338

If you have any concerns about our products,
you can contact us on
ProductSafety@springernature.com

In case Publisher is established outside the EU,
the EU authorized representative is:
Springer Nature Customer Service Center GmbH
Europaplatz 3, 69115 Heidelberg, Germany

Printed by Libri Plureos GmbH
in Hamburg, Germany